WILD About Rocky Mountain Birds

A Youth's Guide to the Rocky Mountain States

by Adele Porter

Adventure Publications, Inc.
Cambridge, Minnesota

This book is dedicated to Elizabeth, Rachael and Byron. Wamlati!
To the children of the Rocky Mountain region, may your wildest wishes come true.

Acknowledgments

Carrol Henderson, Minnesota DNR Nongame Wildlife Program:
Thank you for your continued support and for allowing the use of your photographs of the Handsaker Egg Collection.

Brian Wheeler:
Thank you for sharing your expertise of Rocky Mountain region birds and lands. Your input was most valuable and truly appreciated.

The teachers and students that shared their ideas and support:
Thank you for your invaluable enthusiasm and input.

Emily C., neighbor extraordinaire:
Thank you for sharing your engaging journal notes on the American Robin!

The numerous staff members of the conservation and natural resource departments of the states represented in this book, who willingly provided data, background and supporting facts:
Thank you for your dedication to the stewardship of natural resources and for your willingness to share your knowledge, skills and enthusiasm.

My sincere thanks to the countless professionals and volunteers that have contributed their time, energy and field data to state and federal reports, breeding-bird atlases, bird counts and other citizen science projects. The collaborative efforts of wildlife professionals and volunteers across North America, as well as those at globally important migratory wintering areas, provide vital information to the life histories and population status of birds. These resources have been imperative to the writing of *Wild About Rocky Mountain Birds.*

Edited by Gretchen Jensen, Anthony Hertzel and Brett Ortler

Book and cover design, nest, migration map and habitat map illustrations by Jonathan Norberg

Habitat Café, feather, exterior and interior of bird illustrations by Julie Martinez; range maps and bird silhouette illustrations by Anthony Hertzel; cartoon bird illustrations by Brenna Slabaugh; child's nest drawing by Emily Connick

Photo credits by photographer and page number:
Egg photos: Chester A. Reed, *North American Birds Eggs:* 39 R. L. Ridgway, *Life Histories of North American Birds:* 49 **all other egg photos from the Handsaker Egg Collection taken by Carrol Henderson**
Rick and Nora Bowers: 138 (main), 144 (soaring), 146 (in flight), 158 (winter), 170 (in flight), 180 (gosling) **John Kramer:** 104-105 **Maslowski Wildlife Productions:** 54 (winter) **Johann Schumacher/CLO✲:** 164 (female) **Brian E. Small:** 54 (male, female), 70 (both), 78, 80 (female), 84 (both), 86 (both), 88 (female), 98 (red-shafted), 100 (main), 114, 124, 130, 174 (both) **Alan Stankevitz:** 6 (Great Blue Heron, Northern Saw-whet Owl), 30 (both), 36, 40, 44, 66, 68, 76, 92, 98 (yellow-shafted), 102 (spitting pellet), 110 (main), 116 (both), 120 (both), 122 (main), 126 (flight), 132 (both), 142, 146 (main), 154 (both), 176 (flight), 178 (feeding), 182 (flight), 186 (dinner) **Stan Tekiela:** 7 (Mallard, Indigo Bunting), 13 (American Kestrel), 14 (American Bittern), 32 (female), 42 (both), 46 (both), 48, 50, 52, 56, 60 (hawk nest), 64 (both), 74, 88 (main), 90 (both), 94 (side profile), 102 (main), 106 (flight), 110 (male winter, female), 118, 122 (injury-feigning display), 128 (both), 134, 136, 140 (main, bottom inset), 158 (main), 160 (both), 166 (both), 168 (both), 170 (both), 172 (both), 176 (main), 178 (main, fishing), 180 (main, in flight), 182 (main), 184 (both), 186 (main, flight) **Gijsbert van Frankenhuyzen/DPA✲:** 102 (in flight) **Brian K. Wheeler:** 100 (flight), 138 (female) **Jim Zipp:** 7 (hawk's tail), 72, 80 (main), 82 (both), 94 (main), 96, 100 (juvenile), 112, 126 (main), 138 (wheeling), 144 (main), 156, 162, 164 (main)
✲DPA: Dembinsky Photo Associates; CLO: Cornell Laboratory of Ornithology

10 9 8 7 6 5 4 3 2 1

Copyright 2012 by Adele Porter
Published by Adventure Publications, Inc.
820 Cleveland Street South
Cambridge, Minnesota 55008
1-800-678-7006
www.adventurepublications.net
ISBN: 978-1-59193-320-5

Thundering birds. Booming birds. Drumming birds.
Stomping, whistling and jazzing birds.

ROCKY MOUNTAIN BIRDS

Wildlife is waiting for you in the big neighborhood of the Rocky Mountain region and its forests, grasslands, rock and canyon areas, and wetlands. Put on your boots, bring a friend, and head out the door. It's time to get Wild About Rocky Mountain Birds!

How to Use Your Book

There are hundreds of bird species that live in the Rocky Mountain region of the United States. To introduce you to Rocky Mountain birds, this book features 70 fascinating species. You'll find identification tips and information on each species' favorite foods, interesting behaviors, songs and calls, life cycle, migration patterns and more. Most species in the book nest in the Rocky Mountain region and are fairly common. Some uncommon species have also been included for you to get to know about them and support their needs for survival. Consider yourself a "Super Birder" when you have met them firsthand!

The book is organized by habitat—the type of natural environment a bird calls home. It is divided into four sections, one for each of the region's major habitats: alpine and subalpine, montane and aspen park, grasslands, cliffs and canyons, and wetlands, lakes, rivers and shores. Within each habitat section, you'll find the birds that live there arranged by size—smallest to largest—according to their length and wingspan.

For a list of the species in this book and the pages on which they appear, turn to the Table of Contents (pages 4–5). The Index (page 199) provides a handy reference guide to the species in alphabetical order. A taxonomic listing (scientific classification) of the birds is on page 198.

About Birds The beginning of this book (page 6) shows the amazing characteristics that make birds unique. It explains how each part of a bird is designed to help it survive. You will also find clues to what is wild, and what is a nongame or game bird species.

How to Watch Birds This section (page 14) gives you the detective skills to find birds while being respectful to wildlife and the outdoor habitats that we share!

When to Watch Birds When are the best times and seasons to spy on different birds? This section, starting on page 16, helps you understand why some birds can be seen at certain times of the day or year.

Where to Watch Birds Turn to page 20 to learn about the major land areas in our region of the U.S., and for tips on where to find birds in each one.

Table of Contents

Appendix

About the Author

Watch for these friends!

Birding Tip

Great ideas for
bird watching success.

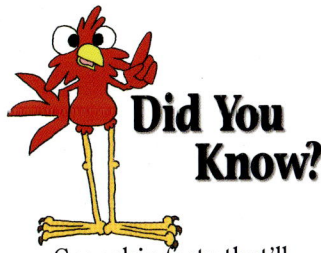

Did You Know?

Gee-whiz facts that'll
WOW the whole family.

Do the Math

Brain-teasing bird math.
(Don't tell, but the answers are
on pages 194-195.)

Gross Factor

Disgusting but interesting
facts guaranteed to make
your parents gag.

History Hangout

Cool details from the past,
such as where a bird's
name comes from.

Unsolved Mystery

Puzzles and oddities that have left
scientists baffled—maybe you'll
discover the solutions.

About Birds

Chickadees, Herons and Hawks. What Makes Us Birds?

Black-capped Chickadee

Great Blue Heron

Cooper's Hawk

Feathers Birds are the only living creatures that grow feathers. They have six basic kinds. Each one helps the bird with a special job: flight, warmth, information reception, protection, balance, or flotation. The color and pattern of a bird's feathers can also help you identify which species you are watching. Learn more about feathers on page 10.

Ears Yes, birds have ears under their cheek feathers. Some owls and hawks have amazing ears. Feathers arranged in a disk around the bird's face funnel sound to its ears, helping it hear better.

Northern Saw-whet Owl

Lungs with air sacs Birds are equipped with two lungs with special balloon-like air sacs that can spread out into other parts of their bodies. This extra capacity allows a bird to store more air, push air through the lungs better and send more oxygen to its cells. This is important during long migration flights.

Osprey

Bones Most birds have strong, flexible skeletons of hollow or semi-hollow bones with many air spaces. This helps them weigh less and—you guessed it—means lighter baggage for flying. For birds that spend a lot of time in the air, this is very important.

Oil Gland To keep its feathers in good condition, a bird spreads oil on its feathers. It gets the oil from the uropygium gland above its rump. The bird rubs oil on its beak, then spreads the oil over its feathers. Cleaning and arranging feathers in this way is called "preening."

Feet Most birds have four toes. Not all, though. Killdeer have just three toes, and all three face forward so the Killdeer can run fast! Toe arrangement can vary. A bird can have three toes in front and one in the back, or two toes in front and two in the back. This arrangement can tell you where the bird lives and how it gets around. You can get more clues about how and where the bird lives by looking at its feet. Are the feet webbed? Do they have large talons (claws)? Some birds have special toes that help them walk upside down, or hang onto a tree while pecking out a hole.

Red-tailed Hawk

Hawk's tail

Woodpecker's tail

Tail How does a bird steer or put on the brakes while flying? By spreading out its tail and adjusting its wing feathers! Each bird species has a tail designed to help it survive. A woodpecker's tail is stiff and pointed. This helps it brace itself against tree trunks while looking for food.

Songs and Calls Birds do not have vocal cords. They have a special voice box called a syrinx. They inflate air sacs to put pressure on the muscles of the syrinx, which makes a range of different sounds. Nearly all birds have some sort of call, but not all birds sing. **Calls** are short and used to signal danger, warn other birds to stay away or announce mealtime. They often sound the same from one species to another. Different bird species can use and understand the same calls.

Songs are sung mostly by males and used to attract a mate or defend their territory. These songs are complex and are only understood by birds of the same species. Try doing what some birds do: sing more than one note at a time, each note at a different intensity and compose 1,000 different phrases! Wow!

Mallard

Bald Eagle

Wings Flying, diving, swooping, hovering, escaping a predator, even landing . . . a bird depends on its wings, which are powered by large, strong muscles anchored to the breastbone. The shape of a bird's wings can tell you a lot about where it lives, what it eats and how it catches its prey. For example, pointed wings indicate a fast flier. Large, broad wings are common among big soaring birds, while birds that maneuver around trees in a forest have short, broad wings.

Crop and Gizzard How does a bird chew food without teeth? For some birds, the food first goes into a sack called a crop, which is located near the esophagus. From there, it is sent into a two-part stomach, where the gizzard grinds it up into smaller pieces. Some birds eat gravel or eggshells (substitute teeth) that stay in their gizzards for grinding hard-to-digest food.

Beak The shape and length of a bird's beak are clues to what and how it eats. How different can beaks be? Spoon, fork, knife, straw, strainer, fish net, tweezers, pliers, nutcracker, saw and chopsticks are a few different styles. Hungry? Select your dinnerware!

American White Pelican

Anatomy

It's easier to identify birds and talk about their characteristics if you know the names of their different parts. The following illustrations will help you understand basic bird anatomy. Because these images are composites of many species, they shouldn't be confused with any actual bird.

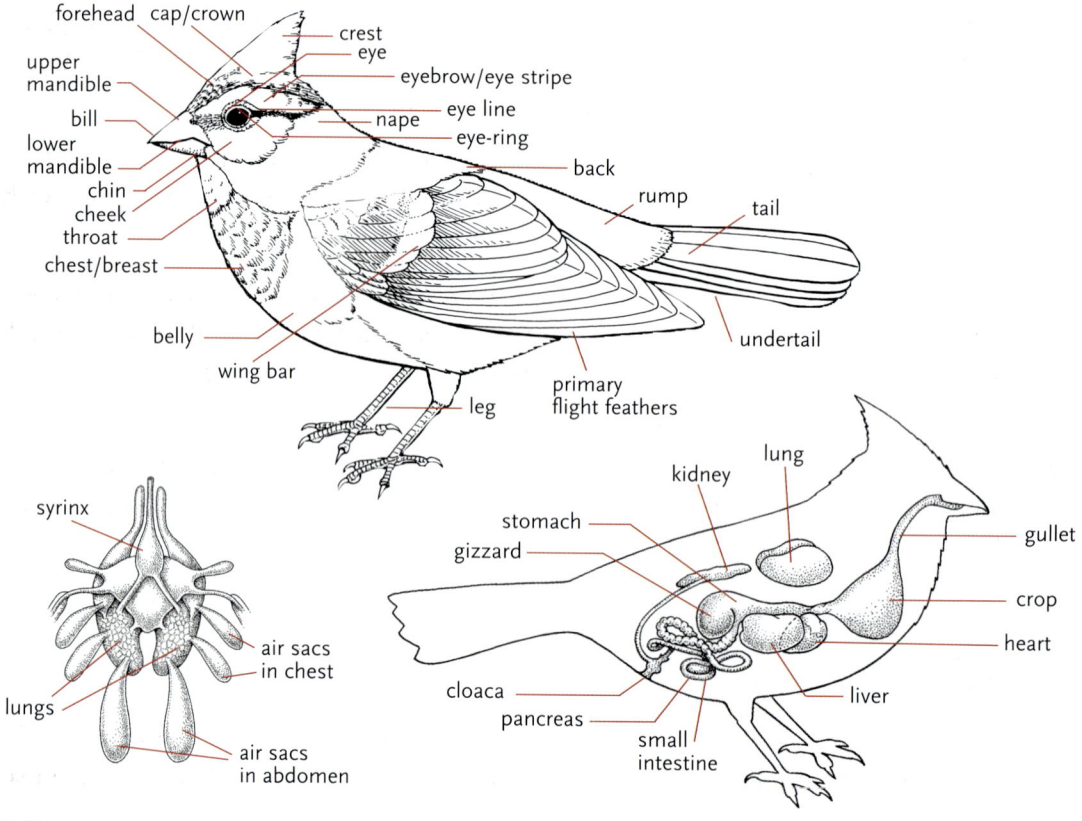

Eggs

Unlike mammal mothers, which give birth to squirming, squalling babies, female birds lay eggs. The shell is made of calcium (the same thing bones are made of) and protects the young bird developing inside it. The shape of the egg makes for a strong shell. It is sturdy enough for parent birds to sit on and incubate (keep warm), yet fragile enough for baby birds to break through at hatching. Some birds lay colorful eggs. The colors can hide the egg from predators or help parents identify imposters.

Almost all parent birds develop a "brood patch" on their chest or belly when incubating their eggs. The feathers either fall off or are plucked out. Blood vessels next to this bare spot help keep the eggs warm. Inside the egg, the yolk is the baby bird's main source of food. The egg white provides water and protein. This food energy, together with a temporary egg tooth, helps the chick free itself from the shell.

Robin eggs

Nests

Bird nests are amazing. Imagine building your house strong enough to survive a storm, large enough for your growing family, insulated—and waterproof. Now, imagine finding all the materials from the natural habitat where you live. Birds do!

Just as there are different kinds of birds, there are different types of nests. Some bird species, including the Killdeer, prefer a simple **ground nest** scraped out of the earth. Birds with such nests may have eggs shaped to spin rather than roll away.

To build a nest that floats on water or balances on a cliff or bridge takes some fancy work. A **platform nest** may be built of small twigs and branches that form a simple base, with a dip in the middle to nestle the eggs.

Cup nests are used by most songbirds. They have a solid base attached to a tree, shrub or ledge. Sturdy sides are made by weaving grasses, twigs, bark or leaves tightly together. A soft inner lining of feathers, fur or plant material keeps the eggs and young birds cozy.

Keeping a nest safe from predators calls for hanging out at the edge. A **pendulous nest** looks like a sock hanging at the end of a tree branch. It takes nearly a week for Bullock Orioles to weave together the fibers of their strong watertight nests. They are such good tailors, it even feels like a soft sock!

Cavity nests are used by woodpeckers, chickadees and many other forest birds. Usually chipped into a tree trunk or branch, cavity nests often have a small entrance hole that leads to an inner room.

Cliffside/riverbank nests are cavity nests that are built into a cliffside or riverbank. For example, the Belted Kingfisher's nest features a long tunnel leading back to the nursery.

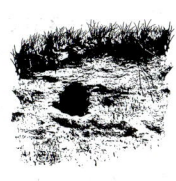

ground nest   platform nest   cup nest   pendulous nest   cavity nest   cliffside/riverbank nest

Feathers

When dinosaurs roamed the Earth there also lived a prehistoric, crow-sized animal with feathers; scientists believe it was related to reptiles, and have named it **Archaeopteryx** (ar-kay-op-tehr-icks) from its fossil remains. *Archaeopteryx* is one of the first known bird species.

Today, birds still have characteristics of their distant relatives. Reptiles have scales of solid keratin. Bird feathers are also formed of keratin, but in strands, which are much lighter. Birds are the only animals on Earth with feathers!

Feathers help a bird fly, stay warm and dry, and protect their skin. Feathers allow birds to swim through the water and fly through the air with less friction (which makes these jobs much easier). For some birds, such as owls, feathers quiet the sound of their flight. Feathers can be camouflaged, to help a bird hide from predators, or occur in bright colors to show off during courtship. Whew—feathers do a lot for birds!

Mallard

What do birds do when their feathers start to get old? They molt (or shed) the old ones and replace them with new feathers one or two times each year. To keep their balance in flight, the feathers are shed a few at a time and in the same place on each side of the body.

Have you noticed the "goose bumps" on the skin of a chicken from the grocery store? The bumps, called papillae, are where feathers grow out of the skin. At the bottom of each of the papillae are ligaments (similar to muscles) that the bird uses to move each feather on its own, an important function when it needs to turn in flight or slow down!

Mountain Bluebird

Did You Know? In herons, the middle foot claw has a comb-like serrated (jagged) edge used as a preening tool. This is called a pectate claw or feather comb. Herons use this claw to keep their feathers in top condition.

CONTOUR FEATHERS: *Zipped in Place*

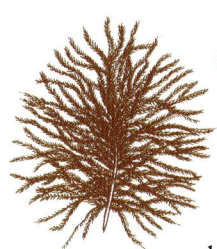

Contour feathers overlap each other to give birds a streamlined body shape (a contour) for less friction, faster flight, and faster diving in the water. Contour feathers are found on the body, wings and tail. Contour feathers have a central shaft (rachis) with vanes on each side. Attached to the vanes are barbs. On each side of the barbs are small barbules that make a "zipper" to hold the feather barbs together. When the barbs unzip, the bird uses its beak to zip them back together while preening.

DOWN FEATHERS: *Keeping Warm*

Down feathers do not "zip" together like contour feathers, but stay fluffy. The air spaces hold the bird's body heat close like a warm blanket. Young birds often have down first, to keep their small bodies warm until their contour and other body feathers grow in. Adult birds' down feathers are located under their contour feathers.

SEMIPLUME FEATHERS: *Support and Warmth*

Semiplume feathers, which are found beneath the contour feathers, are a cross between a contour and a down feather. They have a stiff shaft, but also have soft down vanes that act like extra insulation.

FILOPLUME FEATHERS: *Information Receivers*

Filoplume feathers are tiny, hair-like feathers comprised of a long central shaft tipped with a tuft of barbules. They help a bird adjust the position of its flight feathers. These sensitive feathers move with the slightest breeze, sending information to the nerve cells at their bases. Vibrations from the filoplume feathers tell the bird when to adjust its contour feathers for better flight.

BRISTLE FEATHERS: *Sense, Guard and Guide*

Bristle feathers are stiff, hair-like feathers with a firm central shaft. They are found near the eyes, nostrils and beak, and may help protect the bird's eyes, help it to locate food, and funnel prey (such as flying insects) into its mouth.

POWDER DOWN FEATHERS: *Talcum Powder Protection*

Powder down feathers, found on birds such as Great Blue Herons (page 182) are never shed, but grow all the time. The ends break down into a waxy powder that protects the bird's skin from moisture and damage.

What is Wild?

Is your pet parakeet wild? It may act wild at times, but pets and farm animals are not wild. They are domesticated animals that depend on people for survival. Wild birds find their own food, water, shelter and a place to nest and raise their young.

Wild birds are not owned by people. They are a part of the greater global environment. In the Rocky Mountain region of the U.S., wildlife biologists and managers study wild birds and their habitats. The information is used to make laws that protect wildlife and wild places. Conservation officers make sure everyone follows these rules, and you can help! Law-breakers can be reported to your state's game department or state resources agency (page 196). People that call remain unidentified. Together, we can make sure Rocky Mountain birds are around for a long time.

Leave Wild Things Wild

Wild birds and animals were once considered unlimited resources. They were killed for their meat, feathers and hides without seasons or limits. By the late 1800s, unregulated market hunting (along with habitat destruction) caused many species—from the American Bison to the Great Egret—to almost disappear forever. The Passenger Pigeon, which once darkened the skies with its huge flocks, eventually became extinct.

Fortunately, laws like the Lacey Act and the Migratory Bird Treaty Act helped protect other wild birds before it was too late. These laws governed the harvest of migratory birds, including their

Great Egret

eggs, nests and feathers. Today, many state and federal laws protect wild birds, animals and the habitats they need to survive.

The eggs shown in this book are from a famous collection of eggs gathered by Iowa farmer Ralph Handsaker in the late 1800s and early 1900s. Although wild bird eggs are now protected, in that era collecting eggs was a popular hobby for naturalists. Handsaker's collection consists of nearly 4,000 eggs from 400 species of birds found around the world. It is the focal point of the book *Oology and Ralph's Talking Eggs* by biologist Carrol Henderson. The collection is now at the Peabody Museum of Natural History at Yale University.

It's tempting to enjoy nature by taking it home with us. But it's important to keep wild things wild. Leave eggs, nests and baby birds in their natural habitat.

Game or Nongame Wildlife?

Canada Goose

Wildlife that can be hunted under state law, such as the Canada Goose, is called **game wildlife**. The Department of Natural Resources (DNR) or wildlife management agency in each state in the Rocky Mountain region regulates hunting so it does not threaten game bird populations. For their part, hunters buy licenses and stamps, and pay special taxes on hunting gear; this raises millions of dollars for habitat protection and management that benefits all wildlife.

Birds that cannot be hunted legally are considered **nongame wildlife**. This book is mostly about nongame birds.

Each state or district's resources agency keeps a special eye on hundreds of species of birds, animals, reptiles and amphibians. Donations to state Nongame Fish and Wildlife Funds through a special check-off on state income tax forms help the programs conduct important research, protect habitat and help with other management efforts. Ask your parents to show their support for your state's endangered, threatened and nongame wildlife by purchasing a wildlife habitat license plate for their vehicle and/or making a donation.

What's in a Name? Binomial Nomenclature

Some people call this bird a kestrel; some a sparrow hawk; and still others call it a killy hawk, after its call, "killy, killy, killy." So, which is correct? In our region, the official common name of this small falcon is American Kestrel. But a species' common name can be different from

place to place; especially if the people speak a different language. Scientists saw the problem with common names and decided that each living thing needed a name that was exactly the same all over the world. They developed a system of scientific names called **binomial nomenclature** (by-no-me-all no-men-clay-chur).

American Kestrel

Whether you're in Montana or Madagascar, a bird's scientific name is always in the same language: **Latin**. Scientific names are written in *italic*, or slanted, letters. Each scientific name has two words. The first is always capitalized and is the genus, meaning the big group it belongs in. The second word is not capitalized and is the species. The American Kestrel's scientific name is *Falco sparverius*. Knowing this, you're well on your way to becoming a citizen scientist.

13

How to Watch Birds

We live in a big neighborhood. In the Rocky Mountain region, we share our land with wildlife neighbors that depend on us to treat them with respect and care. Here are some tips for successful wildlife watching and being a responsible next-door neighbor to wildlife.

To Find One, Be One

Your best chance of spying on wildlife is by thinking like a bird.

American Bittern

MOVE SLOWLY AND BLEND IN

Sudden movements may startle wildlife. Take a lesson from the American Bittern, a bird found around shallow wetlands and lake edges. The bittern eats small prey such as crayfish, frogs and fish. It catches them by S-L-O-W-L-Y stalking along water edges. The bittern's best moves are almost as slow as the hour hand on a clock. Bitterns also stand still, watching, until dinner swims a little too close . . . gotcha!

Just as moving slowly can help you see more birds, so can blending in. The bittern knows this, too. Its grass-colored feathers are a great disguise. Because part of being a successful wildlife detective is working unnoticed, it's smart to wear drab-colored clothing. Camouflage patterns that match your surroundings work well. Birds will be less likely to see you, and you may get a better look at them.

SHHH . . . BE QUIET, LIKE AN OWL IN FLIGHT

Some birds have very good hearing. If you talk and make noise, they will hear you coming long before you see them. Great Horned Owls are super hunters partly because they keep quiet. Special feathers help them silently swoop down on mice and other small animals. When you're spying on birds, think like an owl and barely make a sound. Some birds also use their feet to feel the vibrations of your footsteps. Walk lightly if you want to spy a bird before it flies away.

KEEP YOUR DISTANCE

If you saw a giant watching you, would your legs feel shaky? Wildlife can feel like this if you get too close. Binoculars and spotting scopes can give you a close-up view from far away. If you're not using binoculars, hold your head still and move only your eyes. Animals do this to spy on YOU.

Using binoculars

LISTEN UP

Bird calls, songs and other sounds can be hard to hear, especially at a distance. To improve your hearing, cup your hands behind your ears. It's amazing what you can hear now!

Wing marks on the snow

If you don't see any birds right away, look for signs they've been in the neighborhood. These include clues such as wood chips scattered around the base of a tree, holes pecked in a soft or decayed tree, droppings, food scraps and empty seed shells, wing marks on the snow, even a stray feather.

FEEDING TIPS

It's fun to feed birds in your backyard. Check the **Today's Special** listing for each species to learn what each bird likes to eat; some include tips on what to put in your backyard feeders.

Snap Photos Safely

Wild birds and animals can be unpredictable. They sometimes move fast, often without you knowing ahead of time. Keep a safe distance away. Many cameras have a zoom lens that allows you to get close-up photos while staying safe.

You may need to remind the adults with you about this safety tip. If your Mom or Dad thinks it would be cute to have a photo of you standing next to an elk, deer or a Canada Goose, tell them to use the zoom lens and leave you out of the picture.

Souvenir Shopping

Souvenirs help us remember fun times. A photograph, drawing, artwork and your own stories are super souvenirs of time afield. Leave everything else in the outdoor neighborhood—including baby animals that look like they're all alone. Resist the temptation to "rescue" them. Chances are, their parents are nearby.

Look But Don't Touch

Your pet hamster may enjoy being picked up, but wild animals do not. Don't try to pet or touch a wild bird or animal; it may become frightened and bite, peck, or scratch. Keep your distance, especially during nesting season.

If you really want to give wildlife a "hug," build a birdhouse or backyard feeder. Leave our natural habitats the way they were when you found them. Then give yourself a pat on the back for being a responsible wildlife neighbor.

When to Watch Birds

Day, night, summer, winter. **When is the best time to spy on birds?**
Look for the **clues**.

Birds Move When they are the least likely to be seen and caught by a predator; their food is available; they need the most energy and refueling; and when they need to, according to the changing seasons.

DAYTIME = DIURNAL

Birds that are active during the day and sleep at night are called diurnal. Why daytime? Think like the bird. For example, hummingbirds are active during the day because the flowers that hold the nectar they need only open in sunlight.

TWILIGHT = CREPUSCULAR

Many animals are active at dawn (when the sun is just coming up) and at dusk (when the sun is going down). Why dawn and dusk? There is enough light for the animals to see where they need to go, but not enough for some predators to hunt them. At twilight they appear like faint shadows.

NIGHTTIME = NOCTURNAL

Birds that are active at night and sleep during the day are called nocturnal. These animals have special adaptations for being up all night. Owls have excellent hearing and special nighttime and daytime vision.

Journaling and Phenology

Phenology is the study of the seasonal changes and movements of nature. The return of the first robin in spring; the migration of monarch butterflies; the first and last snow of the year; and the first ground squirrel you spy after winter hibernation, are all part of phenology in the Rocky Mountain region of the U.S. Wildlife biologists and ornithologists use phenology records to help them understand the needs and behaviors of birds.

You can be a part of ongoing wildlife studies by keeping a journal. It's as simple as writing in a notebook or on a calendar. Get started with the journal section beginning on page 188. Journals are fun to look back on. Plus, your addition to the records of the Rocky Mountain region of the U.S. could help scientific research. Be a citizen scientist.

Let's start a journal to record your adventures as an outdoor detective!
SEE HOW MANY BIRDS YOU CAN FIND

YOU MIGHT INCLUDE:
- size, shape, field marks
- type of bill and feet
- shape of wings and tail
- feather color and pattern

Sample Journal Entry

Today I was looking in my binoculars and I saw a female robin feeding her chicks. They were in my neighbor's tree on 5/13/12. The chicks were small and gray. They had bright yellow beaks. The female was brown with an orange belly, feet and beak. Her nest was made of sticks and twigs. She was very cool.

OTHER NOTES YOU MAY WANT TO INCLUDE:
- Date, time and habitat
- What the bird was doing (behavior)
- Song/call
- Alone, pair or group of birds
- Flight pattern
- Other signs, like tracks, scat (droppings), nests, eggs, wood chips, wing marks in snow, ice crystals from a snow-borne

188

State Birds

Colorado: Lark Bunting

When the Lark Bunting was adopted as the state bird of Colorado in 1931, the short-grass prairies where it nests were more common, and so too was this sparrow-sized bird. Explore the state's eastern grassland from April to September and get to know the showy black-and-white male and the camouflaged gray-brown female. Listen to their whistling song and you will know why they were chosen to represent this sunny state.

Idaho: Mountain Bluebird (page 82)

Montana: Western Meadowlark (page 118)

Wyoming: Western Meadowlark (page 118)

Seasons

Understanding how the changing seasons affect the birds of the Rocky Mountain region will bring you wildlife watching success.

SPRING

Once the ice leaves the wetlands, lakes, and rivers (generally in March), listen and watch overhead for returning birds. Look for waterfowl and hawks to lead the way. Shorebirds and songbirds arrive in April and May with warblers close behind. Birds that overwinter in the region begin to move to higher elevations. Birds are busy in the spring finding a date and a mate. This is when males defend their territory, sing and do an array of tricks to attract a female. It's a very entertaining time of year!

SUMMER

Summer Gross Factor On hot summer days, some birds excrete waste down their legs to help cool them through evaporation. Gross, but cool!

In summer, birds are busy breeding, nesting and raising their young. Shhh . . . by mid July it quiets down. In some species, males leave the nesting area in late July or early August for a quiet place where they can molt (shed) their bright breeding feathers and grow in duller colored plumage. They are ready for flight in time for migration.

FALL

By July and August, Canadian birds, including shorebirds, begin to pass through on their migration south. Warblers and songbirds are generally next in line. They are joined by some

17

resident birds. Many species begin to group up in large migratory flocks and feed heavily in preparation for migration. During September–November, raptor and waterfowl migration is in high gear along the Central Flyway. Birds that stick around for the winter may take advantage of the more favorable winter conditions at lower elevations and migrate down the mountain rather than migrating south of the Rocky Mountain region entirely.

WINTER

To beat the cold, birds grow an extra layer of feathers for the winter, like putting on a winter coat. Some will also fluff out their feathers to create more air pockets, which trap heat close to their bodies. Others lower their body temperatures at night to reduce the amount of energy (and food) needed to keep warm.

Another strategy is to make a group huddle—there's warmth in numbers! And some birds sit on their legs, or tuck a leg and foot, one at a time, into their warm body feathers.

How do the tiny legs of chickadees keep from freezing in the winter? Instead of having their veins and arteries separated by muscle like we do, theirs are side by side in their legs. The warm blood coming from their heart is right next to the cool blood flowing back to it from their legs. Heat exchanges between them!

Speaking of legs, some birds grow extra feathers around their legs and feet, or extra scales on the outside edge of their feet, for use as snowshoes to stay on top of deep snow!

Because food supplies often run low in winter, some bird species store food in bark cracks, crevices and tree cavities. Others bulk up (gain fat) in the fall in preparation for the extra energy demands of winter, while some bulk up before night and refuel the next day.

Because there is less competition for nest sites and food then, some hardy birds may take advantage of the situation and begin nesting in winter.

Migration

THE ROCKY MOUNTAIN REGION'S FIVE MIGRATION PATTERNS

Boreal migrants live in Canada but come south into the northern U.S. when their northern food supply is short.

Permanent residents are birds that stick it out and stay in the region all year.

Short-distance migrants go just far enough south to avoid the extreme temperatures of Rocky Mountain region winters and return to breed in the spring. They travel to wintering grounds as far south as Texas.

Mid-distance migrants breed in (or north of) the Rocky Mountain region and migrate to wintering areas in Mexico and Central America.

Long-distance migrants breed here, but migrate to wintering areas in South America. These migrants travel up to thousands of miles on their way from the Rocky Mountain region to their wintering grounds.

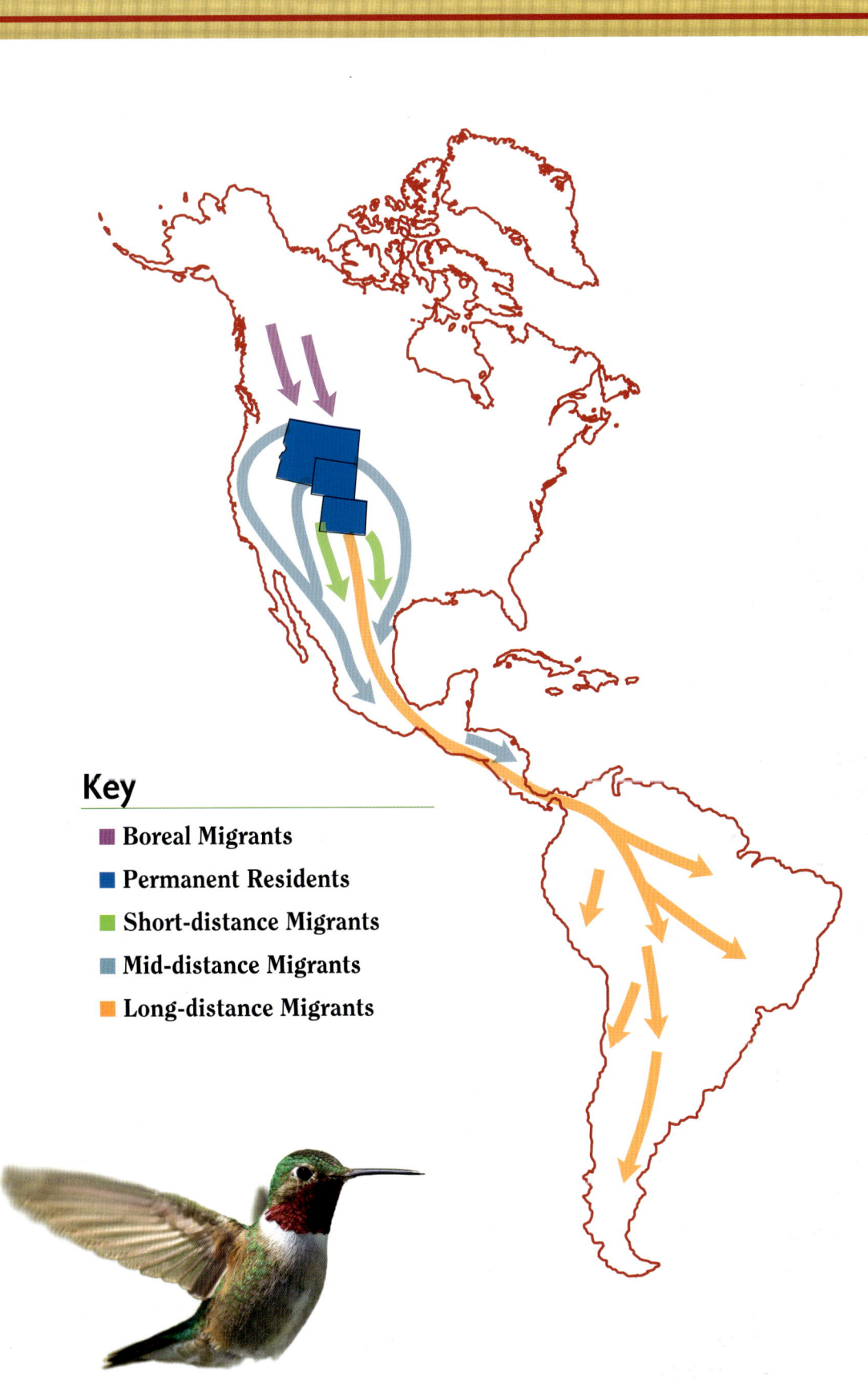

Key

- ■ Boreal Migrants
- ■ Permanent Residents
- ■ Short-distance Migrants
- ■ Mid-distance Migrants
- ■ Long-distance Migrants

Where to Watch Birds

Make bird identification easy on yourself. Narrow down the possibilities by first knowing a bird's habitat. After all, it is of little use looking for a Rock Wren in a lake or a bird that dives in water, like an American Dipper, in a grassland!

Rocky Mountain Region Habitats

Have you noticed that some wild places look different than others? Some have few or no trees at all, others are covered with trees, and some are a mixture of trees, shrubs, grass, or rocky outcrops. That is because the Rocky Mountain region of the U.S. has different types of ecological systems, or habitats. In each of these habitats, a combination of the elevation (the rise in the land), climate (weather, seasons and precipitation), geography, land history and soil support different kinds of wild plants and animals.

Elevation is especially important when it comes to habitats in the Rocky Mountain region. Generally, hiking up a mountain is like going north: every 1,000 feet higher in elevation is similar to traveling 600 miles north. For example, at mid-mountain elevation you find the moderate temperatures and conditions of an aspen parkland forest, but head up the mountain 2000 feet (equal to 1,200 miles north) and you are in the alpine tundra of the mountain peak, with conditions similar to the cold and windswept Canadian tundra. Instead of migrating, some species simply change elevation in order to change habitat. Also, in general terms, the western slopes of the mountain range are wetter than the eastern slopes, where there are greater extremes in seasonal temperatures.

ALPINE TUNDRA is found at the highest mountain elevations above timberline.

SUBALPINE FORESTS are found at mid to high elevations.

MONTANE FORESTS and **ASPEN PARKLAND FORESTS** are found mixed at lower to mid mountain elevations and foothills.

WATER HABITATS are found scattered throughout the region.

GRASSLANDS are found mainly at the base of mountains and surrounding plains while steep **CLIFFS** and **CANYONS** are found throughout the region.

FANTASTIC FOUR

To make identifying bird habitats easier *Wild About Rocky Mountain Birds* has simplified the habitats into four sections based on elevation, moisture and plant communities: alpine and subalpine; montane and aspen parkland forests; grasslands, cliffs and canyons; and wetlands, rivers, lakes and shores. The 70 birds in this book appear in the habitat section where you are most likely to see them. Of course, many can live in more than one habitat and habitats can mingle or overlap. Some birds are able to live almost anywhere. We have called these species "Super Adaptors." Can you find birds in all of the habitats of the Rocky Mountain region?

HIGHS AND LOWS

Most birds are more often found—or easier to see—at different levels in their habitat. For example, you're more likely to see a Wilson's Snipe strutting across a wet meadow than soaring through the air. But just the opposite is true if you're looking for a Cooper's Hawk. To help you know where to look, a large picture at the beginning of each section shows the habitat. Silhouettes of each bird species are placed within it where you're most likely to see them, particularly during the day. The silhouettes don't always indicate where a bird spends most of its time. Some show where the bird is easiest to see. Common Nighthawks can be tough to spot when they are perched amid the gravel of a city roof or a rocky canyon ledge. But they're hard to miss when they fly in hunt of insects at dawn and dusk—especially with their boomerang-shaped wings.

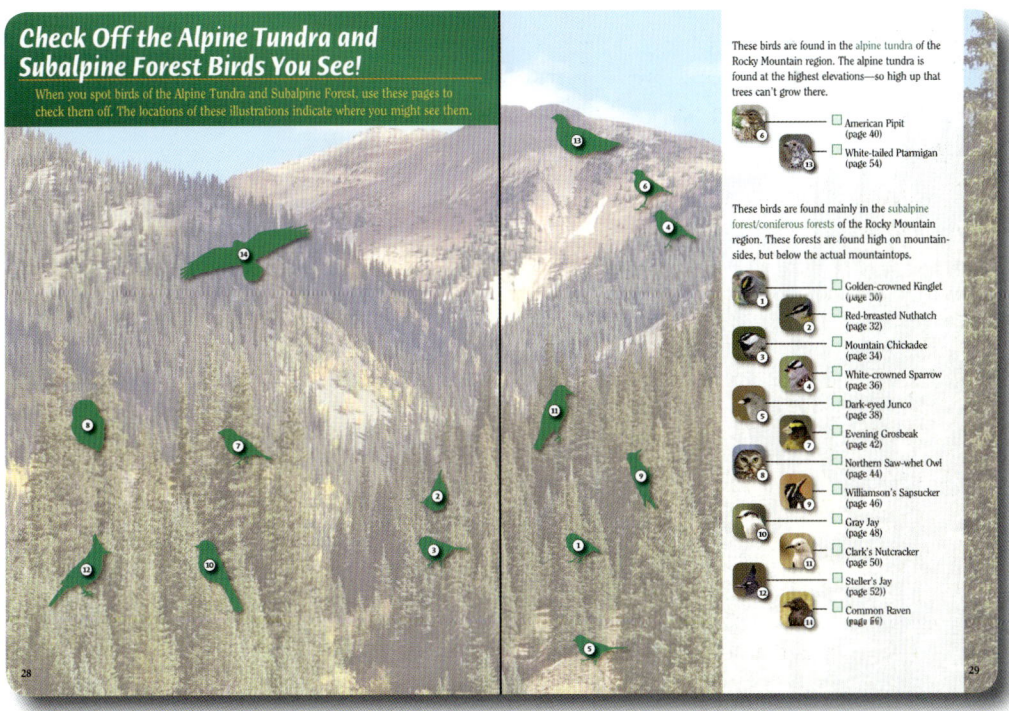

Check Off the Alpine Tundra and Subalpine Forest Birds You See!

When you spot birds of the Alpine Tundra and Subalpine Forest, use these pages to check them off. The locations of these illustrations indicate where you might see them.

These birds are found in the alpine tundra of the Rocky Mountain region. The alpine tundra is found at the highest elevations—so high up that trees can't grow there.

- American Pipit (page 40)
- White-tailed Ptarmigan (page 54)

These birds are found mainly in the subalpine forest/coniferous forests of the Rocky Mountain region. These forests are found high on mountainsides, but below the actual mountaintops.

- Golden-crowned Kinglet (page 30)
- Red-breasted Nuthatch (page 32)
- Mountain Chickadee (page 34)
- White-crowned Sparrow (page 36)
- Dark-eyed Junco (page 38)
- Evening Grosbeak (page 42)
- Northern Saw-whet Owl (page 44)
- Williamson's Sapsucker (page 46)
- Gray Jay (page 48)
- Clark's Nutcracker (page 50)
- Steller's Jay (page 52))
- Common Raven (page 56)

Alpine Tundra and Subalpine Forest

Alpine Tundra and Subalpine Forest

Montane Forest and Aspen Parkland Forest

Grasslands, Canyons and Cliffs Habitat

Wetlands, Rivers, Lakes and Shores

Sample Page

Common Name
The name used most often in the Rocky Mountain region of the U.S.

Scientific Name
Universally identifiable, two-part name originating in Latin or Greek.

Size
Measurements from the bill tip to the tip of the tail and wingtip to wingtip.

Photo
Most large photos are of a male in breeding plumage.

Field Marks
Identifying characteristics, including unique colors, feather patterns, and bill, wing, feet and tail shapes that help you distinguish one species from another.

Birdsong and Other Sounds
Information about calls, songs and other sounds the bird makes—and what they mean.

Hairy Woodpecker
Picoides villosus
Length: 7–10 inches (18–26 cm)
Wingspan: 13–16 inches (33–41 cm)

Male has a red band across the back of head

female

Black above with white center stripe

White underneath

The long, thin white feathers in the middle of its back give this bird its name

Black wings and tail

"Drum, drum." This is used to declare territory, to call out to a mate, call out a location, or to react to an intruder.

Hairy vs Downy
Hairy and Downy Woodpeckers are nearly twins. Look for these clues to tell them apart. The Hairy is larger. Its bill is as long as its head and it does not have any marks on its outer tail feathers. The sparrow-sized Downy is a petite member of the woodpecker family that can find food in smaller spaces than its cousins. Its bill is shorter than its head and it has black wings with white spots. Their drumming patterns sound different and these sounds reflect their sizes. The larger Hairy has a louder, slower, and more irregular drum. Its rattle call is lower pitched and more forceful than the Downy's. Whether you are watching a Hairy or a Downy, you are sure to have a wood-erful time!

88

Bird Facts
Interesting natural history information, bird watching manners and tips for success.

Habitat Café

What a bird eats, how much it needs and when the food is available.

Habitat Café

Yumm . . . bring an order of insects and spiders with a small side order of seeds and fruit, and a sip of tree sap. Hairy Woodpeckers are mainly insectivores. They tap a tree with their bill to find an insect tunnel and then chisel to reach the insects. They rake them in with their long barbed tongue (up to four times the length of their bill). Their tongue is curled inside their head like a tape measure!

SPRING, SUMMER, FALL, WINTER MENU:
Insects and some seeds, fruit

Life Cycle

NEST Both the female and male make the nesting hole in a tree with a decayed center, 5–40 feet above the ground. The outside hole is about 2½ inches high and 2 inches wide. The inside of the nest cavity is 10–12 inches deep and 4½ inches in diameter. The eggs are laid directly on the wood chips.

EGGS About 1 inch long. The parents take turns incubating the clutch of 3–6 eggs for 11–12 days.

MOM! DAD! Altricial. The chicks depend on Mom and Dad to bring meals of regurgitated (spit up) insects until they are ready for whole insects.

NESTLING Woodpecker chicks have a heel pad that protects their feet from the rough nest edges. The pad is shed once they leave the nest.

FLEDGLING The young birds can fly and leave the nest at about one month of age.

JUVENILE The following spring they are mature enough to find a mate, excavate a nest hole, and raise their own young woodpeckers.

Do the Math

How many drumbeats can a woodpecker drum? A lot. If they make 15 drumbeats in one second, how may drumbeats can a woodpecker drum in one minute? Ten minutes? (Put your answer here, _____.) How do woodpeckers drum without getting a big headache? Shock absorbers: strong neck muscles and an extra thick skull help cushion the brain. The answers are on pages 194–195.

When

Diurnal. Hairy Woodpeckers are active during the day and rest at night.

Migration

Permanent resident. Hairy Woodpeckers stay in the Rocky Mountain region of the US all year.

Nesting

Hairy Woodpecker females stay in their nesting territory all year. The male joins her in late winter. They begin actual nesting activity in April–May in the Rocky Mountain region of the US.

Getting Around

How do they stay on a tree while drilling or searching for insects? Their toes are zygodactyl: two toes point forward and two point backward. Their long, curved claws are super for getting a tight grip. Their stiff tail feathers act as a brace against the tree trunk and as a spring to help them move forward as they hitch up a tree. Their flight is undulating (up and down) in a series of wing flaps and then a bound forward.

Where to Look

Look for Hairy Woodpeckers in the deciduous and coniferous forests throughout the Rocky Mountain region.

Year-round Migration	Summer Winter

Montane & Aspen Parkland Forest 89

When

Times when the bird is active. A bird can be active during the night (nocturnal), during the day (diurnal) or at twilight (crepuscular).

Migration

Does this bird migrate or stick around? If it migrates, look here to see when it arrives in spring, when it leaves in fall and where it spends the winter.

Nesting

When the bird starts nesting and lays its eggs.

Getting Around

Find out if this bird flies, hops, glides, dives, wades or soars.

Where to Look

A range map and notes offer tips on specific locations to look. Use the extra space below to write down where you spotted each bird.

History Hangout, Birding Tip, Do the Math, Did You Know? and Gross Factor.

Here you'll find interesting facts, math questions, ideas for better bird watching and gross (but fun) bird facts. (The answers to the math questions are provided on pages 194–195.)

Life Cycle

Includes details about the entire lifespan of the bird, including nesting habits, information about the number and size of eggs each species lays, fun facts about what goes on in the nest and how nestlings and fledgling birds survive, the role of parents (or adults of the same species that act as caretakers) in a chick's early life, and the final stages of adolescence a bird goes through before becoming an adult.

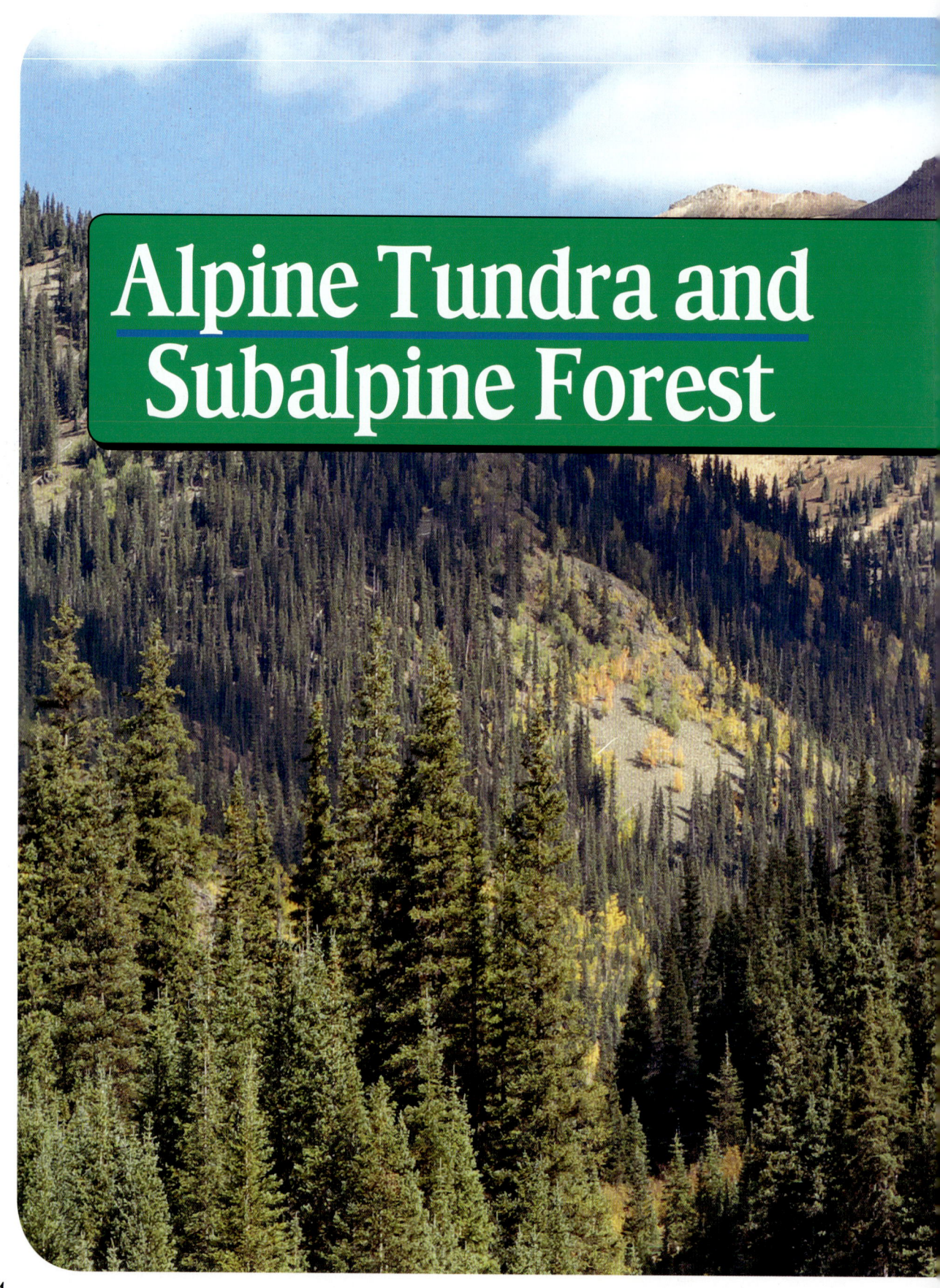

Alpine Tundra and Subalpine Forest

24

Take to the mountaintops to find the amazing birds that have adapted to survive the quickly changing weather, wind, extreme differences in temperatures, and the short summer growing season found in the Alpine Tundra and Subalpine Forest.

Land Before Time

Explore the Rocky Mountains and walk on rock from well before even the dinosaurs! You can read the history written in the mountain rocks and travel back in time 3 billion years. The stories tell of an ancient supercontinent, volcanoes and mountains that formed and then moved or wore away; you can even hold up fossils of inland sea plants and animals, and ancient "basement" rock heaved up to the earth's surface by powerful forces.

More recently, the region's history is dominated by mountains; over the past 180 million years, the land has risen and fallen, and been shaped by the action of the glaciers and of forces from deep within the earth. This is an ongoing process, and time is still working on the Rocky Mountain range of the western United States and Canada. The power of the earth deep underground, wind and water make changes each day.

Above Treeline: Alpine Tundra

The harsh conditions found at the highest elevations (upper heights) of the Rocky Mountains limit life to a small group of plants and animals. The alpine tundra habitat is located above the treeline—no trees live there. The

Alpine tundra

plant life that survives here has adapted to the wind, extreme temperatures, short two-month growing season, and lack of true soil. The flowering plants and grasses are less than 6 inches tall and grow in tight, thick groups. The nearly flat lichens (small, leathery plants) grow on the rocks. There is even a watermelon-pink algae that grows at the edges of melting snow!

The American Pipit is just as amazing: it builds its nest tucked under a rock ledge and eats insects found in the short plants. In a seasonal camouflage act, the summer brown plumage (feathers) of the White-tailed Ptarmigan changes to white once snow covers the mountaintop. The grouse grows feathers on its feet as snowshoes and digs into a snow burrow for a warm snooze.

Treeline: Subalpine Forest

The next level down the mountain in elevation is the edge of the treeline, where the subalpine forests begin. This is the highest point where trees can live on the mountain. The coniferous trees growing at these high elevations are well adapted to the patchy, shallow soils that are low in nutrients, to the short growing season, cold and heavy snowfall.

Subalpine forest

Their shallow roots take nutrients (minerals) from the topsoil. A wax coating protects their needles from the extreme cold and winds. The needles stay dark green and do not all fall off each year. This saves the tree energy and provides more time to turn sunlight and water into plant energy (photosynthesis). Conifers are tough, too: their branches can bend with heavy snowfall.

In the subalpine forests the miniature Golden-crowned Kinglet can be found eating tiny insects from the branches of spruce and fir trees. Clark's Nutcrackers and Steller's Jays are busy hiding pine seeds for winter. New forests will grow from the leftovers. Nesting in tree cavities in the mid-level of the forests are the small Northern Saw-whet Owls, while a Mountain Bluebird scans a subalpine meadow for insects from its forest edge perch.

Hiking the Heights

Mountain Chickadee

Prepare for a true alpine experience at the high elevations of the Rocky Mountains where many of the birds featured in this section can be found. To see them, visit a state or national park or forest for a look at Mountain Chickadees, Red-breasted Nuthatches and White-crowned Sparrows. Be safe about mountain hiking and venture out only with someone that knows the area.

Check Off the Alpine Tundra and Subalpine Forest Birds You See!

When you spot birds of the Alpine Tundra and Subalpine Forest, use these pages to check them off. The locations of these illustrations indicate where you might see them.

These birds are found in the alpine tundra of the Rocky Mountain region. The alpine tundra is found at the highest elevations—so high up that trees can't grow there.

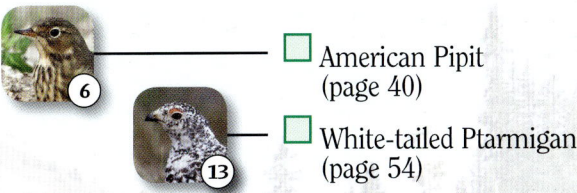

☐ American Pipit (page 40)

☐ White-tailed Ptarmigan (page 54)

These birds are found mainly in the subalpine forest/coniferous forests of the Rocky Mountain region. These forests are found high on mountainsides, but below the actual mountaintops.

☐ Golden-crowned Kinglet (page 30)

☐ Red-breasted Nuthatch (page 32)

☐ Mountain Chickadee (page 34)

☐ White-crowned Sparrow (page 36)

☐ Dark-eyed Junco (page 38)

☐ Evening Grosbeak (page 42)

☐ Northern Saw-whet Owl (page 44)

☐ Williamson's Sapsucker (page 46)

☐ Gray Jay (page 48)

☐ Clark's Nutcracker (page 50)

☐ Steller's Jay (page 52)

☐ Common Raven (page 56)

Golden-crowned Kinglet

Regulus satrapa

Length: 3–4½ inches (8–11 cm)
Wingspan: 5½–7 inches (14–18 cm)

Males have a small yellow-orange king's crown with a black border

Females have a gold crown

Black eye line with white eyebrow

Wings have two white wing bars

Olive green above and pale gray below

"Tsooo-tsooo-tsooo-tsooo-tsooo-tsooo-whip-lipalip!" is the male saying, "This is my territory!"

Royalty in Miniature

Challenge on. Consider it worth honing your detective skills to spy a Golden-crowned Kinglet in the spruce and fir forests of the Rocky Mountains. To succeed, think in miniature. These tiny birds eat tiny insects at the ends of branches and in bark cracks. Weighing no more than two pennies and barely the size of a man's thumb, some kinglets stay all winter. As physics has it, the smaller the animal, the faster it cools. Kinglets maintain a body temperature about 5°F (3°C) higher than most birds, requiring even more heat-making fuel. To survive cold nights, they feed heavily during the day to store energy, huddle in groups, and may lower their evening body temperature.

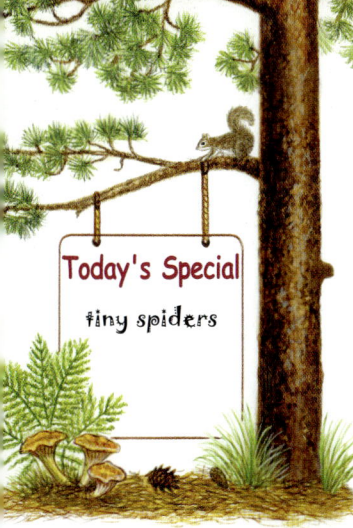

Habitat Café

Yumm . . . bring an order of tiny, soft-bodied spiders, gnats, aphids, beetles, bugs and ants with a side order of sap. Golden-crowned Kinglets are insectivores. Kinglets hop along conifer and shrub branches and even hang upside down to find insects at all levels of the forest, except the ground.

Today's Special
tiny spiders

SPRING, SUMMER, FALL MENU:
🐜 Insects and insect eggs

WINTER MENU:
🐜 Dormant insects

Life Cycle

NEST Both parents build the small, deep, sock-like nest 25–65 feet above the ground, hidden on the end of a spruce or fir branch. They weave birch bark, mosses and lichen together with spiderweb silk and line it with animal fur and feathers. The nest is so narrow that the eggs are laid in layers.

EGGS About ½ inch long. The female incubates the clutch of 5–11 eggs for 14–15 days. The large number of eggs offsets their short average lifespan of 2 years, which is due in large part to extreme winter conditions.

MOM! DAD! Altricial. Mom keeps the young safe by brooding them at shorter and shorter periods as they grow.

NESTLING Chicks are fed spiders and small insects by both parents.

FLEDGLING The stretchy nest expands to hold the growing chicks. There is a limit, and at about 18–19 days of age the chicks squeeze out of the nest pouch.

JUVENILE Golden-crowned Kinglets are mature enough to nest and raise their own young the following spring.

Did You Know?

Kinglets lose heat from their featherless bill, eyes, legs and feet. To keep warm, they fluff out their feathers so that they have an inch-thick layer of insulation. When at rest, they tuck their head and feet into their fluffed feathers. There can be a difference of up to 78 degrees between a kinglet's inside temperature and the air outside of its body. For this thumb-sized animal, that is an amazing feat!

When

Golden-crowned kinglets are diurnal. They feed during the day, rest at night and migrate by day and night.

Migration

Spring Arrival: Mar–Apr
Fall Departure: Sep–Nov
Permanent resident to short-distance migrant. In the fall some join mixed-species flocks and move to lower elevations and some migrate to milder temperatures in the southern U.S. and into northeastern Mexico.

Nesting

Golden-crowned Kinglets begin nesting in May–June in the Rocky Mountain region.

Getting Around

Nearly always in motion, they flit quickly and directly from branch to branch, jerking their wings in nervous flight. To find insect prey, they search underneath leaves, twigs and small branches by hanging upside down.

Where to Look

Subalpine spruce and fir forests of the Rocky Mountain region during nesting season. Some move to the coniferous forests of lower elevations in winter.

Year-round / Migration — Summer / Winter

Red-breasted Nuthatch

Sitta canadensis

Length: 4–4½ inches (11 cm)
Wingspan: 7–8 inches (18–20 cm)

female

Female wears a gray cap and gray eye-stripe; red color below is pale

Blue-gray above and red-cinnamon below

Juveniles look like pale versions of adults

Male wears a black cap

Black eyes hidden in a black stripe; white eyebrow stripe

White chin

"Yank, yank!"
Both male and female make this call.

Fancy Forest Footwork

Head up, head down, turn around . . . How does a Red-breasted Nuthatch perform this fancy footwork? It has specially designed feet and toes. The first toe (hallux) is pointed to the back and the other three toes are jointed at the base and pointed forward. Like a mountaineer uses a pick when climbing up or down a steep slope, a nuthatch uses its hallux (first toe). While one foot is being moved, the hallux on the other foot is mounted into tree bark like a pick for support. When you see a nuthatch upside down and headfirst, be amazed, he/she is an experienced climber!

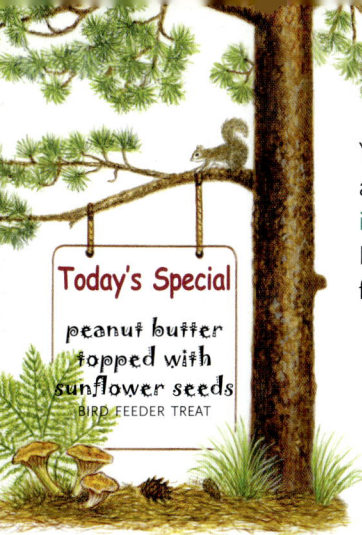

Habitat Café

Yumm . . . bring an order of forest insects and seeds. Red-breasted Nuthatches are insectivores and granivores (seed eaters). Fill your bird feeders with seeds and suet for these backyard visitors.

Today's Special

peanut butter
topped with
sunflower seeds

BIRD FEEDER TREAT

SPRING, SUMMER, FALL MENU:
Mostly insects, some seeds

WINTER MENU:
More seeds than summer, but still mostly insects

Life Cycle

NEST Both parents hollow out a hole in a soft branch or stub of a dead tree, 5–40 feet above the ground. They may recycle a woodpecker hole. This deep hole is built up with shredded bark, grass and leaves. Mom lines the nest with feathers, fur and moss and puts a mat of sticky tree sap around the hole to keep out predators.

EGGS Almost ¾ inch long. The female incubates the clutch of 4–7 eggs for 12 days.

MOM! DAD! Altricial. With gummy resin around the nest hole, parents do not enter the nest after the first week. Instead, the young open their beaks close to the entrance hole for food delivery. Chicks poke their little rumps out of the nest for fecal sac (diaper) pick-up.

NESTLING Just before the young leave the nest, Mom and Dad put clumps of mammal fur on the sticky resin of the entrance hole.

FLEDGLING They leave the nest at about three weeks of age.

JUVENILE They search out other teens to form flocks during winter months.

Gross Factor

What is that white stuff on your car window? Bird droppings. Three kinds of wastes leave a bird's body in one package. The dark part is the feces (food waste from the intestine). The white part includes urates and urine, two kinds of waste filtered from the blood by the kidneys. Birds have the ability to conserve water by making their urine concentrated and chalky rather than liquid. Berry- and seed-eaters may have purple or green droppings. Insect- or animal-eaters often have darker brown parts to their droppings. Gross.

When
Diurnal. They feed during the day and rest at night.

Migration
Permanent resident to short-distance migrant moving around the subalpine forests with the changing seasons. In fall, winter and early spring they move to wooded areas with the most food sources, especially cone seeds. They return to their breeding areas in the spring to nest. In some years, birds from Canada move south into the Rocky Mountain region in search of seeds from cones. These irruptions (large temporary increases in numbers) may occur in 2–3 year cycles.

Nesting
The Red-breasted Nuthatch begins nesting in late April–May.

Getting Around
Zooming through the forests, this bird stops only to pick up a seed or insect. It wedges the seed in a tree bark crack and hacks it open with blows from its sharp bill. Zoooom, it is off again in its fast, short flight to another tree!

Where to Look
The subalpine and montane coniferous forests. Will visit backyard winter bird feeders.

Year-round
Migration

Summer
Winter

Alpine Tundra and Subalpine Forests

33

Mountain Chickadee

Poecile gambeli

Length: 4½–5½ (11–14 cm)
Wingspan: 7–8 inches (18–20 cm)

Black cap,
eye-stripe, bib

White cheeks and
forehead stripe

Males and females
look alike

Gray sides

"Fee—Bee, Fee—Bee!"
is how males say,
"This is MY territory."

Hide-and-Seek

Mountain Chickadees play some serious hide and seek when it comes to surviving the cold temperatures of winter in the high mountains. They hide conifer seeds in late summer and fall and then seek their cached (stored) meal when the weather is too cold or snowy for hunting. They beat the cold with other games as well. Chickadees can gain 10 percent of their weight in body fat before nightfall. They use this fatty fuel overnight and rebuild it again the next day. In another move, their body temperature may lower at night, using far less fuel to stay warm!

Habitat Café

Yumm . . . bring an order of insects, insect larvae and eggs with a side of coniferous tree seeds sprinkled with berries. Mountain Chickadees are omnivorous. They glean insects from coniferous trees and carry them in their small, pointed black bill.

Today's Special
spiders

SPRING AND SUMMER MENU:
 Mostly insects, with some seeds and berries

FALL AND WINTER MENU:
 More seeds, some insects, berries

Life Cycle

NEST The nest cavity is often a natural hole in the soft, rotten wood of a tree trunk, or an abandoned woodpecker hole. The female lines the cavity with wood chips, lichen, grass or moss and then makes a nest cup of animal fur. More fur is snuggled on top of the eggs. They will also use a man-made nest box.

 **EGGS** About ½ inch long. The female incubates the clutch of 7–9 white eggs for 14–15 days. She may eat the eggshells once the chicks have hatched. Yum, calcium.

MOM! DAD! Altricial. Both parents feed the newly hatched, blind and naked chicks. Delivering over 20 meals per hour can keep a parent bird very busy. For each meal there is a fecal sac (diaper) to carry away.

NESTLING The chicks are defended from predators by their parents' loud "Chick-a-Dee" calls.

FLEDGLING At 3 weeks of age, they leave the nest and soon fly. They stay near their parents for another few weeks and beg for food. This works for a while, but in time the parents no longer provide meals.

JUVENILE They leave their parents' area to join a winter flock. They are ready to mate and raise their own young the following spring.

Did You Know?

Do chickadees remember where they store their snacks? Research shows that during the fall, chickadees can produce new brain cells to handle the additional memory needed to recover the cached (stored) food in winter. They likely do not remember where every seed is hidden. This allows other wildlife to benefit from their efforts. During spruce budworm outbreaks, foresters thank the chickadees for all the insects that they eat.

When

Mountain Chickadees are diurnal. They feed during the day and rest at night.

Migration

Permanent residents. During years when food sources are scarce they may move to lower elevations where food is more plentiful. Juveniles are the more common local migrants.

Nesting

Mountain Chickadees begin nesting in April–May in the Rocky Mountain region.

Getting Around

Mountain Chickadees hop from branch to branch. They may cling to conifer needles right-side-up and hang upside down on needles and limbs while searching for insects. Short flights between trees are quick. Look for the chickadee's bill to point up when it lands, making a "V" with its body. It quickly lowers its tail for balance. On cold mornings, they warm in a place out of the wind and in the sun.

Where to Look

Subalpine and montane coniferous forests. They may move to lower elevations in winter to locate food sources. May visit backyard bird feeders all year.

Year-round Summer
Migration Winter

Alpine Tundra and Subalpine Forests

35

White-crowned Sparrow

Zonotrichia leucophrys

Length: 6 inches (15 cm)
Wingspan: 8½–9½ inches (21–24 cm)

White crown with two dark stripes

Dark eye stripe

Pink bill

Male and female look alike

Back and wings with brown streaks

Gray overall with light throat and abdomen

Brown tail and rump

"Whistle, buzz, thrillllll!" A male's song can have its own local sound.

Night Migration

White-crowned Sparrows sleep at night. During migration they become night owls and travel by starlight. Do they sleep during migration? To find an answer, scientists put the sparrows in a laboratory that mimicked the natural light-and-dark cycles of the seasons. The birds' behavior was captured by video and their sleep-wake times recorded. The birds spent less time sleeping at night during the spring and fall seasons, called "migratory restlessness." The loss of sleep did not change how alert they were. Changes in the amount of daylight cause changes in body chemicals, called hormones. Hormone levels may be why some bird species store extra fat and get "restless" just before migration.

Habitat Café

Yumm . . . bring an order of seeds, beetles, bees, bugs and ants with a small side order of berries. White-crowned Sparrows are omnivorous. They will visit bird feeders and need to drink water often. Keep your bird bath filled and fresh!

Today's Special
caterpillars

SPRING, SUMMER, FALL MENU:
 Insects and seeds

WINTER MENU:
 Seeds, buds, grass, fruits with some insects

Life Cycle

NEST The female builds the nest cup on the ground in a clump of grasses or at the base of a bush or low coniferous tree. The outer cup is made of fine twigs, grass stems, conifer needles and moss, and is lined with feathers, fine grasses and mammal fur.

EGGS About ¾ inch long. The female incubates the 4–5 camou-flaged eggs for 12–13 days. She may eat the eggshells once the chicks hatch. Yum, calcium.

MOM! DAD! Altricial. Within ten minutes of hatching, the naked and helpless chicks hold their bills wide open for food. Both parents capture and deliver many high protein (insect) meals. Chick diapers are either eaten by the parents or carried away from the nest.

NESTLING Mom stays on the nest to keep the chicks warm until they grow feathers. When she's off the nest, the chicks huddle together.

FLEDGLING They are ready to leave the nest at 9–10 days of age and run along the ground and take short flights. They are fed by their parents for another week until they can find food on their own.

JUVENILE They are mature enough the following spring to nest and raise their own young sparrows.

Unsolved Mystery

Science is about solving mysteries. Using the same scientific method you use to do a science fair project, scientists pose a question and hypothesis, design experiments to test it and study the results (data). Did the results answer the question or provide clues? What is the conclusion? Scientists use the new information to make our world a better place to live. Detective work is waiting for you. Enter your school science fair and solve a mystery.

When

White-crowned Sparrows are diurnal. They feed during the day and rest at night.

Migration

Spring Arrival: Apr–May
Fall Departure: Aug–Sep
Short-distance migrant to the southwestern United States and northern Mexico. Arrive in the spring to low elevations and then move higher as snow melts. Migrate by day and night.

Nesting

White-crowned Sparrows begin nesting in May in the Rocky Mountain region in areas with a patchy mix of bare ground, grass, and dense, low shrubs. The male may perch and declare his territory on a tall coniferous tree nearby.

Getting Around

White-crowned Sparrows hop from branch to branch and on the ground when searching for food. Scales on the bottom of their feet allow them to grip tree branches.

Where to Look

In the Rocky Mountain region White-crowned Sparrows are found in the mountains at the edge of the alpine tundra, just below timberline in low shrubby bushes and in alpine meadows.

Year-round   Summer
Migration   Winter

Alpine Tundra and Subalpine Forests

Dark-eyed Junco

Junco hyemalis

Length: 5½–6½ inches (14–16 cm)
Wingspan: 7–10 inches (18–25 cm)

pink-sided

Pink-sided Juncos wear a blue-gray hood, are black around the eyes (lores), and have pinkish sides (flanks), and white outer tail feathers

Bill is pale orange-pink

Males are dark gray with a white belly

White outer tail feathers; "Signal of white—a Junco in flight"

"Hack" means "This is my territory." Both males and females give this defense call in all seasons.

Zelda-like Battles

Watch your bird feeders for flocks of 10–20 Dark-eyed Juncos during their fall and spring migration. Pick out the dominant head honcho of the flock. This male sleeks down his head and neck feathers, pushes his neck out and leaps toward other males. The little guys give in or get pecked on the head. Ouch! When two flocks meet, the head honchos may have a battle. The winner is decided in a "head dance." The two males meet face-to-face with legs and heads stretched tall and bills pointed to the sky. *Kew. Kew.* Clawing and using their bills as swords, they have a standoff, spreading their tails like peacocks. Watching this could be better than a game of Zelda. Game on!

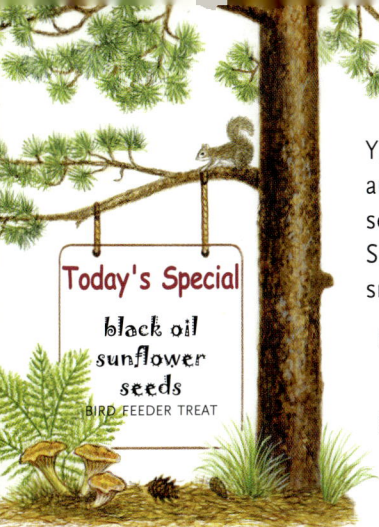

Habitat Café

Yumm . . . bring an order of grasshoppers, ants, beetles, caterpillars, spiders and weed seeds. Dark-eyed Juncos are omnivorous. Scatter white proso millet on the ground or snow. Watch for juncos!

Today's Special
black oil sunflower seeds
BIRD FEEDER TREAT

SPRING MENU:
 More insects than seeds

SUMMER, FALL, WINTER MENU:
 Mostly seeds, some insects

Life Cycle

NEST The female builds the nest cup on the ground hidden in thick weeds or up to 8 feet above the ground in a tree or bush. She weaves grass, bark strips, moss and twigs together for the base of the nest cup. It is lined with fine grass, rootlets and mammal fur.

EGGS About ¾ inch long. The female incubates the clutch of 3–5 eggs for 12–13 days. Mom may help the chicks hatch by pulling the eggshell with her bill. She may eat the shell to help replace the calcium her body used to make the eggs. Eggshells also give her the needed calcium to make a second clutch of eggs.

MOM! DAD! Altricial. Both parents hunt for insects, take turns with diaper duty and defend the nest and young against predators.

FLEDGLING Young leave the nest when they are 1½ weeks of age. In another few weeks they can feed themselves and fly as well as an adult.

JUVENILE Youngsters look like adults, but with more brown than gray. At one year of age, they are mature enough to date, mate and raise their own young.

Gross Factor

Keeping the nest clean is a chore for some songbird parents. Fortunately, chicks defecate (poop) in tidy bags called fecal sacs. Like disposable diapers, fecal sacs have a strong outside liner to hold the droppings. This liner is made up of edible sugars and proteins. The first few days, parents eat the fecal sacs! Does it make them sick? No. During the first days, the chicks do not produce harmful bacteria; once they do, Mom and Dad drop the diapers away from the nest.

When

Dark-eyed Juncos are diurnal. They feed during the day and rest at night.

Migration

Spring Arrival: Mar–Apr
Fall Departure: Sep–Oct
Permanent resident to short-distance migrant. In the fall, juncos move to lower elevations in the Rocky Mountain region and overwinter. Some may migrate to areas as far south as the Gulf of Mexico.

Nesting

Dark-eyed Juncos begin nesting in the forests of the Rocky Mountain region in May. They raise 1–2 broods each year.

Getting Around

Juncos hop forward and sideways on the ground, scratching and foraging for insects and seeds. They fly with steady, quick wingbeats. When flying against the wind, Juncos stay close to the ground. When flying with the wind, they fly higher; this allows the wind to "blow" them along.

Where to Look

Openings in coniferous and mixed woodlands with bushy thickets. Winter bird feeders.

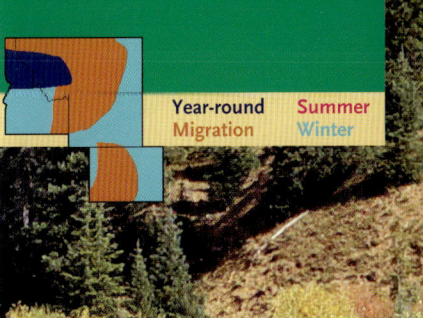

Year-round Migration
Summer Winter

Alpine Tundra and Subalpine Forests

American Pipit

Anthus rubescens

Length: 5½–6½ inches (14–17 cm)
Wingspan: 10½ inches (27 cm)

Slender, short bill with a notch near the tip

Brown above and cream below in summer and white below in winter

Tail has a white edge

Long legs

"Pipitititititi" is a male telling another male flying over, "This is my space!"

Life on the Mountaintop

Take to the mountaintop and you may cross paths with the indomitable American Pipit. The pipit does not have much competition on the high meadows. There is a reason for this: It is cold even on July nights, the winds are fierce and the summer is very short. Anything that grows there does so in double-time. The high meadow wildflowers bloom for only a few weeks a year. This short growing season also dictates a short nesting season. The first pipit egg is not laid until the air temperature stays around 47°F (8°C). Once hatched, the chicks eat their way through a huge growth spurt to be mature enough to move to the lower elevations when the real extremes hit—in winter!

Habitat Café

Today's Special
willow catkins

Yumm . . . bring an order of spiders, flies, grasshoppers, ants, a few seeds and a side order of butterflies with the scratchy wings removed. American Pipits are omnivorous. They may wash aquatic insects before eating them.

SPRING & SUMMER MENU:
🐜 Insects

FALL & WINTER MENU:
🐜 Insects and seeds

Life Cycle

NEST The nest is started by making a shallow scrape on the ground in an alpine meadow. The nest is protected by the overhang of a rock or plant. Dried grasses and sedges are used to make a saucer in the scrape and then it is lined with fine, soft grasses.

EGGS Just over ¾ inch long. The female incubates the clutch of 3–7 eggs for 13–15 days.

MOM! DAD! Altricial. Mom keeps the featherless chicks warm and acts as an umbrella to shade them from the sun and rain.

NESTLING Dad captures insects, beaks them over to Mom, and then she feeds the hungry chicks. This fast food delivery involves about 6 trips per hour the chicks' first day and increases to 29 per hour in another two weeks!

FLEDGLING The camouflaged young exercise their wings just before leaving the nest at two weeks of age. Once out of the nest they fly short distances and take cover in the alpine grasses and plants. Mom and Dad help feed them for a couple weeks.

JUVENILE They leave the family group and form a flock with other young pipits and adults. They are mature enough to nest and raise their own pipits the following spring.

Did You Know?

Songbird eggs are generally laid one per day over a period of a week or so, but all hatch within a day or two of each other. Biologists designed experiments to find out how the eggs might be different depending on when they were laid. Eggs laid last had more of a body chemical called testosterone than the eggs laid first. Higher levels of testosterone cause faster growth and more aggressiveness, helping chicks from the last eggs catch up!

When

American Pipits are diurnal. They feed during the day and rest at night.

Migration

Spring Arrival: Apr–May
Fall Departure: Sep–Nov
Short-distance migrant. During winter, they move in small flocks from alpine meadows to lower altitudes with less snow. They return to the alpine meadows in the spring.

Nesting

American Pipits begin nesting in May on the high rocky tundra slopes above the Rocky Mountain timberline.

Getting Around

Pipits can most often be seen walking or running along the ground while pecking for insects in the low plants. They come with a built-in snow and ice pick, the extra long toenail of their hallux (hind claw). Their strong flight is undulating—an up and down path.

Where to Look

Alpine meadows and open habitat above treeline during the summer and at lower altitudes during the winter months.

Year-round Summer
Migration Winter

Alpine Tundra and Subalpine Forests

41

Evening Grosbeak

Coccothraustes vespertinus

Length: 6½–7 inches (16–18 cm)
Wingspan: 12–14 inches (30–36 cm)

female

Females are dull gray with yellow underneath, white rump and white on their black tail; young look like females with a grayish bill

Male has black cap and yellow "eyebrow"

Yellow belly and undertail

Black wings and tail

"Clee—ip!" is a loud call heard when a group of grosbeaks visit a bird feeder.

Gross Factor of Another Kind

Gross means disgusting, icky. Gross can also mean big and bulky. This is the perfect way to tell about the big, thick bill of the Evening Grosbeak. Why do they need such a big bill? It works like a pair of large, strong pliers to crack open hard seeds, including cherry pits. Grosbeaks toss the outer cherry fruit that you would eat to the side and eat the soft food inside the hard pit. Each spring, the outer yellow layer of their beak falls off, like a snake sheds its skin. A new green bill is a clue that the Evening Grosbeak you are watching is an adult ready to open hard seeds. Crack!

Habitat Café

Today's Special
spruce
budworms

Yumm . . . bring an order of pine, fir, redcedar, elderberry and spruce tree seeds with a side order of caterpillars, spiders and beetles. Evening Grosbeaks are omnivorous. Their bird feeder favorites are safflower seeds, black oil sunflower seeds and peanuts.

SPRING, SUMMER, FALL, WINTER MENU:
Mostly seeds, some insects

Life Cycle

NEST The female builds the loose nest cup 20–60 feet above the ground in spruce and northern white cedar swamps. She weaves together twigs with moss and lichen, lining the inside with rootlets.

EGGS About 1 inch long. The female incubates the clutch of 3–4 eggs for 12–14 days.

MOM! DAD! Altricial. Both parents feed the young by regurgitating (spitting back up) partially digested insect larvae.

NESTLING Starting after the first week, the young eat whole insects and soft seeds on their own.

FLEDGLING Young leave the nest when they are about two weeks of age. Mom and Dad stay around and will shell seeds from bird feeders for the kids.

JUVENILE The teens are adult-sized and able to fly and feed on their own at 3 months of age.

History Hangout

In April of 1823, a young Ojibwe boy heard the strange call of a black and yellow bird that ate the seeds of trees and fruits. The bird was given the Ojibwe name *Pashcundamo* from *pashcaun*, meaning soft, fleshy vegetable. From this the native name Berry-breaker was formed. In 1823, a U.S. agent recording land boundaries heard a bird calling at sunset. Later, in 1825, ornithologist William Cooper named it "Finch of the Evening." However, it calls both in the evening and the day.

When

Diurnal. They are active during the day and rest at night.

Migration

Permanent resident. Evening Grosbeaks stay in the Rocky Mountain region all year, moving to lower elevations during the cold months. Stock your bird feeders; grosbeaks are in large numbers some years and few the next, but nearly always in a group.

Nesting

Evening Grosbeaks begin nesting in May in the Rocky Mountain region.

Getting Around

Birds that spend a lot of time in trees also hop when on the ground. Look for their side-by-side hopping track pattern as you explore the forest floor. Their flight is undulating (up and down).

Where to Look

They are found in the coniferous forests and backyard bird feeders in the Rocky Mountain region of the U.S.

Year-round
Migration

Summer
Winter

Northern Saw-whet Owl

Aegolius acadicus

Length: 7½–8½ inches (18–21 cm)
Wingspan: 16½–19 inches (42–48 cm)

Round head with white facial disk

Tuft of black bristle-like feathers between eyes

Yellow to golden eyes

Brown streaked above with white on crown

Females are larger than males

White with brown stripes below, white spots on wings and tail

The male's rhythmic hooting song reminded early settlers of a whetstone sharpening a saw.

Short feathered legs

I Hear You!

Finding food is a big deal to owls that live in the forests of the Rocky Mountain region. The structure of the Northern Saw-whet Owl's face gives you a clue about how they find small mammals in the darkness of night. Their facial feathers are arranged like a satellite disk. Your ears are the same height on each side of your head. The owl's ears are each at a different level on the outside of their head. To know exactly where a mouse is, the owl triangulates the sound; it detects the slight differences between the times that the sound of the scuffling mouse reaches each ear. On silent wings the owl then zeroes in to capture an unsuspecting meal that's on the move.

Habitat Café

Today's Special
white-footed mice

Yumm . . . bring an order of house mice, deer mice, harvest mice and montane voles with a side order of shrews. Northern Saw-whet Owls are carnivorous. Food may be cached (stored) on branches, and if the food becomes frozen, the owl thaws it by incubating it.

SPRING, SUMMER, FALL, WINTER MENU:
Small mammals

Life Cycle

NEST The Northern Saw-whet Owl does not excavate a nest hole but uses a man-made nest box or the nest cavity of a woodpecker or flicker, 14–60 feet above the ground. They lay the eggs on the leftovers of the previous nest (wood chips, grasses, twigs, moss and old bones) and may place some of their own breast feathers.

EGGS About 1 inch long. The female incubates the 4–7 eggs for 27–29 days.

MOM! DAD! Semi-altricial. Mom broods the white downy chicks for the first 18 days and Dad delivers meals and keeps extra nearby.

NESTLING The larger nestlings may tear the food into smaller pieces and feed their smaller siblings. Mom may begin to help bring food or she may leave to start a new brood.

FLEDGLING The young leave the nest at 4–5 weeks of age and can fly.

JUVENILE The juveniles stay together for another month while Dad continues to bring food. They are mature enough the following year to nest and raise their own young owls.

Did You Know?

Our ears do not hear the full range of sounds that birds make. How do we know? We can see the bird sounds that we hear and don't hear on an electric sonogram and an oscillogram. A sonogram and oscillogram put sound into a printed graph that we can see and study. This allows us to better understand the volume and pattern of a bird's song or call.

When

Northern Saw-whet Owls are nocturnal. They feed during the night and roost during the day, low to the ground in thick vegetation.

Migration

Permanent resident to short-distance migrant. Those that nest at higher elevations may move to lower elevations during winter months. During years when the food supply is scarce in Canada, Northern Saw-whet Owls may move south into the U.S.

Nesting

Northern Saw-whet Owls begin nesting in March in the coniferous or mixed deciduous forests of the Rocky Mountain region of the U.S.

Getting Around

This small owl maneuvers low to the ground around the forest thickets on small, rounded wings. Its wingbeats are fast and quick.

Where to Look

Coniferous forests at mid-mountain elevations during nesting season, moving to lower elevations during cold conditions.

Year-round   Summer
Migration   Winter

Alpine Tundra and Subalpine Forests

Williamson's Sapsucker

Sphyrapicus thyroideus

Length: 8½–10 inches (21–25 cm)
Wingspan: 17 inches (41 cm)

Black head with white mustache stripe

Red throat patch

Yellow belly

Black back, white wing patch

White rump, black tail

Female: brown head, black and white barred all over, black breast, yellow belly, no red throat patch

"Churr."
This call is made mainly by males to declare their territory.

Feathered Engineers

Who has been drilling holes in a nearly perfect circle around the trees? Williamson's Sapsuckers drill neat lines of holes that leak a sweet sap that attracts insects. Sapsuckers then have a two-course meal, insects and sap! Sapsuckers are important members of the ecosystem, called a keystone species. Chipmunks, red squirrels, and House Wrens are just a few of the many wildlife species that use extra sapsucker nest holes. When Golden-crowned Kinglets return in the spring they feed on the sap as well.

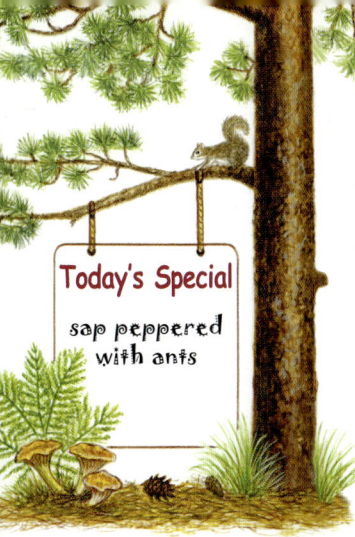

Habitat Café

Yumm . . . bring an order of sap and ants with side orders of fresh fruit and tree bast (inner bark and cambium). Williamson's Sapsuckers are omnivorous. They lap up sap with their brush-like tongue.

SPRING & FALL MENU:
 Mostly sap, some insects and fruit

SUMMER MENU:
 Insects with some sap and fruit

WINTER MENU:
 Fruit with some sap and insects

Life Cycle

NEST The male uses his bill as a chisel to excavate the nest cavity in the soft inside of a coniferous tree about 5–60 feet above ground. He may make a new nest in the same tree for many years. The 1½ inch diameter cavity opening is a tight fit for the parents.

EGGS About 1 inch long. Both the male and female incubate the 3–7 white eggs for 12–14 days.

MOM! DAD! Altricial. Their bright pink, naked skin shows until their first feathers begin to grow in after the first week. They are fully feathered at two weeks of age.

NESTLING The chicks are fed a diet of ants. Dad keeps the nest free of chick diapers and soggy wood chips.

FLEDGLING About one month after the young hatch, the parents coax them from the nest cavity by holding food outside the hole. The young can fly and learn to find insects themselves within a few days of leaving the nest.

JUVENILE They are fully independent in time for fall migration, but watch out for hawks. They chow on young sapsuckers.

Unsolved Mystery

Please pass the dip. When feeding young, parent sapsuckers gather ants and other insects and may then dip them in sap from a sap well. Does this provide extra nutritional value? Dip into this unsolved mystery!

When

Williamson's Sapsuckers are diurnal. They are active during the day and rest at night.

Migration

Spring Arrival: March–May
Fall Departure: Sep–Oct
Short-distance migrant to lower elevations within their breeding range or as far south as Mexico.

Nesting

Williamson's Sapsuckers begin nesting in April–May in the coniferous trees of the subalpine and montane forests.

Getting Around

Sapsuckers climb tree trunks, cling to them while drilling and hop up the large stems as they collect ants. Their flight is undulating (up and down).

Where to Look

Subalpine, montane, and some times aspen-parkland forests, often with spruce-fir, Douglas fir, lodgepole pine and ponderosa pine trees. Moves to lower elevations with colder weather.

Year-round
Migration
Summer
Winter

Alpine Tundra and Subalpine Forests

47

Gray Jay

Perisoreus canadensis

Length: 11–13 inches (28–33 cm)
Wingspan: 18 inches (46 cm)

Short, black bill is used to twist and tug meat from a dead animal

No crest on head

Gray feathers camouflage the jay against the gray bark of a coniferous tree

Pale gray chest

Male and female look alike; juveniles are dark gray

"Koke-ke-keer!" This scolding call can be heard more than a quarter of a mile away.

Hiding the Loot

Have you ever saved your ABC (already been chewed) gum in a favorite spot for later? Then you and the Gray Jay have something in common. Gray Jays have a special throat pouch to carry food in, and an extra-large salivary (spit) gland. They stick their favorite food together with thick and sticky saliva and then glue it to a tree. If they think another jay has discovered their hiding spot, they will move the food to a different place and jam a piece of bark or lichen over it. When the snow blows and hunger hits, a frozen dinner is ready, allowing this robber bird to survive well in harsh, cold winters.

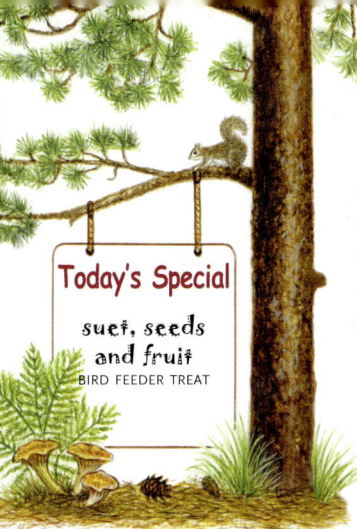

Habitat Café

Yumm . . . bring an order of butterflies, grasshoppers, beetles, bugs, spiders, ticks, mice, voles, the eggs and young of small birds, blueberries, mushrooms, soft seeds and dead animal meat. Gray Jays are omnivorous. They eat almost any small living thing in the northern forest.

SPRING, SUMMER, FALL, WINTER MENU:
 Any available food item

Life Cycle

NEST The female builds the bulky nest cup (8-inch diameter) hidden in the branches of a coniferous tree. It is usually 6–12 feet above the ground. Keep a hold of your tissues, they will hijack them and even cotton swabs for ultra-soft nest lining.

EGGS About 1⅛ inch long. The female incubates the clutch of 2–5 eggs for 16–18 days.

MOM! DAD! Altricial. Both parents feed the chicks and take turns removing the fecal sacs—chick diaper duty.

NESTLING Mom and Dad bring spit-covered "baby food" wads in their cheek pouches. Each glob of food is pushed out of their throats into the chick's gaping beak. The dark brown wads contain insects high in protein. Double yum!

FLEDGLING The young leave the nest at three weeks of age.

JUVENILE Teens stay in the area with their parents until June. The strongest bird chases its brothers and sisters away. When spring comes, Mom and Dad chase away this offspring to live on its own.

Did You Know?

Take a close look for a Gray Jay to give large forest mammals a free cleaning. Jays eat ticks from the animal's hide. There's a black fly . . . gulp. They catch annoying black flies from the perch of their unsuspecting host also. Tasty little morsels.

When

Gray Jays are diurnal. They feed by day and rest at night.

Migration

Permanent resident. They tend to stay in their home territory year after year during all four seasons. A few may move to lower elevations.

Nesting

Gray Jays nest in the coniferous subalpine and montane forests as early as April. An early nesting season gives young Gray Jays time to mature and learn the skills of food caching (storing) before the cold winter begins.

Getting Around

Gray Jays are skilled at sneaking up! They perch near prey and scout out the scene (including the baked beans on your picnic plate). Before you know they're even around, they glide on quiet wings, pick up the loot with their bill, and transfer it to their feet for a quick getaway. These antics have earned Gray Jays the nickname "Camp Robber."

Where to Look

Subalpine and montane forests areas of the Rocky Mountain region of the U.S. Will visit backyard bird feeders.

Year-round   Summer
Migration   Winter

Clark's Nutcracker

Nucifraga columbiana

Length: 10½–12 inches (27 – 30 cm)
Wingspan: 24 inches (61 cm)

White around eyes, on forehead, and chin

Their long, sharp black bill is used to crack open thick-hulled pine seeds

Light to medium gray all over

Black wings and tail

White patch on wings

"Kraaaack" or "I'm over here!" This loud call can be heard over a half mile away.

Forest Planters

Pine trees have a friend among birds. Clark's Nutcrackers plant thousands of pine seeds each year, some of which take root to become part of the pine forests that many animals depend on. Look to the nutcrackers' long, sharp bill for a clue to their success. They use it to open conifer tree cones, remove the seeds, and then make seed storage spaces in the soil. Typically, 3–7 seeds at a time are cached (stored) in one place. The nutcracker may come back up to a year later to get the seeds and carry them in their expandable throat pouch to feed their young. Some of the seeds are forgotten, sprout, and grow. When you see a clump of pine trees in a forest opening, the story of the nutcracker has come to life.

Habitat Café

Yumm . . . bring an order of fresh and stored pine seeds, and a small combo plate of spiders, insects, berries, birds, nestlings and eggs, ground squirrels, chipmunks, toads, voles, some dead meat (carrion), and your picnic scraps. Clark's Nutcrackers are omnivorous. Researchers estimate that in a year's time a single nutcracker can harvest up 129,000 seeds (whitebark pine). Only a red squirrel can beat this number at 875,000 per year!

SPRING, SUMMER, FALL, WINTER MENU:
 Mostly pine seeds

Life Cycle

NEST Both parents build the nest cup on a horizontal limb in a conifer tree 8–45 feet above ground. The base is made of dry twigs and strips of bark. The inner cup is made by quilting bark strips with pine straw and grass.

 **EGGS** About 1 inch long. The parents take turns incubating the clutch of 2–3 eggs for 18–22 days. The off-duty parent finds and delivers pine seeds cached (stored) earlier in the year.

MOM! DAD! Altricial. Parents take 30-minute shifts brooding the chicks for the first 10 days after the chicks hatch.

NESTLING A lunch of slippery pine seeds and liquefied insects is delivered by the parents right into the open mouth and throat of the chicks.

FLEDGLING The chicks stay in the nest for about 20 days but remain with their parents for about 3½ to 4 months.

JUVENILE The family group moves to higher elevations to feed on stores of seeds found with melting snow. Juveniles are able to survive on their own around the time the new seed crop becomes ripe.

Do the Math

Under the Clark Nutcracker's tongue, there is a seed delivery pouch. The nutcracker tosses its head back and points its bill high to slide a seed into the pouch. As the pouch fills, the throat bulges. How many seeds can the pouch hold? Up to 150 pine seeds at a time, or about 20% of the bird's total weight. If you weigh 90 pounds and had a full pouch of seeds that was 20% of your weight, what would the weight of the pouch be? Do the math. Answer on pages 194–195.

When

Clark's Nutcrackers are diurnal. They are active during the day and rest at night.

Migration

Permanent resident. The availability of fresh and cached (stored) seeds determines the movements of Clark's Nutcrackers. In July–Aug they eat new seeds from cones in the subalpine and montane levels. In Sep–Dec they store ripe seeds and move to lower elevations for new seed sources. The stored seeds are used in winter; by late spring they move back to higher elevations as seeds are uncovered with the melting snow.

Nesting

Clark's Nutcrackers begin nesting as early as Jan–Feb in coniferous forest of the subalpine and montane zones.

Getting Around

Their long and pointed wings support their strong flight.

Where to Look

Subalpine and montane forests with pine trees. They live in higher elevations during the warmer months and lower elevations during the colder months, but they can be found at all elevations throughout some years depending on pine seed availability.

| Year-round | Summer |
| Migration | Winter |

Steller's Jay

Cyanocitta stelleri

Length: 12–13½ inches (30–34 cm)
Wingspan: 17½ inches (44 cm)

Black face
and crest

White stripe
above eye

Silver or light blue
streaked forehead

Grayish
throat patch

Bill, legs, and
feet black

"Wah, wah!" or "Danger! Join the mob to chase the intruder away!"

Blue Marauders of the Pines

Steller's Jays look like a hooded band of marauders as they glide single file into the edge of a coniferous forest. They are likely after pine seeds to stuff into their handy throat pouch. Once in the trees and out of the sun, their blue markings fade into the forest shadows. The blue of their feathers comes from light reflecting off of the top of the feathers. Cells near the top, called air vacuoles, scatter and reflect blue light. Cells deeper in the same feather hold melanin, or pigment that give the feather a brown color. This can be seen when light travels through the feather rather than reflecting off of it. Watch for this colorful character in nearby forests and campgrounds.

Habitat Café

Yumm . . . bring an order of insects, pine seeds, acorns, berries, fruits, small vertebrates, and eggs and young of smaller birds. Steller's Jays are omnivorous. Bird feeder treats include suet, sunflower seeds and peanuts.

SPRING, SUMMER, FALL, WINTER MENU:

 Seeds, insects, fruit, some small birds

Today's Special

grubs

Life Cycle

NEST The nest is made in the horizontal branch of a tree close to the trunk. Mud is used to glue sticks, moss and dried leaves into a base. This is lined with rootlets, animal fur, and pine needles.

EGGS Almost 1 inch long. The female incubates the 2–6 bluish-green eggs for 16 days. The male brings her food.

MOM! DAD! Altricial. Both parents feed the chicks and remove the fecal sacs (chick diapers).

NESTLING With their eyes closed and no feathers when they hatch, the chicks have a lot of growing to do.

FLEDGLING The young leave the nest when they are about 16 days of age and are able to run along the ground with fluttering hops. At one month they can feed themselves and fly some distance.

JUVENILE They stay with their parents in a family group in fall and sometimes winter. They are mature enough the following spring to nest and raise their own young jays.

Gross Factor

Do birds have flatulence (pass gas)? The cousin to the Steller's Jay, the Blue Jay, does. Adult jays were observed passing gas by a biologist who was studying them. Now you know even more about bird bodily functions. Word has it that they have a "hiccup" call too. Silly birds.

When

Steller's Jays are diurnal. They feed during the day and they rest at night.

Migration

Permanent resident. Steller's Jays at high elevations may move to lower elevations during the winter.

Nesting

Steller's Jays begin nesting in March in the Rocky Mountain region of the U.S.

Getting Around

Steller's Jays hop on the ground in search of food and climb trees by hopping from branch to branch. They fly short rather than long distances.

Where to Look

Steller's Jays hang out in coniferous and mixed-coniferous forests, near bird feeders, and in parks and campgrounds.

Year-round Migration   Summer Winter

White-tailed Ptarmigan

Lagopus leucura

Length: 12 inches (31 cm)
Wingspan: 22 inches (56 cm)

Scarlet eye combs

In breeding season, males wear a striped brown-black necklace

Winter white plumage changes to grayish-brown in summer

Feathers on legs and toes in winter serve as snowshoes

summer plumage

winter plumage

"Chuur-uur-uur" or "A predator on wings is near—high tail it under a rock!"

Chill Out and Lay Low

White-tailed Ptarmigans live in one of the harshest environments in the Rocky Mountains. Their survival strategy: chill out, lay low, and expend as little energy as possible. Flying takes a lot of energy, so ptarmigans opt to walk. During winter they add a pair of snowshoes by growing a lot of feathers from their legs down to their toes. Ptarmigans don't just walk on the snow, they roost under it, away from the wind and predators. Snow is one of nature's best insulators, with tiny pockets of air that trap the heat of the ptarmigan, like a blanket. Their dense coat of feathers protects them from the strong winds and cold temperatures and changes color according to the season.

Habitat Café

Yumm . . . bring an order of buds, leaves and seeds with a combo platter of flowers, fruits and a few insects. White-tailed Ptarmigans are herbivores.

Today's Special
willow buds

SPRING, SUMMER, FALL MENU:
 Buds, leaves, stems, seeds, fruit, flowers, insects

WINTER MENU:
Buds, stems, seeds

Life Cycle

NEST The ground nest is constructed by the female in a snow-free area protected from the wind. She first makes a scrape in the ground and then makes a nest rim by using her bill and feet to pull plants, leaves and grasses around her body. She repeats this until a shallow nest bowl is made. She does not put lining in the nest, but some of her own white feathers may fall in the middle.

EGGS Over 1½ inches long. The female incubates the 2–7 spotted eggs for 22–26 days.

MOM! DAD! Precocial. As soon as the chicks have hatched and their thick down is dry, they leave the nest to follow Mom to food. If they become separated from her, they send out a "cheerp!" call. When Mom sends out a warning "craaow!" the chicks freeze in place for up to half an hour or until all is well. During the first weeks after hatching, they eat insects along with some flowers and leaves. They gradually adapt to the full adult diet of willow buds and other plants.

JUVENILE By the time they are two months of age, their white winter feathers begin to grow in. They will be completely white by November.

Do the Math

When the air is -27°F above the snow surface, it will be +24°F seven inches below the surface of the snow. How many degrees difference does the layer of snow cause? Do the math: ____ degrees difference. Bring on the snow! Answer on pages 194–195.

Answer on pages 194–195.

When

White-tailed Ptarmigans are diurnal. They are active during the day and rest at night.

Migration

Permanent resident. White-tailed Ptarmigans move to the high elevations of tundra during April and May. In October they move to wintering areas at lower mountain elevations. Ptarmigans from different breeding areas may use the same wintering site.

Nesting

White-tailed Ptarmigans begin nesting in the alpine tundra in June.

Getting Around

White-tailed Ptarmigans are aware that they are food for Golden Eagles, Prairie Falcons and other stealthy predators, so they use a slow, creeping walk close along the ground. When needed, they will run and fly short distances. The males patrol their territory by flying over it now and then.

Where to Look

Rocky alpine tundra often near snowfields and streams with willow plants nearby.

Year-round
Migration

Summer
Winter

Common Raven

Corvus corax

Length: 22–27 inches (56–69 cm)
Wingspan: 4 feet (122 cm)

Heavy, black hooked bill

Glossy black feathers

Shaggy throat feathers

Long, rounded wings with separation between flight feathers

Male and female look alike

Black legs

Wedge-shaped tail

"Rrock, rrock, rrock!" is given by both males and females declaring their territory.

Voice Mail, Raven-style

Calling all ravens—food! A raven sends loud voice mail to let other ravens know the location of food. It won't be long before they arrive. The announcement may also be made at the roost where locals and newcomers gather to exchange the neighborhood gossip. Early morning raven patrols along roadways may turn up fresh roadkill for breakfast. Ravens depend on larger predators to kill and open the body of large prey. Cars and trucks become partners in foraging. Ravens rip off pieces of meat with their hooked upper bill and hammer frozen meat with the sharp, pointed lower bill. They cache (store) food in bite-sized pieces, each in a different location. "Rrock, rrock"—you have voice mail!

Habitat Café

Yumm . . . Bring an order of dead meat (carrion), eggs, insects, small mammals, grains, fruit, garbage. Common Ravens are omnivorous.

Today's Special
carrion

SPRING, SUMMER, FALL, WINTER MENU:
Animal matter and some grains

Life Cycle

NEST The female does most of the work carrying sticks and constructing the 1½–5 foot diameter platform nest high (up to 98 feet) in a tree. The inner nest of smaller twigs and plants is made cozy with fur, shredded bark, grasses, sheep's wool and even paper.

EGGS About 2 inches long. The female incubates a clutch of 3–7 eggs for 20–25 days. The male feeds her and stands guard.

MOM! DAD! Altricial. Hatched naked with only a few gray downy feathers, the chicks look like tiny gremlins. The dinner call to the chicks is one short grunting sound from a parent just before it regurgitates into their open throats.

NESTLING Mom makes soft, comforting sounds and gently preens the feathers around the chicks' eyes with her large, thick bill.

FLEDGLING They leave the nest at 4–7 weeks of age when they can fly short distances.

JUVENILE They are mature enough at 2–4 years of age to raise their own young.

Did You Know?

A big black bird is overhead—is it a raven or a crow? Ravens are two times larger than crows and have a wedge-shaped tail. Crows have a square-ended tail. Ravens have a heavier, stronger bill with an angle on the top and shaggy throat feathers and wing "fingers" too. Listen for the difference between the deep, hoarse "rock" of the raven and the clear "caw" of the crow. Raven or crow—now you know!

When

Common Ravens are diurnal. They feed during the day and rest at night.

Migration

Permanent resident in the Rocky Mountain region of the U.S.

Nesting

Common Ravens begin nesting as early as February and into April in the Rocky Mountain region. Nests may be reused in another year and can become very smelly.

Getting Around

Ravens use deep wingbeats. Look for the long fingers of the outer primary flight feathers of their large wings. How does a raven dive? It tucks in both wings. Dive and turn? Tucks in only one wing. Watch for half-way rolls, full rolls, and in a rare performance, a double-roll. Juvenile ravens may be seen "playing" tug-of-war, king-of-the-hill, sliding in snow and even hanging upside down!

Where to Look

Subalpine, montane, aspen parkland forests and into the lower levels of grasslands in the Rocky Mountain region of the U.S.
· *Super Adaptor*

Year-round
Migration
Summer
Winter

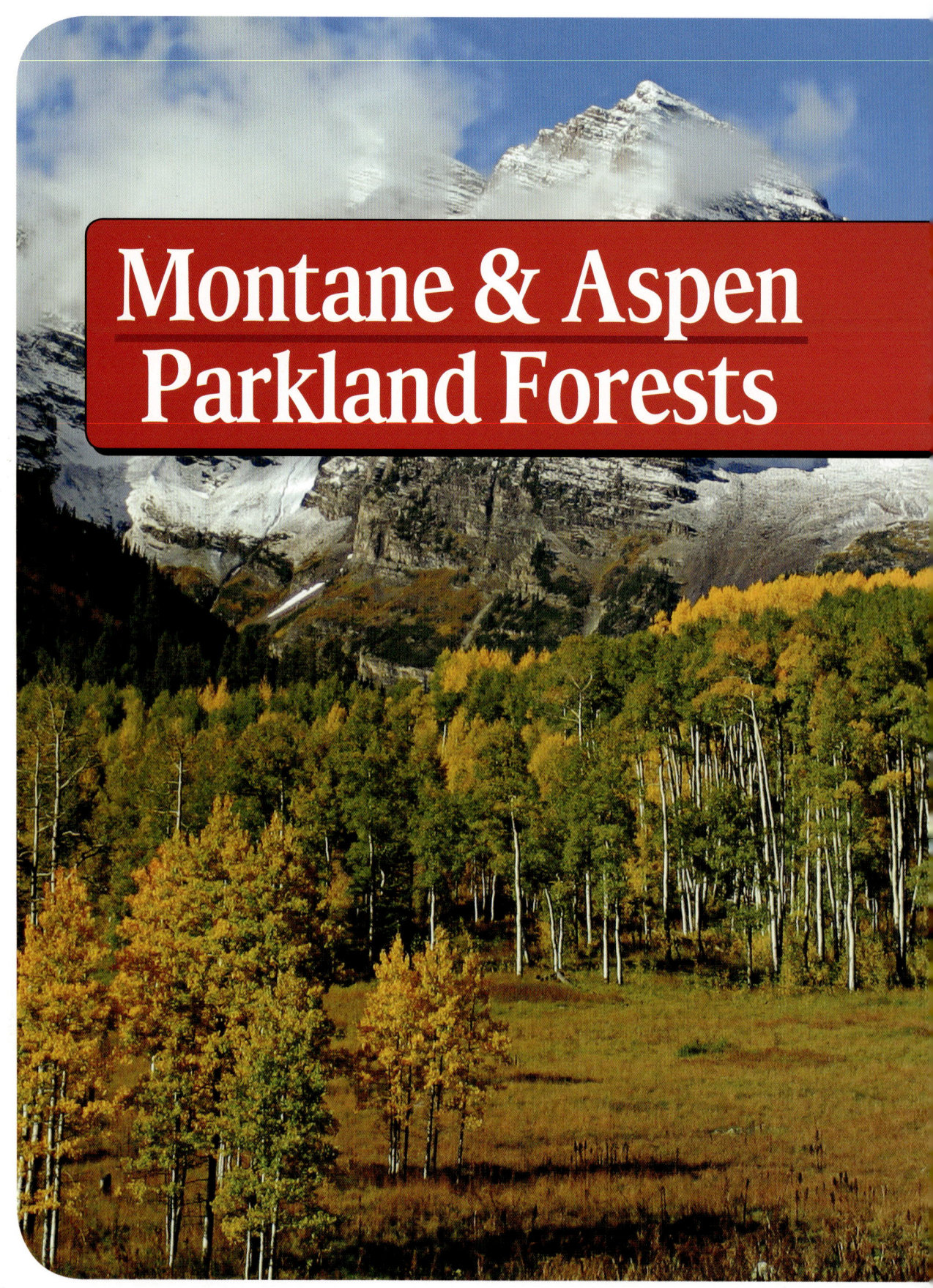

Montane & Aspen Parkland Forests

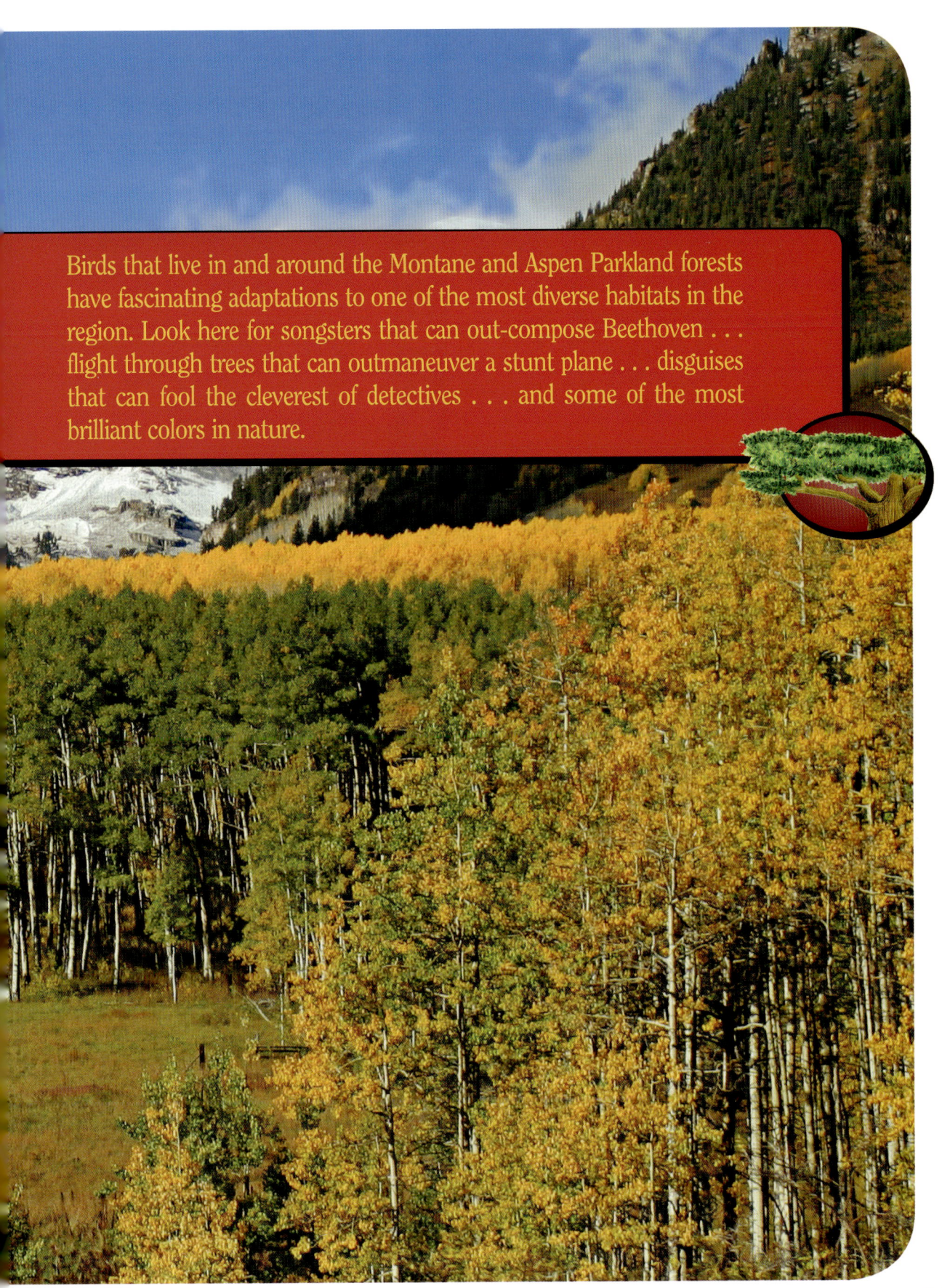

Birds that live in and around the Montane and Aspen Parkland forests have fascinating adaptations to one of the most diverse habitats in the region. Look here for songsters that can out-compose Beethoven . . . flight through trees that can outmaneuver a stunt plane . . . disguises that can fool the cleverest of detectives . . . and some of the most brilliant colors in nature.

Mixing It Up

The mountain forests found just above the grasslands and foothills are known as the montane, which literally means "of the mountains." This level is home to both coniferous and deciduous trees adapted to moderate (mild) conditions. There are a variety of forest types here, depending on which direction the mountain slope faces, the elevation, and any special features. There is rarely a straight dividing line between types of habitats. Usually it's a gradual change.

Douglas fir (wetter areas) and ponderosa pine (drier areas) are the dominant coniferous trees and aspen are the most common deciduous trees from the

foothills up to the mid-mountain elevations, and sometimes higher. Deciduous trees lose all of their leaves every year and grow new ones.

Trees provide buds and seeds that are important year-round food for Black-beaked Grosbeaks and forest mammals that are in turn eaten by Great Horned Owls higher in the food chain.

The forest habitat along mountain streams and rivers is called a riparian habitat. Riparian trees, like cottonwood and willow, are fast-growing, shallow-rooted and can withstand flooding. Here, Western Screech Owls search out tree-hole hideouts to perform their magic tricks and Western Wood-Pewees hawk insects on the wing.

In the forests openings and meadows watch for Broad-tailed Hummingbirds sipping nectar from meadow wildflowers.

Colorful Variety

More bird species live in a forest than a grassland because there are more habitat levels in a forest. It's easier to learn about these birds if you explore the different forest levels.

Hawk nest

The highest level, the top or upper canopy of trees, includes nests of sky-dwellers like Cooper's Hawks.

Birds that hunt for insects on tree branches and trunks, like Hairy Wood-peckers and Northern Flickers, use the middle level of the forest. So do birds that favor the seeds, fruit and nuts found there. Other birds are like tiny carpenters, and build nests in tree cavities (holes), like the House Wren does.

Protective Camo, Amazing Antics

The lower level of the forest is home to birds like Gray Catbirds that eat the seeds, nuts and fruit of forest plants. Birds like Song Sparrows also eat the snails, insects and worms found on the ground. Many of these birds are well camouflaged against the brown and light patterns of the forest floor.

Song Sparrow

Turn the pages to learn more about the birds that make their home in the different levels of the forests. Take this book along on a walk in the forests with a buddy. For a long walk, you'll need an adult. Remember to tell an adult where you are going, who is with you and when you will be back. If your plans change, be certain to tell them right away. Safety first!

Winter Wonderland

You can explore the wilds of the lower elevation Rocky Mountain forests in the winter, too. It's a great time to learn how the hearty birds that live there year-round survive the cold, snow and changes to their food supply. Their adaptations to the cold climate are fantastic! Turn to page 18 to learn more about how birds that stay in the Rocky Mountain region survive winter.

When the snow squeaks underfoot, take a clue from the local wildlife and dress in layers, wear warm boots or snowshoes, take along water and a snack for extra energy and buddy-up with a friend. Be adventurous and, of course, always be safe!

Check Off the Montane & Aspen Parkland Forest Birds You See!

When you spot birds of the Montane and Aspen Parkland, use these pages to check them off. The locations of these illustrations indicate where you might see them.

Broad-tailed Hummingbird

Charadrius vociferus

Length: 3–3½ inches (8–9 cm)
Wingspan: 5 inches (13 cm)

female

Females have speckled throats

Male's throat (a gorget) has a dark rose-colored patch

Iridescent green back

Long body and wings compared to most other hummingbirds

White-tipped inner tail feathers

"Syrrrr-syrrr." This cricket-like trill is made by the male's narrow wingtips during flight displays, courtship and territory defense.

Aerial Acrobat

Broad-tailed Hummingbirds are fearless showoffs. In an attempt to wow females into becoming their mate, males put on an aerial display that includes 60–100 foot climbs, power dives that shift direction within a breath of an awestruck female, and a yo-yo swing dance (called a whisking display) that is so up-close and personal that she may not be able to make a move of her own. If this doesn't get her full attention, surely the loud trill of his wings and accompanying vocals will. A male on a mission, he may carry on with 43–96 dives per hour to woo her, wow her, and render her totally hum-less.

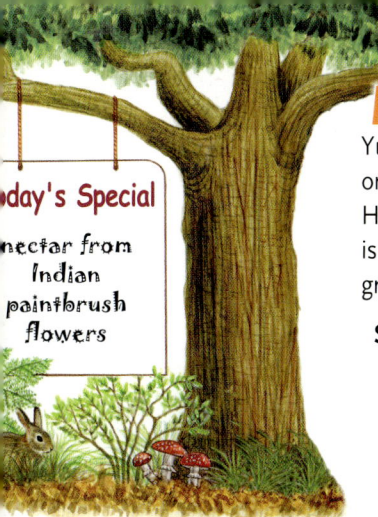

Habitat Café

day's Special

nectar from
Indian
paintbrush
flowers

Yumm . . . bring an order of nectar with a side order of small insects and spiders. Broad-tailed Hummingbirds are omnivorous. Their tongue is longer than their bill, with a forked tip and grooves for the nectar to follow.

SPRING, SUMMER, FALL, WINTER MENU:

 Mostly nectar from flowers with a few insects and spiders

Life Cycle

NEST The female builds the small cup nest on a low tree branch protected by an overhanging limb or bend in the trunk. She constructs the nest of plant down, pieces of bark, lichen and moss, with spider webbing on the inside so the nest looks like part of the tree.

EGGS About ½ inch long. The female incubates the 2 white eggs for 16–19 days.

MOM! DAD! Altricial. The tiny chicks each weigh less than a single chocolate chip when they hatch! Mom feeds them protein-packed gnats and aphids. By the end of their first week, they have increased their mass by six times. Mom shields the chicks from rain, wind and cold.

NESTLING By the time the chicks are two weeks old, they exercise their wings, perch on the rim of the nest, and attempt their first flights.

FLEDGLING They leave the nest at about 3–4 weeks. Mom increasingly ventures from the young. This may encourage them to capture their own insects and find nectar.

JUVENILE They are mature enough the following spring to nest and raise young.

Birding Tip

In our region, there are at least four species of hummingbirds. In the north, look for the Rufus and Calliope Hummingbirds during the summer. The busy Black-chinned Hummingbird can be seen throughout the region during migration. Attract them to your yard by planting tube-like flowers and filling a nectar feeder. Make nectar by boiling one cup of white sugar with four cups of water for one minute. Change the nectar often.

When

Broad-tailed Hummingbirds are diurnal. They are active during the day and rest at night.

Migration

Spring Arrival: Apr–May
Fall Departure: Aug–Sep
Mid-distance migrant to the mountains of central Mexico. They double their body mass just before their migration to wintering areas. These extra stores of energy are used to fuel their migration flight.

Nesting

Broad-tailed Hummingbirds begin nesting in June in the Rocky Mountain region. Nesting season in the alpine meadows is at the same time that the flowers bloom.

Getting Around

They can fly forward at up to 29 miles per hour, backwards and even upside down. Their wings beat about 50 times per second while at a nectar feeder. Hovering saves valuable energy, as does resting at perches between feeding flights.

Where to Look

Often found in open subalpine meadows at high elevations and in montane valleys. Also lower elevations, including foothills.

Year-round   Summer
Migration   Winter

House Wren

Troglodytes aedon

Length: 4–5 inches (11–13 cm)
Wingspan: 6 inches (15 cm)

Fairly long, slender,
down-curved bill for
picking up insects

Short wings that
are curved in on
the underside

Males and females
are brown above and
light brown below

Narrow tail that
is held up, down,
or fanned out
depending on the
signal

"Tsi, tsi, tsi,
oodle-oodle-oodle-oodle."
When the male's warbling song
becomes shorter and quieter,
it is a sure sign that
the chicks have hatched.

Carpenter of the Forest

The pocket of a scarecrow's overalls, an overturned clay flowerpot, a boot left outside, a mailbox, an abandoned woodpecker hole, a deep crack in a rotten tree—all are used by House Wrens for a house. Watch wrens long enough and you can add to this remarkable list. Building and putting up backyard wren houses is the best invitation you can give to these small birds. Males prepare 2–7 houses for a female to choose from. Before she arrives, he is busy spring cleaning, bringing in furniture (small twigs) and setting out snacks (spider egg cases and larvae). How will you know which house is "Home Sweet Home?" When the female adds grass and feather pillows to her favorite cozy house.

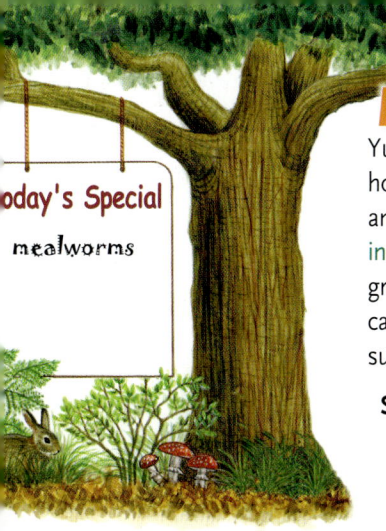

Habitat Café

Yumm . . . bring an order of leafhoppers, grasshoppers, crickets, caterpillars, beetles, moths, ants, bugs and spiders. House Wrens are insectivores. The parents will eat snail shells for grit and feed snail shells to their chicks for the calcium content. They will come to yard feeders supplied with wiggly mealworms.

SPRING, SUMMER, FALL, WINTER MENU:

 Almost entirely insects

Today's Special

mealworms

Life Cycle

NEST The female finishes the nest started by the male and makes an average of 300 trips to the nest in only a few days. She lines the nest with grass, fur, hair and feathers.

EGGS About ¾ inch long. The female lays one egg each day for 6–8 days. Mom begins full-time incubation after the last egg is laid and continues for 12–15 days. The eggs hatch on the same day.

MOM! DAD! Altricial. At first, Dad "beaks" the insects over to Mom and she feeds the chicks. After the first days, they both feed the chicks, remove fecal sacs (diaper duty) and carry the sacs away from the nest.

NESTLING The downy chicks stay in the nest about two weeks.

FLEDGLING After leaving the nest, the chicks are fed insects by their parents for another two weeks.

JUVENILE In summer, wrens leave the shrubby nest site and prepare for migration in the safety of a more thickly forested area. On their spring return, they are mature enough to date, mate and set up house for their own young.

Did You Know?

How do bird eggs stay warm? Incubating parents have a brood patch. This bare spot on the bird's belly has many blood vessels close to the skin's surface. During incubation, the blood flow to this area increases, making it a real "hot spot." The parent sits with the eggs directly under the brood patch. Once the job of keeping eggs and chicks warm is finished, feathers regrow and the brood patch disappears.

When

House Wrens are diurnal. They feed during the day and rest at night.

Migration

Spring Arrival: Apr–May
Fall Departure: Sep–Oct
The House Wren is a short- to mid-distance migrant to the southern U.S. and Mexico.

Nesting

In the Rocky Mountain region, House Wrens begin nesting in May. They raise 1–2 broods each year. Watch for wrens in your neighborhood; nest territories are ½–¾ of an acre in size, or an average city block.

Getting Around

House Wrens hop on the ground and fly from bush to bush in search of insects. Their longer flights are straight and steady. If a wren's tail is straight up, the bird feels excited or in danger. Tail down means it is comfortable. A male with a fanned out and lowered tail, head held forward, and fluffed up back feathers, is defending his territory.

Where to Look

Open shrubby woodland and habitat edges, including backyards and parks all over the Rocky Mountain region.
· *Super Adaptor*

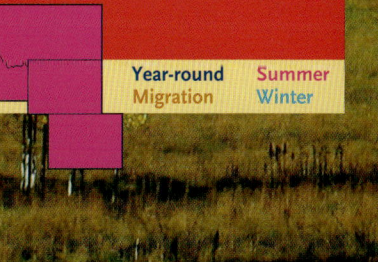

	Year-round	Summer
	Migration	Winter

Warbling Vireo

Vireo gilvus

Length: 5 inches (12–13 cm)
Wingspan: 8½–9 inches (22–23 cm)

Olive-gray
all over

Male and female
look alike

Underside is white
to cream colored

"Oodle-oo, oodle-ooo, oodle-ee." The males sings this bright song while courting females and during migration.

Signs in the Forest

Imagine walking in a forest with signs hanging from the trees advertising exactly where forest birds can be found. One reads: American Robin is defending his family's nest from this branch. Another says: Hairy Woodpecker is drumming here to attract a female and declare his territory. Close your eyes and listen to the forest sounds and you will hear the advertisements. The Warbling Vireo is a forest bird more easily heard than seen because it hangs out in shrubs and trees and is easily hidden from view. What is not camouflaged is their cheerful song: If the vireo's song was a color it would be bright red. Males sing to females in the spring, leaving oo-oo-oodles of advertisements for you to find!

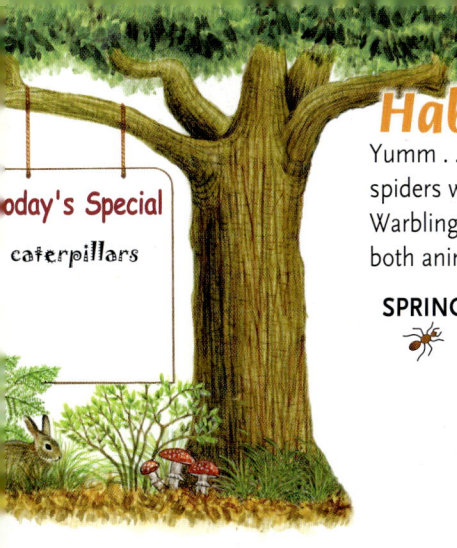

Habitat Café

Yumm . . . bring an order of insects and spiders with a side order of small fresh fruit. Warbling Vireos are omnivorous. They eat both animal and plant matter.

SPRING, SUMMER, FALL, WINTER MENU:
 Insects, spiders and few small fruits

Life Cycle

NEST Both the female and male build the cup nest in the fork of a tree or shrub branch within 12 feet of the ground. They weave leaves, strips of bark, grass and feathers together with spiderwebs. The nest is lined with soft plant stems and animal hair.

EGGS About ¾ inch long. The male sings while he and the female take turns incubating the clutch of 3–5 eggs for 11–16 days. A Brown-headed Cowbird female (page 120) may deposit an egg in the nest which the vireos may or may not incubate and raise.

MOM! DAD! Altricial. At the time the chicks hatch, their only feathers are a few tufts of down on their dark yellow skin.

NESTLING Both Mom and Dad take turns staying at the nest with the chicks and making feeding expeditions. They have a special call that they utter to signal it is time to change places.

FLEDGLING The young perch on the nest edge and eventually leave at about 14 days of age. Adults provide food for approximately 2 weeks.

JUVENILE They are mature enough on their return from wintering grounds the following spring to nest and raise their own young vireos.

Did You Know?

Bird bones are so light that their feathers may weigh more than all of the bones in their skeleton. This includes species that migrate long distances. In 1927, Charles Lindbergh, the first person to fly an airplane nonstop from New York to Paris, France, sat in a wicker chair to keep the weight low in his canvas-covered airplane. He only took sandwiches, survival gear, and two canteens of water with him. He even tore off the edges of his map! Keep it light for a fuel-efficient flight!

When

Diurnal. Warbling Vireos are active during the day and they rest at night.

Migration

Spring Arrival: Apr–May
Fall Departure: Aug–Oct
Medium- to long-distance migrant, flying by night to wintering areas in western Mexico and northern Central America. They are in danger of hitting tall structures (including communication towers) during their nocturnal migration flights.

Nesting

Warbling Vireos begin nesting in May in the forests of the Rocky Mountain region.

Getting Around

Warbling Vireos hop along branches, searching for insects under and on leaves.

Where to Look

Look for Warbling Vireos in open and mixed-deciduous forests, often with aspen trees. They will also venture into campgrounds, city parks and backyards.

Year-round   Summer
Migration   Winter

Yellow-rumped Warbler

Dendroica coronate

Length: 4½–5½ inches (12–14 cm)
Wingspan: 7½–9 inches (19–23 cm)

female

Black face with a yellow throat and cap

Blue-gray above with black sides

White wing patches

Yellow spots on each side of chest

Yellow rump

"Tuwee-tuwee-tuwee!" From the top of a tree the male sings, "Come and be my partner, female."

Warbler Watch

Warblers are small, quick, flitting birds. There are scads of warbler species, and the Yellow-rumped Warbler is a common one. To get to know it, start in the spring as warblers migrate in waves through North America. Go to a local forest where you can spend an hour or two. Take your notebook and binoculars, and then settle into a comfortable spot where trees and plants provide camouflage. Listen. Look for leaves that move when others are still. Look at the ends of branches where the tree's flowers and new leaves are popping out—there are tiny insects buzzing there that the warblers eat. Send your information to the Cornell Lab of Ornithology's "Warbler Watch" and be a part of science.

Habitat Café

Yumm . . . bring an order of ants, grubs, caterpillars, bark beetles, flies, aphids and spiders with a side order of berries. Yellow-rumped Warblers are omnivorous, they eat both plant and animal matter.

SPRING & SUMMER MENU:

 Insects and some small fruits and berries

FALL & WINTER MENU:

 Small fruits and berries and some insects

Life Cycle

NEST The female builds the deep cup nest on the branch of a conifer tree near its trunk about 20 feet above ground. She uses bark, twigs and plant down for the base and lines it with soft animal hair and grasses. To protect the eggs from rain, sun and predators, she weaves feathers into the nest rim that arch above the nest's center.

EGGS Nearly ¾ inch long. The female incubates the clutch of 3–6 eggs for 12–13 days.

MOM! DAD! Altricial. The chicks do not have feathers when they hatch, but within the first week their feathers begin to grow.

NESTLING Both Mom and Dad feed the chicks insects and remove the fecal sacs (chick diapers). They deposit the sacs away from the nest to deter lurking predators like red squirrels and Common Ravens (page 56).

FLEDGLING The young leave the nest at 10–14 days of age and make short practice flights.

JUVENILE The following spring they are mature enough to nest and raise their own quick-winged warblers.

Unsolved Mystery

When 14-year-old Jim Gilbert saw the first American Robin of the year on his front lawn he marked it on a calendar. The next year he checked the calendar to see if the robins had returned at the same time. They had. Jim then added other seasonal events to his journal. Jim had no idea that 50 years later his notes would be a part of an international effort to study the effects of global climate change, but that is exactly what has happened. Your notes are important too—be a part of science!

Diurnal. Yellow-rumped Warblers are active during the day and rest at night.

Migration

Spring Arrival: Apr–May
Fall Departure: Sep–Oct
Short to mid-distance migrant to the southwestern United States and Mexico.

Nesting

Yellow-rumped Warblers begin nesting in late May and June in the coniferous and mixed forests of the Rocky Mountain region.

Getting Around

Warblers are small, active birds that are built for catching insects with their short, thin bill and short wings. Yellow-rumped Warblers are perch gleaners: they capture insects by searching the stem, leaves and bark of their perch and then flit to another perch. They are quick in their pursuit and will flit before you can blink twice!

Where to Look

Yellow-rumped Warblers spend the summer months in the coniferous forests and the winter months in mixed forests and thickets.

Year-round Summer
Migration Winter

Chipping Sparrow

Spizella passerine

Length: 5–6 inches (12–15 cm)
Wingspan: 8 inches (21 cm)

Black eye-stripe and between eyes and beak (lores)

Brown crown

White "eyebrow" line

Black bill

Female similar to male

White belly

Gray rump and chest

"Chip. Chip. Chip." Chipping Sparrows get their name from the chip call that signals a threat is near, or "Chicks, I am here with food!"

Little Brown Birds: Sparrows

Little brown birds are everywhere: by the sidewalk on the way to school, in the bushes, city park, along the roadside and at the edges of ponds. Are they all the same kind of bird? Yes and no. They may all be sparrows, but different species (kinds). Sparrows might seem the same at first glance, but with a closer look and listen they can be as easy to tell apart as your classroom friends. Take note of the shape and color of the top of their head, bill, any color patches and streaking, as well as where they hang out, their behavior, and their songs and calls. Get to know the four sparrows detailed in this book and you are on your way to making some fun friends!

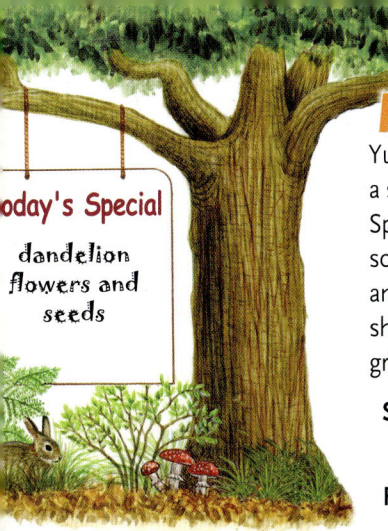

Habitat Café

Yumm . . . bring an order of grass seeds with a summer side order of insects. Chipping Sparrows are omnivorous. They run, hop and scratch on the ground to find seeds, insects and grit (small pieces of sand, stone or snail shells). Grit stays in their crop and helps to grind seeds for easier digestion.

SPRING & SUMMER MENU:

 Seeds and some insects

FALL & WINTER MENU:

 Seeds

Life Cycle

NEST The female builds the small nest cup in a coniferous tree (often spruce), a vine, or a shrub just 3–10 feet above the ground. She uses dead grass, plant roots and stems for the nest cup basket, and then lines it with fine, soft grass and animal hair.

 **EGGS** Nearly ¾ inch long. The female incubates the clutch of 2–5 eggs for 11–14 days. The male makes soft "chips" to let her know he is coming to the nest with food.

MOM! DAD! Altricial. The featherless chicks make their own way out of their egg.

NESTLING The chick that can reach its open bill up the highest usually gets the most food from Mom and Dad.

FLEDGLING At about 9–13 days of age the chicks climb to the rim of the nest and hop onto tree branches.

JUVENILE The young group into flocks in late summer and early fall in preparation for migration. They are mature enough the following spring to nest and raise their own chipping chicks!

Birding Tip

How close is too close? You are minding your wildlife manners when your presence does not change an animal's behavior. If an animal does notice you, move slowly and quietly away. Make a wildlife-watching blind in your backyard with items from home (sheets, tent). Camouflage your hideout and journal about your wild neighbors. Journal on pages 188–189 or visit www.birdsforkids.com for downloads.

When

Diurnal. Chipping Sparrows are active during the day and they rest at night.

Migration

Spring Arrival: Mar–Apr
Fall Departure: Sep–Nov
Short-distance migrant. Chipping Sparrows migrate along high ridges in flocks of 3–40 in the spring and 25–1,000 in the fall to areas in the southwestern U.S. and northern Mexico.

Nesting

Chipping Sparrows begin nesting in April and May in our region of the U.S.

Getting Around

Chipping Sparrows have several flight patterns. In open areas their flight is rapid at up to 20 mph and undulating (up and down). In close spaces they use short and direct flights and hop when on the ground.

Where to Look

Chipping Sparrows live in open coniferous and deciduous forests and brushy edges. They have adapted to living in urban places as well: city parks, gardens and backyards. They will visit bird feeders stocked with millet, cracked corn, milo and even suet.
· *Super Adaptor*

Year-round   Summer
Migration   Winter

Montane & Aspen Parkland Forest

Black-capped Chickadee

Poecile atricapillus

Length: 5–6 inches (12–15 cm)
Wingspan: 6–8 inches (16–21 cm)

Short, small, black bill shaped like a cone

Black cap and chin

White breast and belly

Gray back

Females and males look the same

Long tail

"Chickadee-dee, Chickadee-dee-dee" means "Hey, I'm over here!" "Fee-bee, fee-bee" is often a male saying, "This is my space!"

A Tiny Bird With Mighty Adaptations

The forests are home to a tiny, yet mighty, survivor. The Black-capped Chickadee stays in the Rocky Mountain region of the U.S. all year. They have adapted to the cold, snowy winters by lowering their body temperature at night. This helps them use less energy so they can skip the extra trip for a midnight snack. During the day, chickadees fill up on high-energy foods and stash snacks for later use. A deer hunter watched a group of chickadees each carry away about one pound of deer fat in a single day! They stuffed and pounded it with their small pointed bills into every tree bark hole and crack they could find. That is a mighty job for a tiny bird.

Habitat Café

Yumm . . . bring an order of caterpillars and the eggs of gypsy and codling moths. A friend of the forest, they eat moths that are destructive to some trees. Black-capped Chickadees are insectivores.

SPRING, SUMMER, FALL MENU:
 Mostly insects, some seeds and berries

WINTER MENU:
 Insects and an equal amount of seeds, berries and fat

Life Cycle

NEST A hole is made in the soft, rotten wood of a tree, 4–10 feet above ground. The female lines the nest with rabbit fur, moss, feathers and even the soft threads of insect cocoons. A chickadee uses a different nest each year, whether it makes its own, uses a man-made nest box, or recycles a cavity made by woodpeckers.

EGGS About ½ inch long. The female incubates the clutch of 6–8 eggs for 12–13 days. The male brings food.

MOM! DAD! Altricial. Both Mom and Dad feed the young and remove the fecal sacs (chick diapers), which are covered in a slippery coating. This makes the job of taking them out of the nest much easier!

NESTLING The young leave the nest when they are just over two weeks old.

FLEDGLING Their pink feet and bill soon turn black and they look just like Mom and Dad.

JUVENILE Juveniles stay with their parents for about a month and then join a small winter flock. At one year of age, they are mature enough to date, mate, nest and raise their own young.

Birding Tip

When you slice a summer melon and carve an October pumpkin, save the seeds for backyard birds. First, spread the seeds on a pan to dry. Then, place the dry seeds on the ground or in a feeder. Birds need water too. Fill an empty milk jug with water, make a tiny hole in the bottom, and hang it directly above a bird bath or pool of water. Birds are attracted to the sound of dripping water.

When

Diurnal. Chickadees are active during the day and rest at night.

Migration
Permanent resident. In winter, chickadees form groups of 6–10 birds, breaking up into pairs in spring. On cold winter nights they may squeeze into their own small tree hollow or share a large tree cavity or roost box with up to 50 birds.

Nesting
Chickadees begin excavating nest holes in April–May, with egg laying and incubation following about two weeks later.

Getting Around
Look for a flash of lighter color on the tips of their gray wings in flight. When they need to escape a predator they can change directions in just three-hundreths of a second! How do they stay hanging upside down while picking insects off the underside of a tree branch? They have special leg muscles. They creep up and down tree trunks and hop from twig to twig.

Where to Look
Deciduous and mixed forest with open edges all over the Rocky Mountain region. Set out black oil sunflower seeds in feeders and watch for chickadees to visit.

Year-round	Summer
Migration	Winter

Montane & Aspen Parkland Forest

75

Song Sparrow

Melospiza melodia

Length: 4½–6½ inches (12–17 cm)
Wingspan: 7–9½ inches (18–24 cm)

Gray conical bill for eating seeds

Brown with gray and black streaks above

Large brown spot on chest

White throat and underneath with black and brown streaks

Males are larger than females

"Sweet, sweet, sweet." The male declares his territory or attracts a female with 2-3 identical notes and then a cheery jumble.

Uno, 4M and the Backyard Science of Margaret Morse Nice

On a spring day in 1928, Margaret Morse Nice met Uno and 4M, two male Song Sparrows having a territory battle in her Ohio backyard. Margaret was determined to watch Uno for several hours each day to discover exactly what he did and how he did it. What followed changed the basic understanding of one of the most common sparrows in North America. She discovered that the males sang about 260 songs per hour and that each male had his own unique variation of the species' song pattern. Margaret trailed and documented generations of Song Sparrows in her neighborhood for 14 years—she was hooked! Some of the facts on these pages are the result of her discoveries. Thank you, Margaret.

Habitat Café

Yumm . . . bring an order of insects and seeds with a side order of fresh fruit and berries. Song Sparrows are *omnivorous*; they eat both plant and animal matter.

SPRING & SUMMER MENU:
 Mostly insects and other small invertebrates

FALL & WINTER MENU:
 Mostly seeds and fruit, some insects

day's Special

ants
racked corn/
millet
BIRD FEEDER TREAT

Life Cycle

NEST The female builds the open nest cup on the ground, hidden in grasses or a low shrub. She weaves an outer basket with grass, weed stems, leaves and strips of bark. It is lined with fine grass.

EGGS About ¾ inch long. The clutch of 3–5 eggs is incubated by the female for about 12–13 days. When Brown-headed Cowbirds (page 120) are in the area, the nest of the Song Sparrow is often host to their eggs. When a cowbird is at or near the nest, Song Sparrows may stop building and abandon the nest, or send the cowbird packing.

MOM! DAD! Altricial. Parents feed the chicks insects, like spiders and aphids, and eat or remove the fecal sacs (the chicks' diapers).

NESTLING The chicks have a fast growth spurt in their first week— they grow feathers, open their eyes, stand up, and start to beg for food.

FLEDGLING They leave the nest at about 8–10 days of age but are dependent on their parents for another 2–3 weeks.

JUVENILE They are mature enough on their return the following spring to nest and raise their own young.

Unsolved Mystery

Try this backyard science. Find a Song Sparrow in your neighborhood and follow it, just as Margaret Morse Nice did. Take note of how many times and where the bird sings, its behavior and interactions with other birds. Can you tell a difference in the songs of individual Song Sparrows? Return to watch the bird—is it in the same area? Can you tell where its territory begins and ends by watching territory battles? Try this with backyard birds like wrens and robins. Explore the outdoors!

When

Diurnal. Song Sparrows are active during the day and rest at night.

Migration

Permanent resident to short-distant migrant to snow-free wintering areas lower in the mountains, plains and urban areas.

Nesting

Song Sparrows begin nest construction in April in the Rocky Mountain region of the U.S. They may raise 1–3 broods per season.

Getting Around

Song Sparrows make a short, flitting, direct and low flight between perches in low trees or shrubs. They run when on the ground and sometimes walk with a skip.

Where to Look

In the Rocky Mountain region of the U.S., Song Sparrows are found from the elevations of the montane and aspen parkland forests, to shrubby edges, open habitats near water, wetlands, fields, pastures, lake edges, roadsides, and even city parks and backyards.
· *Super Adaptor*

Year-round
Migration

Summer
Winter

Montane & Aspen Parkland Forest

Western Wood-Pewee

Contopus sordidulus

Length: 5½–6 inches (14–16 cm)
Wingspan: 10 inches (26 cm)

Peaked, crested head shape of a flycatcher

Dark gray-brown above, light below

Male and female look similar

White bars on long wings

Small feet

"Pe-ee, come to me." Male chatting with female.

Lightning Quick

Wood-Pewees are in the flycatcher bird family, and the name is fitting. Pewees position themselves for mealtime success. They sit silent and still on a perch near a forest or stream opening where it's easy to see flying insects against a background of sky or forest. All the while they are on the lookout for their next meal. Once a flying insect is detected, the pewee leaves the perch in a floating glide toward its unsuspecting prey. Then, in a shift to lightning-quick speed it hawks the insect out of midair. Biologists call this "aerial hawking." The pewee returns to its perch to gobble uneaten prey.

Habitat Café

Yumm . . . bring an order of the flying insect combo plate: moths, bees, wasps, flies, ants, beetles and bugs. Western Wood-Pewees are insectivores. They eat a diet of insects.

SPRING, SUMMER, FALL, WINTER MENU:

Insects

Life Cycle

NEST The female builds the small nest cup on a forked tree branch (often aspen) generally 15–40 feet above the ground. Spiderwebs are used to hold together the nest base of plant stems, grasses and bark. The nest inside is made cozy with feathers, plant down, and fine grass. The outside of the nest is camouflaged with bits of moss and bud scales.

EGGS Nearly ¾ inch long. The female incubates the clutch of 2–4 eggs for 12–15 days.

MOM! DAD! Altricial. The newly hatched young give squeaky peep calls to beg Mom and Dad for food. For the first few days they are fed insect soup (regurgitated, spit-up insects).

NESTLING Mom spreads her wings over the pink and nearly feather-less chicks to shield them from rain and sun. By the end of the first week their feathers begin growing.

FLEDGLING The young leave the nest at just over two weeks of age.

JUVENILE At one year of age, they can nest and raise their own young pewees.

Did You Know?

A bird's nest is an incubator for the eggs and a crib for the growing chicks. It needs to be camouflaged, weather resistant, and made with materials from the bird's habitat. For forest song-birds like the Wood-Pewee, spider silk is a wise choice. It is strong, light and elastic. Spider dragline silk is only a tenth the diameter of a human hair with nearly twice the strength of steel (weight-for-weight). Spiderman and Wood-Pewees have a common superpower: spider silk!

When

Diurnal. Western Wood-Pewees are active during the day and rest at night.

Migration

Spring Arrival: Apr–May
Fall Departure: Aug–Sep
Mid- to long-distance migrant to the tropical forests of Central and South America.

Nesting

Western Wood-Pewees begin nesting in May–June in the Rocky Mountain region of the U.S.

Getting Around

Western Wood-Pewees have the long and slim wings of an excel-lent flier. Their wings power flight maneuvers to capture flying insects for food. Their small feet are a clue that they spend little to no time hopping or walking on the ground.

Where to Look

Look for Western Wood-Pewees in open coniferous, deciduous and mixed forests and forest edges, often near an area with water where flying insects are in large supply.

Year-round
Migration

Summer
Winter

Western Tanager

Piranga ludoviciana

Length: 6½–7½ inches (16–19 cm)
Wingspan: 11½ inches (28 cm)

female

Females are duller in color than males and without red head feathers

Bill dull yellow

Black and yellow with a reddish head

Legs and feet bluish gray

"Pir-ri pir-ri pee-wi pir-ri pee-wi." Males sing this song in spring and summer to say, "This is my space."

Color Me Bright

If the Western Tanager was your school mascot you'd be waving a red, yellow and black banner. Bird feathers have pigments that give them color. White feathers do not have pigment. There are three main kinds of feather pigments: cartenoids (red, orange, yellow), melanins (black, brown, pale yellow) and porphyrins (red, brown, green, pink). The red of the male Western Tanager's head feathers has a complicated origin. It comes from a chemical found in the needles of a pine tree. Insects eat the pine needles. The tanager then eats the insects. The chemical inside the insect bodies is processed by the tanager and becomes just the right combination to make the rare red pigment rhodoxanthin.

Habitat Café

Yumm . . . bring an order of insects with a side order of fruit and berries. Western Tanagers are omnivorous. They eat both plant and animal matter. Attract wildlife to your yard or common space by planting cherry and apple trees, berry bushes and canes, and other fruit-bearing plants.

SPRING & SUMMER MENU:
 Insects and some fruit

FALL & WINTER MENU:
 Insects and fruit

day's Special

stink bugs

Life Cycle

NEST The female builds the loose nest bowl just 3–10 feet above the ground in a coniferous tree, a vine or a shrub. She uses dead grass, plant roots and stems for the nest basket and then lines it with fine, soft grass and animal hair.

EGGS Nearly 1 inch long. The female incubates the clutch of 3–5 eggs for about 13 days.

MOM! DAD! Altricial. The parents work as a team with Dad delivering food (every 30 minutes at first and by the end of the first week, every 15 minutes) and Mom feeding the chicks regurgitated (spit up) insect soup until they are ready for solid food.

NESTLING After the chicks are fed, they maneuver to the edge of the nest, wiggle their tail, and deposit a fecal sac (chick diaper). Mom and Dad try to catch any falling sacs before they hit the ground and then carry them away so predators don't know chicks are in the area.

FLEDGLING At 11–15 days old the chicks leave the nest to the safety of a nearby tree. Parents may feed them for another couple weeks.

JUVENILE They are mature enough the following spring to nest and raise their own young tanagers.

Birding Tip

Not all Western Tanagers look exactly alike. The color of their head can range from light orange to deep red. They live over a wide area with different food sources that affect their diet. This may be the reason for the differences in the yellow, orange and red colors between birds.

When

Diurnal. Western Tanagers are active during the day and rest at night.

Migration

Spring Arrival: Mar–May
Fall Departure: Aug–Oct
Mid-distance migrant. Western Tanagers migrate by night at high altitudes to wintering grounds in Mexico and Central America.

Nesting

Western Tanagers begin nesting in May in the Rocky Mountain region of the U.S.

Getting Around

Their flight is fast and straight with rapid wingbeats. They hop on the ground and use their wings to help them jump between branches.

Where to Look

Western Tanagers live in the open coniferous and mixed coniferous-deciduous forests of the Rocky Mountain region of the U.S. Look for them in open areas, orchards and city parks during migration.

Year-round   Summer
Migration   Winter

Mountain Bluebird

Sialia currucoides

Length: 6½–8 inches (16–20 cm)
Wingspan: 14 inches (36 cm)

female

Female: blue wings, tail and rump; blue-gray above, gray below

Black eye, bill and legs

Darker blue above, lighter blue below

"Eee-ee-e."
This soft warbling song can be heard at all times during the day.

Building for Success

Bluebirds need tree cavities for nesting. An older or rotting tree is a wildlife hotel complete with buffet dining. The number of bluebirds dropped with the loss of habitat. In the western United States, folks have teamed up to build bluebird nesting boxes and place them along forest edges and other habitats that bluebirds need for catching insects and raising their young. Success happens. As a result, the number of Mountain Bluebirds in the region has increased. You can become a part of this success story by planting and leaving valuable habitat and building and monitoring your own bluebird nesting boxes.

day's Special
beetles

Habitat Café

Yumm . . . bring an order of insects with a side order of small fruits sprinkled with seeds. Mountain Bluebirds are omnivorous. They eat both plant and animal matter. Put wiggly mealworms in a low to mid-level feeder and watch for a blue visitor.

SPRING & SUMMER MENU:
 Insects with some fruit and seeds

FALL & WINTER MENU:
 Fruit and seeds with some insects

Life Cycle

NEST The female builds the nest of conifer needles and grasses in a natural tree cavity made by other birds, such as woodpeckers, or in nesting boxes.

EGGS Nearly 1 inch long. The female incubates the clutch of 4–7 pale blue eggs for about 13 days. The male feeds the incubating female for the first week after the chicks hatch so she can remain on the nest and keep the chicks warm.

MOM! DAD! Altricial. The chicks are fed soft-bodied insects, like caterpillars, and are eased into eating grasshoppers and spiders.

NESTLING Their growth is quick and they can make their first, clumsy flights by the time they are ready to leave the nest.

FLEDGLING They are coaxed from the nest between 18–21 days when parents hold an insect just out of reach from within the nest. When their parents sound an alarm, they freeze in place or duck down in the grass. They have mock battles with adults to learn to defend territory.

JUVENILE At one year of age they are mature enough to nest and raise their own young.

Birding Tip

Be a part of the success story of Mountain Bluebirds by building and monitoring a nest box or by volunteering for a local or state project. For nesting box plans and to learn about projects in your area visit the North American Bluebird Society at www.nabluebirdsociety. org. The Colorado Bluebird Project has a goal of creating a trail of bluebird nest boxes across the entire state! Learn more at www.denveraudubon.com/bluebird.htm

When

Diurnal. Mountain Bluebirds are active during the day and rest at night.

Migration

Spring Arrival: Feb–Apr
Fall Departure: Sep –Nov
Short-distance migrant. Mountain Bluebirds gather in family groups in late summer and then larger flocks that move to wintering areas at lower elevations. Some bluebirds travel to wintering areas in the southern U.S. and as far as Central Mexico.

Nesting

Mountain Bluebirds begin nesting in April–May in the Rocky Mountain region of the U.S.

Getting Around

Mountain Bluebirds forage on the ground for insects and swoop from their perch to catch flying insects. They can hover and make quick turns, but their usual flight has a fluttering appearance.

Where to Look

Look for Mountain Bluebirds in open forests and their edges and in mountain meadows and grasslands up to alpine tundra and subalpine elevations.

Year-round   Summer
Migration   Winter

Montane & Aspen Parkland Forest

83

Bullock's Oriole

Icterus bullockii

Length: 6½–7½ inches (17–19 cm)
Wingspan: 12 inches (31 cm)

Younger males resemble females, which are greenish-yellow with a black throat

Older males have bright black head, eye stripe, throat, and back

Large white wing patch

Yellow-orange face and underneath

"Cut cut cudut whee up chooup." The male sings this musical warble from a tree to attract a female and declare his space.

Backyard Buffet

If you live in an area with large cottonwood or willow trees, then you have a fair chance of hearing and seeing Bullock's Orioles. Increase your chances by setting out grape jelly, sliced apples, grapes and oranges. Orioles also feed on nectar. Add variety to your backyard buffet with protein-packed mealworms and nuts. Leave out the lawn chemicals that can travel through the food chain and cause harm to both people and wildlife. Next, plant their favorite fruit sources like cherry trees, elderberry, blackberry, raspberry, mulberry and juneberry shrubs. Finally, lure orioles in with nesting materials: yarn, string, animal hair and plant down. Sit back and enjoy your new neighbors!

Habitat Café

Yumm . . . bring an order of moth and butterfly larvae, crickets, grasshoppers, beetles and spiders with a side order of fresh fruit and nectar. Bullock's Orioles are omnivorous. Some birds see UV light and many ripe fruits reflect UV light but the leaves around them do not. This allows them to zero in on their next snack!

SPRING & SUMMER MENU:
 Insects with some nectar and fruit

FALL & WINTER MENU:
 Nectar with some fruit and insects

Today's Special

nectar at nectar feeders

Life Cycle

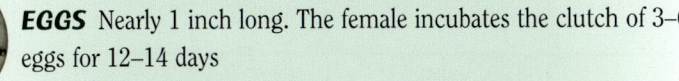

NEST The female weaves the pouch-like nest on the tip of a high and drooping tree branch. She hangs loops of plant fibers and long grass around the branch. Plant silk is woven through the loops to make a hanging sock 4–14 inches deep. The pouch is lined with soft wool, grass and animal fur. Set out brightly colored string, yarn or fabric strips in your yard and she may weave them into her work of art!

EGGS Nearly 1 inch long. The female incubates the clutch of 3–6 eggs for 12–14 days

MOM! DAD! Altricial. Both Mom and Dad feed the chicks and remove the fecal sacs (diaper duty).

NESTLING Chicks have pinfeathers poking through by the end of their first week.

FLEDGLING The young leave the nest about two weeks after hatching.

JUVENILE They stay with their parents for a few days. At times, the young from a few nests join together in a crèche (group) and are fed by the various parents. After a few days they may join a group of orioles and prepare for migration.

Did You Know?

In their Costa Rican wintering grounds, orioles feed on the fruit and insects found in both the tropical lowland forests and on coffee plantations. Planting Inga trees between the rows shades the coffee trees and makes more habitat for wildlife. Migratory birds depend on habitat around the world for their survival. Well done, Costa Rica!

When

Diurnal. Bullock's Orioles are active during the day and rest at night.

Migration
Spring Arrival: Apr–May
Fall Departure: late Aug–Sep
Mid- to long-distance migrant. Bullock's Orioles migrate in small flocks at night to their southern wintering areas in western Mexico and as far south as central Mexico and northwest Costa Rica.

Nesting
Bullock's Orioles begin nesting in May in the Rocky Mountain region of the U.S. They nest in large trees at the edge of a forest that borders a river, lake or other water area (called riparian habitat).

Getting Around
Bullock's Orioles use full wing strokes in their direct and strong flight. They take short hops in trees when searching for insects (foraging). They can even hang upside down to eat fruit and weave their nests!

Where to Look
Look for Bullock's Orioles in open forests with large cottonwood, sycamore and willow trees situated near water habitats.

Year-round   Summer
Migration   Winter

Montane & Aspen Parkland Forest

Black-headed Grosbeak

Pheucticus melanocephalus

Length: 7–7½ inches (18–19 cm)
Wingspan: 12½ inches (32 cm)

female

Female brown with striped head, sides and back

Black head

White wing patches, yellow underwing patch

Cinnamon orange underneath with yellow belly patch

"Cherry-whip, chip-cherry-chip." This robin-like song is sung by both the male and the female.

Black-white tail

Global Warming and Birds

Black-headed Grosbeaks, like other migratory birds, depend on habitat around the globe for survival. How does global warming affect birds? Is spring migration becoming earlier and fall migration later? Are nesting ranges moving north? Birds belong to a complex food web. Birds that nest in North America take advantage of the summer increase in insects (protein) to fuel their chicks' fast growth. This timing has evolved over thousands of years into a synchronized pattern of events. How does global warming affect the food web? Be a part of science and help find the answers. Join the National Audubon Society's "Great Backyard Bird Count" to record events in the natural world.

Habitat Café

Yumm . . . bring an order of insects and fruit. Black-headed Grosbeaks are insectivores and frugivores (fruit-eaters). They glean insects from high in the trees and in the lower shrubs and bushes.

SPRING, SUMMER, FALL, WINTER MENU:

 Insects and fruit

Life Cycle

NEST The male may help the female as she builds the cup nest in the fork of a tree or shrub just 4–12 feet above the ground.

EGGS About 1 inch long. Both the female and male incubate the clutch of 2–5 eggs for 12–14 days.

MOM! DAD! Altricial. The featherless, orange-skinned chicks weigh about as much as a penny. Their call for food is, *hur-ee-up!*

NESTLING The chicks are fed and kept warm by each parent in turn.

FLEDGLING They leave the nest at about two weeks of age. They stay under cover for another couple of weeks until they can fly and protect themselves from predators.

JUVENILE Females are mature enough to mate and nest the following spring, but males must wait another year as it takes the young males two years to gain adult plumage.

Did You Know?

On a moonlit September or April night when you lay quietly in your room, open the windows wide, pull your pillow to the windowsill and listen. The sky is alive. You may even hear the faint migration calls of some of the hundreds and thousands of birds passing overhead. Each species has a call they use during migration to communicate. It's a wonder that anyone can think of sleep on nights with wildlife on the move in the starry sky—the stuff of dreams!

When

Diurnal. Black-headed Grosbeaks are active during the day and rest at night.

Migration

Spring Arrival: Apr–May
Fall Departure: Aug–Oct
Mid-distance migrant. Black-headed Grosbeaks migrate to wintering areas in central and southern Mexico.

Nesting

Black-headed Grosbeaks begin nesting in May in the Rocky Mountain region of the U.S.

Getting Around

Black-headed Grosbeaks hop from branch to branch on the ground. Their fast-winged flight has a slight up and down bounce to it.

Where to Look

Black-headed Grosbeaks live in a variety of habitats, all of which include large trees and a lower layer of shrubs near clearings or water.

Year-round   Summer
Migration   Winter

Hairy Woodpecker

Picoides villosus

Length: 7–10 inches (18–26 cm)
Wingspan: 13–16 inches (33–41 cm)

female

Male has a red band across the back of head

Black above with white center stripe

White underneath

The long, thin white feathers in the middle of its back give this bird its name

Black wings and tail

"Drum, drum." This is used to declare territory, to call out to a mate, call out a location, or to react to an intruder.

Hairy vs Downy

Hairy and Downy Woodpeckers are nearly twins. Look for these clues to tell them apart. The Hairy is larger. Its bill is as long as its head and it does not have any marks on its outer tail feathers. The sparrow-sized Downy is a petite member of the woodpecker family that can find food in smaller spaces. Its bill is shorter than its head and it has black wings with white spots. Their drumming patterns of these two birds reflects their sizes. The larger Hairy has a louder, slower and more irregular drum. Its rattle call is lower pitched and more forceful than the Downy's. Whether you are watching a Hairy or a Downy, you are sure to have a wood-erful time!

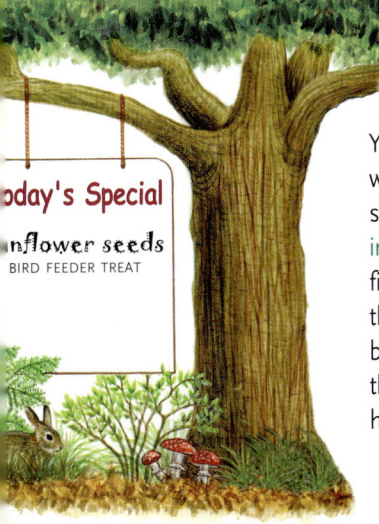

Habitat Café

Yumm . . . bring an order of insects and spiders with a small side order of seeds and fruit, and a sip of tree sap. Hairy Woodpeckers are mainly insectivores. They tap a tree with their bill to find an insect tunnel and then chisel to reach the insects. They rake them in with their long barbed tongue (up to four times the length of their bill). Their tongue is curled inside their head like a tape measure!

SPRING, SUMMER, FALL, WINTER MENU:
 Insects and some seeds, fruit

Life Cycle

NEST Both the female and male make the nesting hole in a tree with a decayed center, 5–40 feet above the ground. The outside hole is about 2½ inches high and 2 inches wide. The inside of the nest cavity is 10–12 inches deep and 4½ inches in diameter. The eggs are laid directly on the wood chips.

EGGS About 1 inch long. The parents take turns incubating the clutch of 3–6 eggs for 11–12 days.

MOM! DAD! Altricial. Mom and Dad bring meals of regurgitated (spit up) insects until the chicks are ready for whole insects.

NESTLING Woodpecker chicks have a heel pad that protects their feet from the rough nest edges. The pad is shed once they leave the nest.

FLEDGLING The young birds can fly and leave the nest at about one month of age.

JUVENILE The following spring they are mature enough to find a mate, excavate a nest hole, and raise their own young woodpeckers.

Do the Math

How many drumbeats can a woodpecker drum? A lot. If they make 15 drumbeats in one second, how may drumbeats can a woodpecker drum in one minute? Ten minutes? (Put your answers here, _____.) How do woodpeckers drum without getting a big headache? Shock absorbers: strong neck muscles and an extra thick skull help cushion the brain. The answers are on pages 194–195.

When

Diurnal. Hairy Woodpeckers are active during the day and rest at night.

Migration

Permanent resident. Hairy Woodpeckers stay in the Rocky Mountain region of the U.S. all year.

Nesting

Hairy Woodpecker females stay in their nesting territory all year. The male joins her in late winter. They begin actual nesting activity in April–May in the Rocky Mountain region of the U.S.

Getting Around

How do they stay on a tree while drilling or searching for insects? Their toes are zygodactyl: two toes point forward and two point backward. Their long, curved claws are super for getting a tight grip. Their stiff tail feathers act as a brace against the tree trunk and as a spring to help them move forward as they hitch up a tree. Their flight is undulating (up and down) in a series of wing flaps and then a bound forward.

Where to Look

Look for Hairy Woodpeckers in the deciduous and coniferous forests throughout the Rocky Mountain region.

Year-round   Summer
Migration   Winter

American Robin

Turdus migratorius

Length: 8–11 inches (20–28 cm)
Wingspan: 12–16 inches (31–40 cm)

female

Females not as brightly colored as males

Gray above with very dark head, wings and tail

White eye-ring and white chin

In flight, look for the white between their tummy and tail

Young have speckled breast and white flecks on their dark backs

"Red" breast— brown to dark red-orange

White tips on outer tail feathers

Brown legs

"Cheerily, cheer-up, cheer-up, cheer-up, cheerily, cheer-up!" This cheery song is sung during the time of nesting and incubation.

Squirmy Worms & Super-sized Storage

When you see an American Robin with its head turned to the side and looking with one eye at the ground, it is probably ready to pounce on an insect with its yellow bill. Rather than eat it right away, the robin may store the food in its stretchy esophagus to digest later. Robins eat about 14 feet of earthworms in one day. At this rate, how many feet of earthworms could a robin eat in a week? Do the math (answer on pages 194–195). In the winter, robins pack their esophagus full of berries before the sun goes down. They digest food from this storage space when their body needs a snack before morning. Delicious!

Habitat Café

Yumm . . . bring an order of earthworms, beetles, grasshoppers, larvae, crickets, spiders, berries and other fruits. American Robins are omnivorous. They need more protein-rich insects during egg-laying and molting season than in the winter.

SPRING, SUMMER, FALL MENU:
Mostly fruit and berries, lots of insects

WINTER MENU:
Mainly fruit and berries, some insects

Life Cycle

NEST The female builds the nest in the fork of a tree, on a fence post, a window ledge, or a man-made nesting platform. The outside of the nest is made with dead grass and twigs. To get just the right shape, she uses the bend of her wing and presses from the inside. Next, she carries mud in her bill for the inside. She turns her body in the hollow of the cup for the final fitting. The nest is lined with soft, dead grass.

EGGS About 1 inch long. The female incubates the clutch of 3–4 bright blue eggs for 12–14 days.

MOM! DAD! Altricial. The chicks hatch without feathers. Their skin is so thin that you can see the inside of their tiny bodies.

NESTLING The chick that begs the soonest, stretches its neck the highest and holds it beak closest to the parent gets food first. During the first 10 days, each nestling gets 35–40 feedings per day.

FLEDGLING They leave the nest at about 2 weeks of age and stay on the ground, fed mostly by Dad while Mom prepares for the next brood. Leave fledglings for their parents to care for, and keep your cat inside.

JUVENILE In late August, juveniles form a flock and prepare to migrate south.

Birding Tip

Make a small mud puddle in your backyard. (It's a good idea to ask first.) Watch from afar as a female robin takes mud for building her nest. When you see a mud-covered female, you'll know her nest is nearby. Set out bright colored yarn and string. She may use this in her nest, too!

When

American Robins are diurnal. They feed during the day and rest at night.

Migration

Spring Arrival: Mar–Apr
Fall Departure: Sep–Nov
Short-distance migrant. Winters in southern states in areas without snow cover and with plenty of food, such as fruit from shrubs. May travel as far south as Mexico.

Nesting

American Robins begin nesting in April–May. They raise 1–2 broods each year. Most nest within 25 miles of their birthplace.

Getting Around

Robins are speedy, using their sturdy leg muscles to run and hop in the grass. You may see them stop and look around quickly for prey or predators, and then they are off running. During migration, robins are fast, straight fliers, with their pointed wings (20–36 mph). They use their medium-length tail for steering through trees during a quick escape.

Where to Look

Most of the Rocky Mountain region, in areas with open woods, forest edges, farm windbreaks, parks or backyards.
· *Super Adaptor*

Year-round   Summer
Migration   Winter

Gray Catbird

Dumetella carolinensis

Length: 8–9 inches (21–24 cm)
Wingspan: 9–12 inches (22–30 cm)

Black crown
and forehead

Dark gray above and
lighter gray below

Straight bill with
long bristle feath-
ers at the base
to help in insect
foraging

Long black tail
with rust color
underneath

Female and male
look similar

"Mew." This cat-like call
is given by both the
male and female to send
predators packing.

Mew, Mew

A friend asked me to help find a cat stuck in a thicket. In his words, "The poor thing must have been after all the birds in there." Perched in the berry thicket was a Gray Catbird singing his song collection, which includes calls of a tree frog, a cat, lawn equipment and 44 other species of birds. Gray Catbirds produce song from both the left and right chamber of their syrinx. Both sides have the same range but generally the left syrinx produces the lower frequency notes, like a pianist who divides the playing between the right and left hands. Invite catbirds to your yard with plantings of plum, Amur maple, honeysuckle and chokecherry. Add blackberry and raspberry plants and you can picnic too!

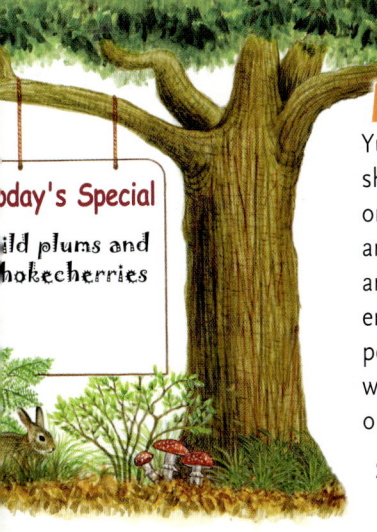

Habitat Café

Yumm . . . bring an order of fruit from wild shrubs, vines and berry canes with a side order of insects and seeds. Gray Catbirds are omnivorous, they eat both plant and animal matter. They visit backyard bird feeders stocked with grape jelly, sliced apples, peanuts, raisins, broken walnuts and mealworms. Place feeders near shrubby thickets or create a brush pile nearby.

SPRING, SUMMER, FALL, WINTER MENU:
 Mostly fruit with some insects, seeds and nuts

Life Cycle

NEST The female builds the deep cup nest in a vine, shrub or low tree 3–10 feet above the ground. She gathers grape or cedar bark, twigs, grass and stems. She then weaves a nest basket and lines it with fine rootlets.

EGGS About 1 inch long. The clutch of 3–5 eggs is incubated by the female for about 12–13 days. Dad guards the nest.

MOM! DAD! Altricial. Mom and Dad feed the nestlings protein-packed insects to fuel their early growth spurt.

NESTLING Direct sun can be hot on the tender skin of a partially feathered nestling. Parents create a sun umbrella by perching on the rim of the nest and spreading their wings.

FLEDGLING The young leave the nest about 10 days after hatching but continue to be fed by Mom and Dad for nearly two more weeks.

JUVENILE The young are mature enough on their return from wintering areas the following spring to nest and raise their own young.

Do the Math

Bulk up! Gray Catbirds increase in muscle and body mass to prepare for fall migration. The pectorals, the muscles that power the down flap of their flight, increase in size by nearly one-third. They also need the muscle to carry the extra fat reserves that fuel migration. How much extra? They add about half their body mass (weight). If you weighed one-and-a-half times what you do now, what would you weigh? (See answers on pg. 194–195.)

When

Diurnal. Gray Catbirds are active during the day and rest at night. However, they are one of the few songbirds that sing into the night.

Migration

Spring Arrival: April–May
Fall Departure: Aug–Oct
Short- to mid-distance migrant to the southern U.S. or as far south as Panama and the West Indies. They generally travel just far enough south to find fruit from trees and shrubs.

Nesting

Gray Catbirds begin nest construction in May.

Getting Around

Catbirds maneuver through and just above a thick tangle of shrubs with a combination of hopping and short flights of even wingbeats. During courtship (dating), the male fluffs his feathers and chases an equally fluffed up female.

Where to Look

Look to the scientific name of the Gray Catbird for a clue to their habitat. *Dumetella* means "small thickets," which describes the thick, brushy undergrowth in deciduous forests, edges, parks, backyards and overgrown fields where catbirds nest and find food.

Year-round	Summer
Migration	Winter

Mourning Dove

Zenaida macroura

Length: 9–13½ inches (23–34 cm)
Wingspan: 15–18 inches (37–45 cm)

side profile

Small head

Males have a rosy colored breast

Light gray above and buff below with black spot on wing and tail

Young are mottled with white wingtips

Short, red legs and fleshy, red feet

Females have a tan breast and brown crown and are smaller than males

"Coo-oo, OO-OO-OO." The male's call to attract a female. Try this. Blow softly across the neck of an open bottle. It will sound similar to a dove.

Long tail that comes to a point

Cooing All Over the United States

Coo-oooo-oo-oo . . . You may wake up to the soothing coos of a love-struck Mourning Dove in Idaho, Montana or Colorado. You may hear the whistle of their wings on a ranch in Wyoming. Mourning Doves are Super Adaptors, able to live in many different habitats all over the U.S. As long as they can find seeds to eat and cover to nest in, Mourning Doves will be in our cities, ranches, farms, parks, and suburban neighborhoods. Spread cracked corn on the ground. A cooing neighbor may come close enough to sketch, photograph, or to simply enjoy their coo . . . mpany.

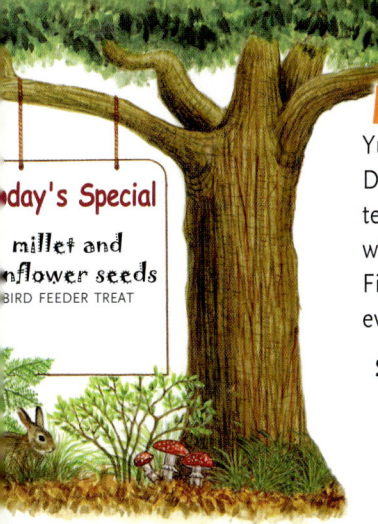

Habitat Café

Yumm . . . bring an order of seeds. Mourning Doves are herbivores. They eat seeds scattered over short grass, and from bird feeders with a perch. At times, they will eat insects. Fill your backyard bird bath; birds need water every day!

SPRING, SUMMER, FALL, WINTER MENU:

 Almost all seeds

Life Cycle

NEST The nest is built in a tree or shrub, in an old nest of another bird, such as a robin, on the ledge of a building, or on the ground. Both parents make the flimsy platform nest of twigs and line it with finer twigs.

EGGS About 1¼ inches long. For over 2 weeks, Dad incubates the 2 eggs during the day and Mom takes the night shift.

MOM! DAD! Altricial. For the first week, Mom and Dad feed the young crop milk. This bird baby formula is a secretion from their crop that has water, nutrients (including high levels of vitamins A and B) and a higher protein and fat content than human or cow's milk! Seeds are gradually added at an increasing rate each day.

NESTLING At least one parent stays at the nest at all times.

FLEDGLING Young leave the nest at about two weeks of age. They continue to be fed some seeds by Dad in decreasing amounts until they are about one month of age, when they forage for seeds on their own.

JUVENILE Juveniles flock with other immature doves and move to areas with plentiful food, such as fields of harvested wheat.

Did You Know?

Mourning Doves pick up as many seeds from the ground as their bi-lobed crop will hold. The seeds are digested later in the safety of their nesting and roosting site. A bird's crop is a large sac at the bottom of the esophagus. How many seeds can a Mourning Dove's crop hold? The highest number recorded was over 17,000 bluegrass seeds!

When

Mourning Doves are diurnal. They feed during the day and rest at night.

Migration

Spring Arrival: Apr–May
Fall Departure: Oct–Nov
Permanent resident to short-distance migrant. They move to warmer areas in the cold months because their fleshy feet are easily frostbitten. Some travel as far as Mexico, but some Mourning Doves may overwinter in the Rocky Mountain region.

Nesting

Mourning Doves begin nesting in the Rocky Mountain region in April and may continue through August. They raise 1–4 broods per year.

Getting Around

Mourning Doves walk or run on the ground when foraging for food rather than hopping. In flight, Mourning Doves are swift, changing direction and altitude quickly.

Where to Look

Most of the wooded areas of the Rocky Mountain region, except deep, thick forests. Look for Mourning Doves in your neighborhood!

· *Super Adaptor*

Year-round   Summer
Migration   Winter

Western Screech-Owl

Megascops kennicottii

Length: 7–10 inches (19–25 cm)
Wingspan: 19–24 inches (48–61 cm)

Ear tufts mimic sticks

Yellow eyes

Male and female look alike, females generally larger

Gray to brown-gray

Large feet and feathered toes

Makes a variety of calls, including a double trill, a bark, a whinny, a chirp, a screech, and a bouncing ball call.

Magicians Among Us

Magicians live in the trees of the western forests. One may even live near your yard, school or local park. You will need to learn their magic tricks to find them. Under the veil of darkness, Western Screech-Owls perch on a limb to stalk their next meal. When the light of day materializes, they hide in the chamber of a tree or a hollow limb, perhaps staring right at you. What is their secret to being invisible? They sit straight up to look like tree bark, raise their ear tufts like tree sticks, squint their eyes to mere slits, and hold their feathers and wings tight against their body. If you are very close, they may shift sideways and raise a wing like a cloak of invisibility, covering all but their eyes. Abracadabra!

Habitat Café

Today's Special

mice

Yumm . . . bring an order of mice, voles, songbirds, squirrels, bats, rabbits, snakes, toads, frogs, crayfish, salamanders, beetles, moth larvae, crickets, grasshoppers, cicadas and fish. Western Screech-Owls are carnivorous. Active at night, they capture prey with their feet.

SPRING, SUMMER, FALL, WINTER MENU:

 Small mammals, birds, insects, reptiles and crustaceans

Life Cycle

NEST True recyclers, screech-owls lay their eggs on old flicker nests or those of other birds in a tree or limb hollow, or a stump, about 5–30 feet from the ground. The eggs are laid on the contents of the nest floor: old leaves, rotted wood, or leftovers from previous renters.

EGGS About 1½ inch long. The female incubates the clutch of 3–5 eggs for 26–30 days. The male stays near and brings food.

MOM! DAD! Altricial. The chicks depend on Dad for the first three weeks to bring food and Mom to tear it into bite-sized pieces.

NESTLING They practice their first vocals, making eerie trills into the night. If threatened they stretch their wings, hiss, and sway back and forth.

FLEDGLING At about four weeks all the chicks leave the nest on the same night for a nearby limb or tree. Mom and Dad stay near and bring food for about 2 months while they practice being predators, pouncing on objects and learning to cache food.

JUVENILE At one year of age, they can nest and raise their own woodland magicians. Poof!

Did You Know?

You can make a simple nest box for screech-owls. Use lumber about ¾ inch thick; 2¾-inch-diameter entrance hole, its bottom 10 inches above floor; front-sloping lid 2 inches above entrance hole, overhanging 1 inch, hinged at back, hooked at side; floor 7 x 7 inches with nail-sized drain holes in bottom corners. Place the box 10–13 feet high on a tree trunk in a shady area about 100 feet from any other owl nest box or cavity. Sprinkle about 1 inch of dry leaf litter on the bottom. Have fun!

When

Nocturnal. Western Screech-Owls are active at night (nocturnal) and sometimes at dawn and dusk, called crepuscular.

Migration

Permanent resident. Western Screech-Owls stay in the Rocky Mountain region of the U.S. all year.

Nesting

Western Screech-Owls begin courtship in January–February and nesting in March–April in the Rocky Mountain region of the U.S.

Getting Around

Screech-Owls are sit-and-wait predators that fly low through the forest in a steady flight. To capture prey on the ground, they walk, hop or run.

Where to Look

Look for Western Screech-Owls in open forests, particularly in open forests near water at low elevations. They can be found in urban and suburban parks and neighborhoods where there are nesting and roosting trees available.

Year-round
Migration

Summer
Winter

Northern Flicker

Colaptes auratus

Length: 11–12 inches (28–31 cm)
Wingspan: 16½–20 inches (42–51 cm)

yellow-shafted

Long bill

Brown area around eye

Male has a red mustache, called a malar

Black bib on tan breast with black spots

Gray-brown with dark bars on back

Flight feathers have red shafts

White rump patch shows in flights

Male defends his space with a loud "wik wik wik wik" with at times, 30–40 "wiks" in one rolling call

Anteater-on-Wings

What eats the most ants of any North American bird? What member of the woodpecker family rarely pecks? The Northern Flicker. Rather than peck wood out of a tree for a nest hole, Northern Flickers choose a rotten tree and dig out the punky (soft) wood. They generally don't use their bill to peck for food either. Anteaters-on-wings, flickers probe the forest soil with their bill and snap ants up with their 3-inch-long, sticky tongue. Invite flickers by keeping dead trees as wildlife hotels. Build and place nest boxes filled with sawdust too. Once flickers come and nest, you may have long-time lodgers. They often return to the same site each year!

Today's Special

Carpenter ants, suet and raisins

BIRD FEEDER TREAT

Habitat Café

Yumm . . . bring an order of ants and beetles with side orders of grasshoppers, topped with wild fruits and berries, a few seeds and nuts. Northern Flickers are omnivorous, eating both plant and animal matter. A researcher counted some 5,000 ants in just one flicker!

SPRING & SUMMER MENU:
 Mostly insects with some fruits and berries

FALL & WINTER MENU:
 Berries of trees, shrubs and vines with some insects

Life Cycle

NEST Both the male and female dig away wood in a dead or dying tree, called a snag. Flickers also use fence posts, poles and nest boxes packed with sawdust. The nest tree is generally located near anthills.

 EGGS About 1 inch long. The clutch of 5–8 eggs is incubated by both parents for about 11–14 days.

MOM! DAD! Altricial. Parents store ant larvae in their crop and deliver this lunch to their young by spitting it back up.

NESTLING A peck on the chick's heel or rump is a signal from Mom and Dad that it is diaper duty time. Parents eat the sacs for the first ten days and carry the sacs away from the nest from then on.

FLEDGLING The young leave the nest when they are nearly four weeks of age and generally in the order that they hatched.

JUVENILE Watch for flicker families filling up on ants near anthills in late summer. At one year old, flickers are able to drum-and-date, mate and raise their own family.

Did You Know?

An important part of the forest ecosystem, flicker nests are recycled by American Kestrels and some ducks. European Starlings are a different matter. They will barge into an active flicker nest, take out the eggs and set up house. Red squirrels will kill young flickers in the nest. Buzzzzzz . . . beware. When threatened, young flickers mimic the sound of a swarm of bees. So long, predators!

When
Diurnal. Flickers are active during the day and rest at night.

Migration
Spring Arrival: Apr
Fall Departure: Sep–Oct
Short-distance migrant flying mostly by night to wintering areas in the southern U.S. Some flickers may overwinter in the Rocky Mountain region.

Nesting
Flickers begin egg laying in May in the Rocky Mountain region in areas with dead and dying trees or in nest boxes. Flickers defend their breeding and nesting territory by noisily drumming on a variety of objects, including trees, poles and metal objects.

Getting Around
Flickers hop when on the ground or on a tree or limb. Their flight is up-and-down, called undulating. The stiff tail is used as a prop when drumming.

Where to Look
Forest edges and open woodlands bordering fields. Two subspecies overlap in the region: the Yellow-shafted and the Red-Shafted Northern Flicker. The color under their wings, tail, and the shafts of the flight feathers will help determine the subspecies in your area.

Year-round   Summer
Migration   Winter

Montane & Aspen Parkland Forest

Cooper's Hawk

Accipiter cooperii

Length: 14½–15½ inches (37–39 cm)
Wingspan: 24½–35½ inches (62–90 cm)

Red eyes

soaring

juvenile

Gray above;
underside is
white with
rust-colored bars

Immature: yellow eyes;
brown back with brown
streaks on breast and belly

Females are one-third
larger than the males

Short, rounded
wings for cruising
around trees

"Cak-cak-cak!"
This call is given by
males and females when
the nest is in danger or
the bird is excited.

Long gray tail with black
bands and a white tip

Small Birds Beware—Accipiter in the Area!

The eyes have it. Cooper's Hawks have eyes so large there is little room left in their skull to move them. Hawks move their entire head from side to side and up and down to get a full range of vision. They are equipped with a monocle, a pair of binoculars and a telescope! Monocular vision allows each eye to see a separate image. The bird can scan and search for prey. Once located, binocular vision (both eyes seeing forward) allows the bird to judge the distance and depth of moving prey. Telescopic vision then allows the hawk to zero in on prey by making the image larger. Small birds beware—a Cooper's Hawk with eyes nearly as large as its stomach may be spying on you!

Habitat Café

Yumm . . . bring an order of Mourning Doves, robins, Blue Jays, starlings, chipmunks, rabbits, squirrels and mice with a side of frog. Cooper's Hawks are carnivorous. During nesting season, prey may be cached (stored) in a roost tree.

SPRING, SUMMER, FALL, WINTER MENU:

 Mainly birds, with a few mammals, reptiles, amphibians and insects

Today's Special

bats

Life Cycle

NEST The male and female build the bulky twig and stick nest 20–60 feet high in a deciduous or coniferous tree. The 2-foot-wide nest is lined with small chips or flakes of bark.

EGGS About 2 inches long. The female incubates the clutch of 4–5 eggs for 24–36 days.

MOM! DAD! Altricial. Mom broods the young for the first two weeks. She spreads her wings as an umbrella.

NESTLING Dad brings the food and Mom tears the prey into bite-sized pieces. Parents carry away food pellets and uneaten food. Diaper duty? Not in this nest. The young are able to scoot to the rim of the nest and take care of this stinky job on their own.

FLEDGLING The young leave the nest when they are about one month old. Mom and Dad continue to bring food for nearly two more months.

JUVENILE At two years of age they are ready to date, mate and raise their own young.

Do the Math

In a study of a Cooper's Hawk nest, researchers found that it took an average of 66 robin-sized prey to raise one young hawk to the age of six weeks. How many prey would parent hawks need to capture for a family of three chicks over six weeks? Four chicks? Five chicks? Where do they find prey? Watch your bird feeders for a Cooper's Hawk shopping for a meal—and they do not eat bird seeds or suet! Answer on pages 194–195.

Answer on pages 194–195.

When

Cooper's Hawks are diurnal. They feed during the day and rest at night.

Migration

Spring Arrival: Apr–May
Fall Departure: Sep–Oct
Short- to mid-distant migrant following along mountain ridges to the southern United States, Mexico, and as far south as Central America.

Nesting

Cooper's Hawks begin nesting in April–May.

Getting Around

Cooper's Hawks fly low to the ground in a series of fast wing-beats and then a swift glide. Gliding saves energy, and uses 1/20 the energy of normal flight.

Where to Look

Deciduous and mixed deciduous-coniferous forests, often near a river or lake. They hunt along forested edges.

Year-round   Summer
Migration   Winter

Montane & Aspen Parkland Forest   101

Great Horned Owl

Bubo virginianus

Length: 18–25 inches (46–63 cm)
Wingspan: 3–5 feet (101–145 cm)

in flight

spitting pellet

Very large, yellow eyes

Ear tufts; the only large Rocky Mountain region owl with long, feathered ear tufts

Hooked beak to tear the muscles and bones of prey

Facial disc of feathers funnel sound waves to their ears for extraordinary hearing

Both males and females have brown, black and cream lines over most of their body, with a white bib

Females are heavier and larger than males

"Who-hoo-ho-oo?" or, "This is my territory." Hooting duets between paired males and females can be heard from January until the first eggs are laid.

Flying Mousetrap

The hooting of Great Horned Owls can wake you up just about any season and anywhere in the Rocky Mountain region, whether you are tucked under your winter covers or watching summer fireflies light your room. Winter is the best time to listen for owls, but I've been driven to giggles on summer nights, listening to young owls practicing their whooing. *Super Adaptors*, they live in cities, rural farming areas and places in between. They need a large tree for nesting and plenty of mice, rabbits, squirrels and skunks for the taking. The full menu includes stray cats and animals as large as porcupines! Hear a Great Horned Owl in the night and know that this flying mousetrap is hard at work in your neighborhood.

Habitat Café

Yumm . . . bring an order of mice, rabbits, hares, ground squirrels, muskrats, squirrels, pocket gophers, snakes, small birds, pheasants, ducks and geese. They may take animals as large as raccoons, skunks, porcupines, or Great Blue Herons. Great Horned Owls are carnivorous.

SPRING, SUMMER, FALL, WINTER MENU:
Mostly mammals, a few birds

Life Cycle

NEST These big owls do not make their own nest. They use a hollow tree cavity or an old hawk, crow, heron or squirrel nest in the top of a tall tree. Owls may line the recycled nest with some of their own feathers. They will also nest in a man-made nest base.

EGGS About 2 inches long. The female incubates the clutch of 2–3 eggs for 28–33 days. She does not leave the eggs for more than a few minutes at a time, to keep them from freezing.

MOM! DAD! Altricial. Cold, wind and snow mean that Mom broods the young downy chicks for the first three weeks. Dad brings food. As feathers replace the down, Mom leaves to hunt too.

NESTLING Able to feed themselves at about four weeks of age.

FLEDGLING At six weeks of age, young owls venture out to nearby branches. Their first test flights begin the following week.

JUVENILE Teenage owls stay with their parents during the summer and set out to find their own territories in late fall and early winter. At 2 years of age, they are able to mate and raise their own young.

Gross Factor

What does an owl do with the bones and fur of their eaten prey? It forms them into a pellet and spits them back up. You'll know you're under an owl roost when you find gray, 2–3-inch pellets. Break open a compact pellet and you may discover the tiny bones of a mouse, the jawbone of a rabbit, spine sections of a gopher, or the beak of a starling, all surrounded by undigested fur.

When

Nocturnal. Feeds at night and rests during the day. At times, they will hunt during the day.

Migration

Permanent resident. Stays all year in the Rocky Mountain region of the U.S. Many predators fly south for the winter, leaving Great Horned Owls to take advantage of less competition for prey.

Nesting

One of the earliest nesting birds in the region, it begins nesting in February. This adaptation may provide them with enough time for the young to mature and lets them take advantage of greater food availability.

Getting Around

Silent flight. An extra fuzzy covering over the flight feathers quiets the rush of air over the short, wide, powerful wings. It tucks its head in and holds its wings straight out, alternating strong wingbeats with glides. On the ground, it walks in alternating steps.

Where to Look

Look for Great Horned Owls in open areas, perched on poles, fence posts, trees and rock outcrops, scanning for food.
· *Super Adaptor*

Year-round / Migration — Summer / Winter

Grasslands, Cliffs
and Canyons

The habitat margins of open sky and land are home to hardy and spectacular birds. Some birds living in open areas have adapted to small niches along roadsides and field margins while others need large unbroken grasslands, pastures or canyon lands to survive.

Open Sky and Land

The backbone of the great Rocky Mountains stretches north from Idaho and Montana all the way south to Colorado. The mountains serve as a

barrier, blocking the moist air traveling from the Pacific Coast. This moisture is dropped on the west side of the mountains, leaving the east side of the mountains in what is called a "rain shadow," an area with little moisture. The land flattens eastward into the great open prairies that once hosted huge herds of buffalo. Today in the wide-open areas of grass and field, Northern Harriers perform aerial dances and food exchanges as precise as circus acrobats. Perched on a fence post, a black-bibbed Western Meadowlark rehearses his flute-like whistles. In the next field over, a Vesper Sparrow sings in the evening while overhead a Red-tailed Hawk zeroes in on a jackrabbit for a meal.

Cliffs and Canyons

Volcanoes, earthquakes and millions of years of wind and water erosion have created spectacular cliffs and canyons in the Rocky Mountain region.

The wildlife that lives here seeks out shade from the sun, shelter from the winds, and cover from predators. The spaces between rocks and boulders become premium nesting and roosting sites. Incubating its eggs in the shade and safety of cliff walls are Prairie Falcons and lower down are the nests of Cliff Swallows. Building a sidewalk to its nest in the rocky outcrops is the small and energetic Rock Wren.

Look to the open sky for Turkey Vultures riding an updraft over a

Prairie Falcon

nearby river. They are easy to identify by their broad wings with leading flight feathers that look like long, outstretched fingers. As they glide close to the ground to locate their prey with their sense of smell, they rock from side to side. Another large predator, the Golden Eagle zeros in on a jackrabbit from over a mile away.

Incredible Critters

Plants and animals that inhabit open areas have adaptations to survive the harsh conditions of the summer heat and winter cold, the lack of moisture, and strong winds. American Goldfinches don't migrate south. They put on a coat of extra feathers and stay for the winter, feeding in large flocks. American Kestrels scan the roadsides until snow covers the ground and then head to warmer areas to find prey. While they are away, consider building a kestrel nest box and placing it in an appropriate grassland habitat. Monitor the nest box over the spring and summer and record the activity. You can then share your results with state and national organizations that collect bird data (see pages 196–197 for a listing). Providing for the needs of wildlife and being a part of science is great fun!

American Goldfinch in winter plumage

Public areas and those managed by private organizations, such as The Nature Conservancy, are great places to spy on birds. You can also find birds along the margins of roadsides and field edges across most of the region. For up-to-date information on where to find birds in your area check out the Ornithologists' Union and Audubon Club in your state; most sponsor field trips, educational programs and breaking news on the locations of resident and migratory birds. Head outdoors. Wildlife is waiting for you in the open spaces of the Rocky Mountain region.

Check Off the Grasslands, Cliffs and Canyons Birds You See!

When you spot birds in the open spaces of the Rocky Mountain region, use these pages to check them off. The locations of these illustrations indicate where you might see them.

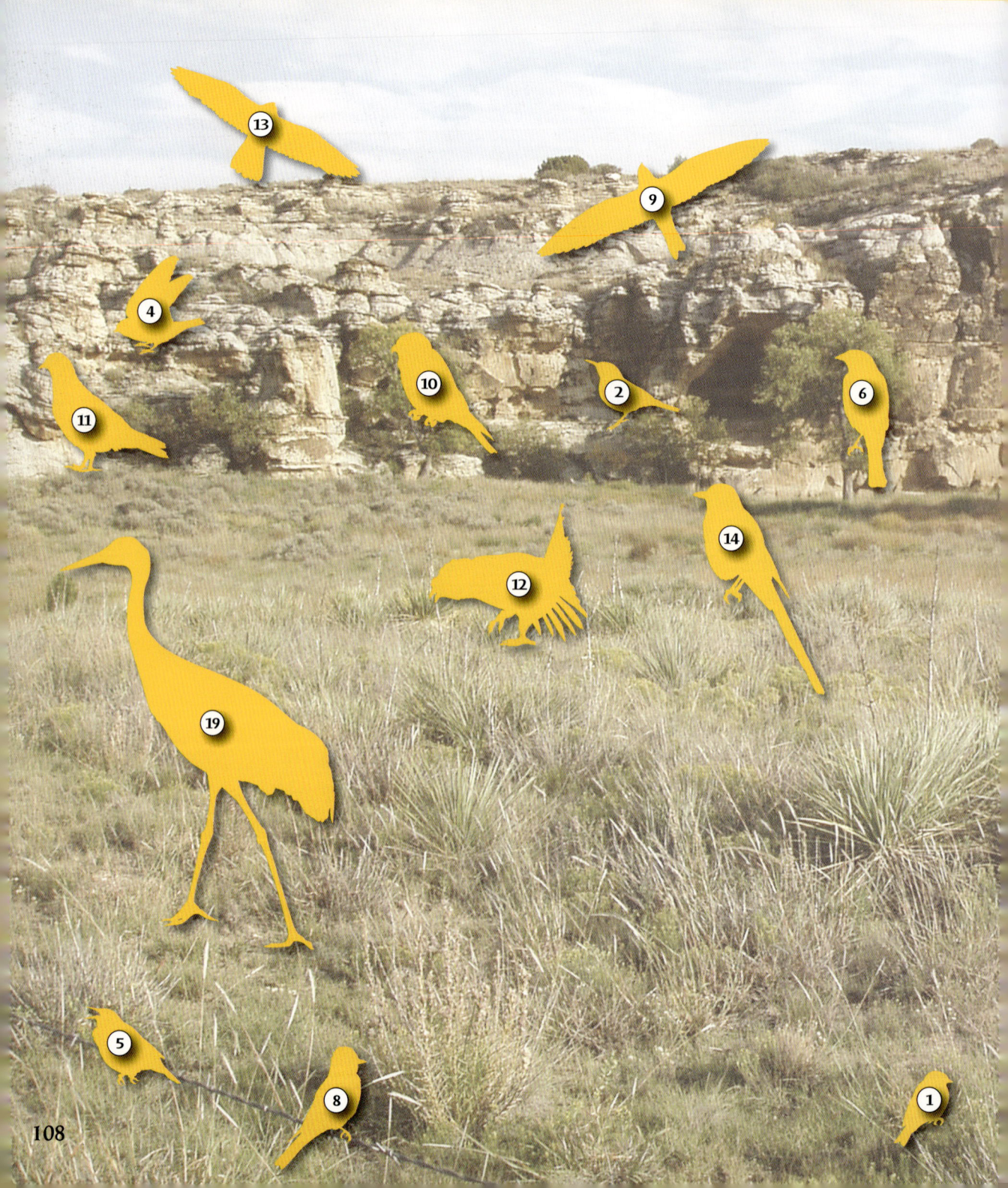

American Goldfinch

Spinus tristis

Length: 4–5 inches (11–13 cm)
Wingspan: 7½–8½ inches (19–22 cm)

male winter

female

Black cap

The male is bright yellow in summer, olive-green in winter

Females are olive-green with pale yellow chest and throat, and no black cap

White rump

"Po-ta-to-chip!" means "This is my space!" (Sounds like a squeeze-toy.)

Black tail is notched

Leap-Frogging Goldfinch

Cold, wind, ice and snow send many birds packing their feathers and heading south for the winter. They are looking for warmth and food. American Goldfinches stay. They have adapted to chilly winters and the change from the large food supply of summer to a limited winter store of seeds. In fact, they can make winter feeding look like a group game. Taking turns in leap-frog fashion over mass seed sources is an efficient (energy-saving and safe) way for goldfinches to feed in large winter flocks. This rolling motion over a field helps to protect the flock from predators. Your turn!

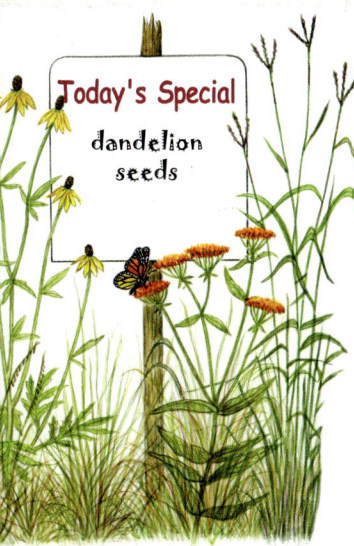

Today's Special
dandelion seeds

Habitat Café

Yumm . . . bring an order of thistle seed and spring tree buds peppered with aphids. Fill your backyard bird feeder with Nyjer thistle seed. American Goldfinches are mostly granivorous; they feed on seeds and grains. They use their cone-shaped bill to break open seeds.

SPRING, SUMMER, FALL, WINTER MENU:
Mostly seeds, a few insects

Life Cycle

NEST The female builds the cup-shaped nest 2–20 feet above the ground in the fork of a thistle, a shrub, or a deciduous tree. With spider silk, she weaves a nest base to the support branches. Next, rootlets are woven in. Soft thistle down is added last. The nest is so compact (tight), it can hold water like a cup!

EGGS Almost ¾ inch long. The female incubates the 4–6 eggs for 12–14 days. The male feeds her regurgitated (spit-up) food from his crop. Gross, but it works!

MOM! DAD! Altricial. Both mom and dad feed the young. For the first four days Dad feeds Mom, and then she feeds the chicks.

NESTLING Feathers replace the chicks' down when they are about one week old, nearly the time they are ready to leave the nest.

FLEDGLING Young goldfinches continue to be cared for by the male for three more weeks. They can then forage for seeds on their own.

JUVENILE Juveniles have feather colors and patterns similar to an adult female. They group with other goldfinches and move to areas with plenty of food. In one year, they can nest and raise their own chicks.

Did You Know?

Most parent birds feed their young a diet of high-protein insects. American Goldfinches feed seeds to their young. When Brown-headed Cowbirds lay their eggs in the nest of a goldfinch, the cowbird chicks do not survive (for more about cowbird habits, see page 120). The seed diet does not have enough protein for cowbird chicks to live. The goldfinch chicks then have the full attention of their parents.

When
Diurnal. American Goldfinches are active during the day and rest at night.

Migration
Permanent resident to occasional short-distance migrant. The American Goldfinch may move to southern regions of the U.S. during harsh winters. Some stay as year-round backyard visitors throughout the U.S. Rocky Mountain region.

Nesting
The American Goldfinch begins nesting as early as May–June or as late as July in the Rocky Mountain region. Many wait until thistle and milkweed plant down are mature and fluffy for use in their nest.

Getting Around
The male flies in spiral circles over the nesting area. He sings his most impressive "po-ta-to-chip." Two or three males join, each circling in crisscross paths, like fluttering bright-yellow butterflies. Biologists call this behavior a Butterfly Flight Pattern.

Where to Look
Open grasslands, rural fields, shrub edges, and backyards throughout most of the Rocky Mountain region.

Year-round   Summer
Migration   Winter

Grasslands, Cliffs and Canyons

Rock Wren

Salpinctes obsoletus

Length: 5–6 inches (12–15 cm)
Wingspan: 9 inches (23 cm)

Grayish-brown

Male and female have
similar plumage

Rusty brown rump

Brown tail with
black bars

Light underneath

"Tic-ear!"
Both males and females do a body bob when using this call. They are telling intruders to skedaddle, beat it.

Paving the Way Home

The Rock Wren is all about rocks. It lives in the cracks of rock piles in the Rocky Mountains. It is the same color as its rock-strewn habitat. This small energetic bird even builds a rock sidewalk up to the doorstep of its nest. The female builds the nest on the ground in a crack (gap) on a hillside, often under a rock that is hanging out. The male then pitches in to build a sidewalk. They use between 100 and 500 rocks that are as small as a lima bean or as large as a half-dollar coin. The reason for the rocky path has stumped scientists. Rock Wrens have paved the way for exciting detective work. Try your skills at solving this mystery.

Today's Special
spiders

Habitat Café

Yumm . . . bring an order of crickets, grasshoppers, beetles, moths, leafhoppers, ants and other ground-dwelling insects with a small side order of seeds. Rock Wrens are insectivores. They use their long and slender bill to capture insects.

SPRING, SUMMER, FALL, WINTER MENU:
Insects

Life Cycle

NEST The nest is made in the hollow or crack of a rock wall or sometimes a building. The female makes a 4–8 inch diameter nest base of grass, sticks and small pieces of wood and then lines it with feathers, fur, insect cocoons, soft plant down and even spider silk.

EGGS Nearly ¾ inch long. The female incubates the 4–6 eggs for 12–16 days.

MOM! DAD! Altricial. Both parents feed the helpless chicks.

NESTLING Parents are kept very busy. They have been seen making 240 food deliveries to a nest in just one day!

FLEDGLING The young are coaxed from the rocky nest by their parents at about two weeks of age and often hide under a nearby rock. Predators like snakes and raptors lurk nearby.

JUVENILE They are fed by Dad for a week after they leave the nest and stay near their parents for another month or so.

Unsolved Mystery

It's exciting to learn first-hand about the Rock Wren. Start with writing down your questions and then go to an area where Rock Wrens live. Observe all that they do. Make detailed notes and drawings and take photos. Share your experience and knowledge with others. The information from kids all over the West can help solve the mysteries of this feisty friend of rocky places.

When

Diurnal. The Rock Wren is active during the day and rests at night.

Migration

Spring Arrival: May
Fall Departure: Sep
Permanent resident to short-distance or partial migrant. Rock Wrens generally stay in their location all year but some may move from higher to lower elevations or to locations to the south during winter months.

Nesting

Rock Wrens begin nesting in April–May in the Rocky Mountain region of the U.S.

Getting Around

Rock Wrens are ground birds that run after their insect prey. They quickly step-hop from rock to rock. They use fast and steady wingbeats in their direct flight.

Where to Look

Rock Wrens live in open, sunny and dry habitats where there are piles of rocks. Areas with cliffs and slopes are popular.

Year-round   Summer
Migration   Winter

Grasslands, Cliffs and Canyons

113

Vesper Sparrow

Pooecetes gramineus

Length: 5–6 inches (13–16 cm)
Wingspan: 9½ inches (24 cm)

Larger, lighter colored and shorter tail than Song Sparrow

Pale, grayish-brown above and light below with dark streaks all over

White outer tail feathers

Their musical song starts with 2-4 notes, then a slur (sounds melted together), and lastly trills (very fast notes) that sound like a flute.

Songster of the Evening

Vesper means evening, the time when night is beginning. The Vesper Sparrow sings during the day and into the evening in open fields, meadows and grasslands. When we sing, sound comes from our vocal cords. When a bird sings it comes from a voicebox, or syrinx. The syrinx has two different rooms, called chambers. Messages from the left side of the syrinx go to the left chamber while messages from the right side go to the right chamber. With two different chambers, one bird can sound like two birds singing at the same time. Birds control how loud the sound is by filling air sacs. The air sacs lean just a little or a lot on the muscles of the syrinx, determining volume. Sing on sparrows!

Today's Special
grasshoppers

Habitat Café

Yumm . . . bring an order of the insect combo with a side order of seeds and grains. Please pass the grit, too. Vesper Sparrows are omnivorous.

SPRING, SUMMER, MENU:
 Insects and some seeds

FALL, WINTER MENU:
 Seeds, with some insects

Life Cycle

NEST The female builds the nest in a sunken area in the ground, hidden by the plants around it. She weaves dried grass, animal hair and rootlets to make a nest basket. The nest is then lined with fine grasses, animal hair, feathers and sometimes pine needles.

EGGS Over ¾ inch long. The female incubates the 3–5 eggs for 12–13 days.

MOM! DAD! Altricial. The pink-skinned and helpless chicks are kept warm by Mom, called brooding. Both parents feed the chicks a diet high in insects. Insects have a lot of protein. Chicks need protein to make bones, muscles and many other things.

NESTLING Parents lead predators away from the nest by faking injury.

FLEDGLING The young leave the nest after 9–10 days, but need Mom and Dad for another 3–4 weeks. Dad takes over if Mom starts another brood of chicks.

JUVENILE They are mature enough the following spring to nest and raise their own young sparrows.

History Hangout

John Burroughs was a naturalist, a scientist that studies the natural world and how all the parts work together. In 1885 he wrote *Wake-robin*, a book about his adventures with birds. He included a sparrow common in fields that sang a very sweet song. "His song is most noticeable after sundown, when other birds are silent; for which reason he has been aptly called the vesper sparrow . . . the poet of the plain, unadorned pastures." The name Vesper Sparrow was first given by another naturalist, Wilson Flagg.

When

Diurnal. Vesper Sparrows are active during the day and rest during most of the night.

Migration

Spring Arrival: Mar–Apr
Fall Departure: Aug–Sep
Short-distance migrant. Vesper Sparrows go only as far south as they need to find winter weather where they can survive. Some stay in their home area and others overwinter in the south.

Nesting

Vesper Sparrows begin nesting in April–May in the Rocky Mountain region of the U.S.

Getting Around

Vesper Sparrows are ground birds that move through grasses and plants in quick runs and hops. They fly using quick, sharp moves that show their outer white tail feathers. Dust baths help them to get rid of feather mites and other uncomfortable bird conditions.

Where to Look

Another name for the Vesper Sparrow is "grass sparrow," after its favorite habitat. Look for them in open grasslands, mountain meadows, fields, roadsides, and other dry, open habitats with places to perch and with short, patchy grasses and other plants.

| Year-round | Summer |
| Migration | Winter |

Grasslands, Cliffs and Canyons

Cliff Swallow

Petrochelidon pyrrhonota

Length: 5 inches (13 cm)
Wingspan: 11–12 inches (28–30cm)

Blue back

Male and female look similar

White triangle on forehead

Orange rump

Square tail

Chestnut-colored throat, neck

White underneath

"Chur, chur!" or, "Hi, it's me, your mate (or parent, or offspring)."

Social Swallows

Cliff Swallows are a social bunch. They nest in colonies with up to 3,000 nests, gather in groups at mud holes to collect mouthfuls of nest mud, and fly in groups to eat swarming insects. Young swallows gather in crèches (large groups) and flying teams after they leave their parents. Being social has its advantages. Swallows can learn directions to an insect picnic from their neighbor. Predators find it hard to attack with hundreds of swallows on the lookout. But, with many nests and chicks in the same place how do parents tell them apart? Swallow parents use a system of voice ID to tell their own chicks from all the other famished, begging chicks. "Son, I'd recognize your voice anywhere!"

Today's Special
mosquitoes

Habitat Café

Yumm . . . bring an order of flying insects and a side order of more flying insects. Cliff Swallows are insectivores. To get the latest scoop on where a group of swallows is feasting, a swallow watches for a neighbor to return with food and then follows it to the feeding frenzy.

SPRING, SUMMER, FALL, WINTER MENU:
Flying insects

Life Cycle

NEST Both the male and female build the gourd-shaped mud nest under the overhang of a cliff, bridge or building, in a colony of other Cliff Swallow nests. They gather 900–1200 mud pellets (a mouthful equals a pellet) to make the nest exterior. The nest is lined with grass, feathers or hair. It takes 1–2 weeks to build the nest.

EGGS Over ¾ inch long. Both the female and male incubate the 2–6 eggs for 15 days.

MOM! DAD! Altricial. The chicks' insect dinner is delivered in a bolus, a compressed ball, which is put into their open mouth.

NESTLING With so many nests and chicks in a colony, parents need a chick ID system. They can identify their own young by their unique begging calls by two weeks of age.

FLEDGLING The young leave the nest at about three weeks of age.

JUVENILE By the time they reach 6 weeks of age they can fly like an adult and are independent. The following spring they are mature enough to nest and raise their own young swallows.

History Hangout

In 1819–1820, Major Stephen Long led an expedition to the Rocky Mountains. On July 19th, Cliff Swallows were seen along the rocky bluffs of the Arkansas River. He noted, "This species attaches its nest in great numbers to the rocks in dry situations, under protecting ledges. It is an active bird, flying about the vicinity of the nest in every direction. In many of the nests we found young hatched." Sharing this same habitat were golden-mantled ground squirrels, rattlesnakes and bright blue Lazuli Buntings.

When

Diurnal. Cliff Swallows are active during the day and rest at night.

Migration

Spring Arrival: Mar–Apr
Fall Departure: Aug–Sep
Long-distance migrant. Cliff Swallows join groups of hundreds or thousands and fly during the day to wintering areas in South America, as far as Argentina.

Nesting

Cliff Swallows begin nesting in May–June in the Rocky Mountain region of the U.S.

Getting Around

Champions on the wing, they reach heights of 200 feet, speeds of 25–50 feet per second and make instant turns to catch insects. These talented fliers only touch ground to collect mud for their nest. Look for their downward slanted wing when they glide—they are the only swallow with this flight profile.

Where to Look

Look for Cliff Swallows at the lower elevations of the Rocky Mountains in open canyons and river valleys with cliffs and overhangs. They have adapted to urban settings that have bridges, culverts and building overhangs near feeding areas.

Year-round   Summer
Migration   Winter

Western Meadowlark

Sturnella neglecta

Length: 6½–10 inches (16–25 cm)
Wingspan: 16 inches (41 cm)

Long, pointed bill

Males are larger and females are not as brightly colored

Black "V" on chest

Bright yellow breast and belly

Short tail with white edges in flight

Long legs and toes

"Whistle!" or "Danger!" means stay low to the ground and freeze!

Woolly Mammoths and Meadowlarks

What do they have in common? Fossil records show that they both lived in North America over 10,000 years ago. Woolly Mammoths are extinct; there are no more Woolly Mammoths living on earth. Meadowlarks are still here, but with continued habitat loss their numbers continue to fall. Male meadowlarks use 5–7 acres of grassland for their breeding territory (space). What can you do? In rural areas, set aside a large grassy area free of chemicals and predators. Wait to mow, hay or graze the area until after nesting season. Include a tall post for a meadowlark to stretch its bill to the sky and sing. Set up your spotting scope. Watch and listen for a new black-bibbed neighbor!

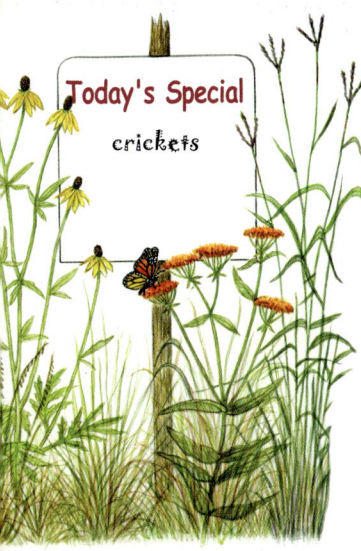

Today's Special
crickets

Habitat Café

Yumm . . . bring an order of beetles, weevils, cutworms and grasshoppers with a side order of fruit peppered with seeds. Meadowlarks are omnivorous. They eat plant and animal matter. They probe for grubs and worms by "gaping" (putting their closed, pointed bill in the ground and opening it).

SPRING, SUMMER, FALL MENU:
 Mostly insects, some seeds

WINTER MENU:
 Mostly fruit and seeds, a few insects

Life Cycle

NEST The female builds a dome-like nest in a grassy field. A deep spot in the ground is filled with large grasses and then lined with fine, soft grasses. A dome is built over the top by weaving together plants growing around the nest. An opening is left on one side of the nest with a path through the grass for coming and going.

 EGGS About ¾ inch long. The female incubates the 3–5 pale eggs for 13–14 days. If the nest is disturbed, the female will leave and not go back to incubate the eggs. Respect the need for safe nesting.

MOM! DAD! Altricial. Mom does most of the feeding. Dad does not go to the nest. He may catch insects and "beak" them over to Mom.

NESTLING Nestlings need to eat more than half of their body weight in food each day. Mom averages 100 trips per day to gather insects for her famished brood.

FLEDGLING With long, quick legs and the ability to hide in plants, the young leave the nest at about 1½ weeks of age. Their parents feed them for two more weeks, until they can fly.

JUVENILE They look like their parents but with spots instead of a black bib on their chest. The following spring they are mature enough to nest.

Did You Know?

Each meadowlark male has his own collection of songs. Meadowlarks only learn songs during a certain period of time when they are young. If they do not hear the song of a Western Meadowlark during this learning window, they will adopt a song from another bird species. Meadowlarks have even taken on the song of a Northern Cardinal!

When

Diurnal. Meadowlarks are active during the day and rest at night.

Migration

Spring Arrival: Mar–Apr
Fall Departure: Oct–Nov
Permanent resident to mid-distance migrant. Western Meadowlarks spend winter months in areas with temperatures above 10 degrees, going as far south as Mexico. In spring, males arrive 2–4 weeks ahead of females to set up territories.

Nesting

Western Meadowlarks begin nesting in April–May in the Rocky Mountain region of the U.S.

Getting Around

Meadowlarks walk and run on the ground. When a female meadowlark nears her nest, she walks closer to the ground to hide from predators. Their flight is a glide followed by quick wingbeats. They can fly 20–40 miles per hour.

Where to Look

Open grasslands, hayfields, pastures and grassy roadsides.

Year-round **Summer**
Migration Winter

Brown-headed Cowbird

Molothrus ater

Length: 7½–9 inches (19–23 cm)
Wingspan: 9–12 inches (23–30 cm)

Short conical bill

Glossy black
with brown
head and neck

female

Female is smaller than
male and has gray or
brown plumage

Fairly long
pointed wings

"Glug glug glee." Males sing
this song and if another
cowbird is near, they bow.

Buffalo Birds

The buffalo that once roamed the open prairies were not alone. Brown-headed Cowbirds followed them, eating both the insects they kicked up and insects living in their dung. Cowbirds didn't have time to stop and nest. Instead, they laid their eggs in the nests of birds that live where the prairie and forest meet. A female cowbird lays up to 40 eggs each year, none of which she hatches. Forest-edge nesters like Song Sparrows are recipients of cowbird eggs. Cowbirds do not reimburse the host species for incubation, meals and around the clock chick-care. Host species have adapted strategies in turn. They push the cowbird eggs out, build over the top, abandon the nest, or accept the eggs and raise the young.

Today's Special
grasshoppers

Habitat Café

Yumm . . . bring an order of grain and weed seeds with a side order of insects. Brown-headed Cowbirds are omnivorous, they eat both plant and animal matter. Buffalo and cattle allow cowbirds to hitch a ride while the birds eat the blood-sucking flies that feed on them.

SPRING, SUMMER, FALL, WINTER MENU:
Mostly seeds and crop grains with some insects

Life Cycle

NEST The female does not form a brood patch for incubating; rather, she lays her eggs in the nest of one or more of 144 host species. She locates a nest by watching for the host female to leave her nest. Laying eggs in multiple nests increases the cowbird's success by spreading out the risks.

EGGS About ¾ to 1 inch long. The eggs hatch after about 11–12 days, often before the eggs of the host species.

MOM! DAD! Altricial. The chicks hatch completely dependent on their host parents for food and warmth. They are usually larger than the host bird chicks.

NESTLING One way to survive is to be the biggest, loudest beak in the nest. As a result, cowbird chicks grow faster than the host species.

FLEDGLING The young leave the nest 8–13 days after hatching. They stay nearby while the host parents feed them for another week or so.

JUVENILE The young join a large group with other cowbirds, black-birds, grackles and starlings to prepare for migration. They are mature enough the following spring to lay their eggs in another species' nest.

Did You Know?

To fool host parents, female cowbirds will remove an egg from the host nest before they lay their own egg inside. This behavior may limit the number of eggs in the host nest to a manageable level for the parents to incubate and feed. Most of the host species are not harmed by the arrangement as they have adapted over time to accommodate the loss to their own species. However, species that have very specific habitat and food requirements, such as the Kirkland's Warbler (found in Michigan), can be threatened by cowbird parasitism.

When

Diurnal. Brown-headed Cowbirds are active during the day and rest at night.

Migration

Spring Arrival: Mar–Apr
Fall Departure: Sep–Oct
Short-distance migrant to areas in the southern United States. They travel about 500 miles between their spring and wintering areas. Flocks of mixed blackbirds travel at about 30 miles per hour. At this speed, how long does it take a flock to travel 500 miles between a spring and winter area? Do the math!

Nesting

Brown-headed Cowbirds begin laying their eggs in the nest of host species in April–May.

Getting Around

Cowbirds search for seeds and insects by walking and running on the ground. When singing, a male ruffles his back feathers, spreads his tail, lifts and spreads his wings, and bows. He then wipes his bill. Males may perform this together—what a sight!

Where to Look

Cowbirds can be found in many habitats. Look in low trees of grasslands, fields, pastures, edge habitats and brushy thickets.
· *Super Adaptor*

| Year-round | Summer |
| Migration | Winter |

Killdeer

Charadrius vociferus

Length: 8–11 inches (20–28 cm)
Wingspan: 18–19 inches (46–48 cm)

injury-feigning display

Olive-brown

Rusty orange rump patch is seen when tail is spread

Both the male and the female have two black bands across their breast

White underside

Long legs for wading in the shallow water and running fast

"Kill—deer, kill—deer!" or, "Sound the alarm! Danger near!"

Best Drama Award

The Killdeer spread out and crushed on the ground in front of you looks like a dying bird. It limps along with a broken wing. Watch it long enough and the wing may suddenly heal. Is the bird injured? No, it is a smart, tricky bird that has just lured you, a potential predator, away from its young. This behavior is called an "injury-feigning display." The Killdeer fakes an injury to protect its young. Your part in this drama is that of a responsible outdoor neighbor. Watch the nesting area from afar with a spotting scope or binoculars. Your reward will be more Killdeer to watch in the future.

Today's Special
crayfish

Habitat Café

Yumm . . . bring an order of grasshoppers, beetles, earthworms, ticks, and mosquito larvae with a side of green tree frog. Killdeer are omnivorous.

SPRING, SUMMER, FALL MENU:
 Mostly insects, crustaceans and amphibians, some seeds

WINTER MENU:
 Entirely insects and crustaceans

Life Cycle

NEST The nest is a simple low scrape in the ground. It is lined with pebbles, gravel or wood chips that help keep the eggs from rolling away with wind and rain. They will also nest on flat rooftops and in gravel parking lots.

EGGS About 1½ inches long. Both the male and female incubate the 4 camouflaged eggs for 24–25 days. Killdeer eggs fit together tightly with the pointed end to the center. This helps the eggs stay warm and not roll away.

MOM! DAD! Precocial. Parents do not feed the chicks. As soon as the chicks have hatched and their down is dry, the parents lead them to feeding areas. Parents brood the young for the first few days and guard them for the first ten days. Chicks can swim across small streams.

FLEDGLING If a predator comes near, chicks lay low and freeze. Some will raise their legs above the grass to look like a stem or stick. Killdeer stay with their parents and siblings until they can fly at 3–4 weeks of age.

JUVENILE Killdeer are mature enough on their spring return to nest and raise their own young. Juveniles have one black neck band.

Did You Know?

Nesting on a rooftop can be dangerous. Killdeer in this situation can be creative when it is time to lead their newly hatched chicks to food. One pair of Killdeer parents called to their chicks from the ground near the base of a rain gutter. The chicks heard the parents call to come down from the roof and they used the rainspout as a slide.

When
Killdeer are diurnal. They feed during the day and rest at night. Migrate by day and night.

Migration
Spring Arrival: Mar
Fall Departure: Sep–Nov
Mid- to long-distance migrant. Killdeer migrate south in flocks of up to 30 birds to Central and South America.

Nesting
Killdeer begin nesting as early as March and April in the Rocky Mountain region of the U.S.

Getting Around
Killdeer have a standard ground move: run a short ways, stop, bob their head and run again. They keep their body straight while their long legs are a blur of motion. In flight, they are strong and fast at speeds of 28–35 miles per hour. Adult Killdeer can swim in fast-flowing water.

Where to Look
Originally a shorebird found on mud flats and sandbars, the Killdeer has adapted to open habitats: fields, grazed pastures, golf courses, gravel parking lots, flat rooftops, soccer fields, airports and playgrounds.
· *Super Adaptor*

Year-round   Summer
Migration   Winter

Western Kingbird

Tyrannus verticalis

Length: 8–9½ inches (20–24 cm)
Wingspan: 14½–16 inches (37–40 cm)

Gray head with hidden red "king's" crown. When excited, the male raises his head feathers to show off his crown.

Dark gray mask

Gray breast

Males, females and juveniles look very much alike

Light yellow underside

Dark gray wings and black tail

"Pwee—T" is a male announcing his territory patrol or telling an intruder to hightail it away from the nest.

Tyrant of the Air

Tyrants are bullies. *Tyrannosaurus rex* dinosaurs are thought to have bullied other dinosaurs, earlier in earth's history. *Tyrannus verticalis*, the Western Kingbird, is known today for bullying bigger birds to claim its territory and protect its young. If a hawk, crow or owl flies even 100 feet above a Western Kingbird nest, watch out. The kingbird will mount a full aerial attack that includes chasing and crashing into the bigger bird from above while screeching, *Buzzzzz*! The predator is . . . out of there.

Habitat Café

Yumm . . . bring an order of grasshoppers, crickets, bees, flies, bugs and ants. Western Kingbirds are omnivorous. They feed on insects during the breeding season in North America and mostly fruit in their Mexican and Central American wintering grounds.

SPRING, SUMMER, FALL MENU:

 Almost entirely insects, some berries

WINTER MENU:

 Mostly fruit, a few insects

Life Cycle

NEST The female and male build the 6-inch-diameter cup nest 8–40 feet above the ground on a shrub or tree branch, fence post, utility pole or other man-made structure. The base is made of plant stems, twigs, rootlets and is lined with soft cottonwood down, wool, feathers, hair, or grass leaves.

EGGS Nearly 1 inch long. The female incubates the clutch of 3–5 eggs for 12–14 days.

MOM! DAD! Altricial. Both Mom and Dad help feed the young. The parents kill the prey, mostly flying insects, and remove the stingers from bees and wasps before feeding them to the young. Ouch!

NESTLING The chicks hatch naked with see-through skin and their eyes closed. After the first few days, feathers begin to form.

FLEDGLING The young normally leave the nest when they are able to fly weakly, at about 2–2½ weeks of age.

JUVENILE On their return the following spring, they are mature enough to nest and raise their own young kingbirds.

Did You Know?

Western Kingbirds wait on their perch for a flying insect to come near. They snatch it from the air in a short, quick flight called hawking. How does a bird overcome gravity to fly? How does it fly against drag, the resistance of the air flowing over its body in flight? Wing shape and physics. If you haven't studied flight yet, turn to page 192 for a wing up on lift and *Bernoulli's Principle*.

When

Western Kingbirds are diurnal. They are active during the day and rest at night.

Migration

Spring Arrival: May
Fall Departure: late Aug–early Oct
Mid-distance migrant to wintering areas in southern Mexico and Central America. They migrate during the day, alone or in small kingbird flocks.

Nesting

Western Kingbirds begin nesting in late May–June in the Rocky Mountain region of the U.S.

Getting Around

Western Kingbirds perch on plants, fence posts or branches. The male does a courtship "tumble flight" to impress and bond with a female at dawn or dusk. First, he flies high in a fluttering flight. Next, in short glides and acrobatic tumbles, he falls to the earth and his perch, Red Baron style. Good grief!

Where to Look

Look for Western Kingbirds in open and edge areas often near water. Suitable habitats often have nearby cottonwood trees for perching and nesting as well as structures like fences, power lines and poles.

Year-round
Migration
Summer
Winter

Grasslands, Cliffs and Canyons 125

Common Nighthawk

Chordeiles minor

Length: 9–9½ inches (22–24 cm)
Wingspan: 21–22½ inches (53–57 cm)

Female has buff throat and no white tail band

Small bill and enormous, wide mouth that opens like an insect net

Large, flattened head with large eyes

White throat patch

White tail band

Long, slender, pointed wings with round white patch

The male makes a booming sound during dives. It is caused by air rushing through the wingtips

High Fly Over Left Field

The baseball game ended as dark set in. Dazed insects swirled around the parking lot light. *Scheer-zoom*, a sound echoed through the warm summer air like fireworks exploding. *Scheer-BOOM*. A dark bird with a white patch on each pointed wing dove to the ground. The Common Nighthawk turned to the sky faster than we turned our head. Nicknamed the "bullbat" for its bat-like flight, this wonder bird is not a hawk, but a member of the nightjar family. Their eyes have a special part that reflects light, the *tapeta lucidum*, and it works like a pair of night vision goggles. This male nighthawk was either defending a nest or in a high fly over left field showing off to a female.

Today's Special
Flying queen ants

Habitat Café

Yumm . . . bring an order of mosquitoes and flying beetles with a side order of bugs. Common Nighthawks are insectivores. They hawk insects in flight at dawn and dusk. Their dinner menu includes a list of more that 50 species of flying insects!

SPRING, SUMMER, FALL, WINTER MENU:
 Flying insects

Life Cycle

NEST Nighthawks nest in open fields, gravel beaches, on rock ledges, or in open burned forest. They also nest on gravel rooftops. The eggs are laid on the surface without any nesting material. Males may dive and boom over the nest. With their wide mouths open, they hiss, fluff their feathers and beat their wings at intruders. They are a scary sight indeed.

EGGS About 1 inch long. The camouflaged female incubates the clutch of 2 eggs for 16–19 days.

MOM! DAD! Semi-precocial. The young are covered with some down when they hatch but still need the warmth of Mom or Dad for the first two weeks.

NESTLING Dinnertime! Dad delivers regurgitated insects to the hungry chicks before sunrise and again after sunset.

FLEDGLING The chicks take their first flight at 18 days of age and by 4 weeks they are first-rate fliers.

JUVENILE Juveniles join a migratory flock at 7 weeks of age to travel on one of the longest migration routes of any North American bird.

Did You Know?

The number of nighthawks in some urban areas has taken a dive. Researchers put the reason in part on the change from gravel roofing to synthetic, slippery roofing surfaces. By simply placing a gravel pad in the corner of a flat, non-gravel roof, you can provide a nesting area for nighthawks. Consider nighthawks a handy neighborhood insect patrol. The stomach of a nighthawk has been found to hold about 500 mosquitoes, or over 2,000 flying ants!

When
Crepuscular. Common Nighthawks are active at dawn and dusk.

Migration
Spring Arrival: May
Fall Departure: Sep–Oct
Long-distance migrant. The Common Nighthawk flies in flocks of up to 1,000 to wintering areas in South America. During their long journey they catch and eat insects both low to the ground and at higher elevations.

Nesting
The Common Nighthawk begins nesting in May–June.

Getting Around
Watching a nighthawk gracefully loop back and forth to catch insects on the wing is a great way to spend a summer evening. Look both high and low. Male nighthawks will climb up to 500 feet and then circle down through the air to catch dinner with their built-in insect net (very wide mouth).

Where to Look
Open grasslands, prairies, fields, rock outcrops, clearings in forests and burned forest areas. They have adapted to living in open city areas where they can nest on flat gravel rooftops.
· *Super Adaptor*

| Year-round | Summer |
| Migration | Winter |

American Kestrel

Falco sparverius

Length: 9–12 inches (22–31 cm)
Wingspan: 20–24 inches (51–61 cm)

Black-and-white face pattern

Markings on the back of the head look like a pair of false eyes, or "ocelli"

Hooked, sharp beak

Narrow body, long tail

female

Females have red-brown wings and seven to nine dark bands across the tail and a brown-streaked breast; females are larger than males

Juveniles look like adults with dull colors

♪ "Killy, killy, killy" means "Stay away!" ♪

Build It and They Will Come

Build a kestrel nest box and place it on a tree or a pole near a grassy area with small mammals, insects and a few snakes for good measure, and these small falcons may come. In the Rocky Mountain region, both kestrel nesting boxes and trees with hollow cavities found along the edges of open areas provide important structures for kestrels. Be involved. Build a nest box for kestrels. Ask your Audubon club for the best place to hang a nest box. Include a hinged lid to carefully check the inside of the box during nesting season and keep a record of the number of eggs, young and adults. Make an older tree in your yard a wildlife tree and watch these handy neighbors as they eat unwelcome insects and rodents!

Today's Special
mice

Habitat Café

Yumm . . . bring an order of mice, snakes, lizards, caterpillars, beetles, dragonflies, crickets and a few small birds and animals. American Kestrels are carnivorous. Kestrel parents plan for the kids' extra snacks and poor weather conditions by caching (storing) prey.

SPRING, SUMMER, FALL MENU:

 Mostly insects, some birds and animals

WINTER MENU:

 All small animals

Life Cycle

NEST Kestrels prefer to nest in a woodpecker hole or natural tree cavity at the edge of a wooded area. With the loss of nesting habitat, they have adapted to using nest boxes near their food. They do not bring in nesting materials but may add feathers. A few wood chips may be placed in the bottom of a nest box.

 EGGS About 1½ inches long. The female incubates the 4–5 eggs for 30 days. The male takes over when the female leaves for a short time each day. Both have a "brood patch," an area on the belly without feathers. Putting a bare belly to eggs keeps them warm.

MOM! DAD! Altricial. Both Mom and Dad help feed the young.

NESTLING The brown-gray chicks stay in the nest for 30 days.

FLEDGLING Parents feed the young for the first two weeks after they leave the nest.

JUVENILE The first year is the hardest for birds to survive. According to research, only 4 out of 10 kestrels reach their first birthday.

Gross Factor

How do some bird species determine the most productive hunting areas? They see the urine trails left by their prey. The urine of voles and other small mammals contains nitrogen components (chemical parts) that reflect ultraviolet (UV) light. Many birds, but not people, can see UV light and can detect the small mammal runways marked by urine along the ground!

When

American Kestrels are diurnal. They feed during the day and rest at night.

Migration

Spring Arrival: Apr
Fall Departure: Sep–Oct
Permanent resident to mid-distance migrant. Some kestrels stay year-round in the Rocky Mountain region or until snow covers the ground and prey is hard to find. Some migrate as far south as Mexico and Panama.

Nesting

American Kestrels begin nesting in April in the Rocky Mountain region of the U.S.

Getting Around

Kestrels hover in one place by facing into the wind with their wings spread. Their boomerang-shaped wings have a notch in the outer three primary feathers to aid in hovering. The tail is used as a rudder to steady the bird while it searches for prey below. Kestrels perch on utility lines and poles and look for prey.

Where to Look

American Kestrels hunt for prey along rural and urban roadways, pastures and open fields with access to a natural perch, nesting tree or nest box.

Year-round   Summer
Migration   Winter

Rock Pigeon

Columba livia

Length: 12–14 inches (30–36 cm)
Wingspan: 19½–26½ inches (50–67 cm)

Bluish-gray, white or
rusty brown all over

Two dark bands on
pointed wings

Dark tail band

Short red-pink
legs and feet

Their song is a "purring" sound from the throat followed by a "coo."

Squabs and More Squabs

Pigeons may be the rabbits of the bird world: they produce squabs (pigeon chicks) at a fast pace. Nesting goes on in all seasons with 6–7 broods a year. Even in winter they can be found with a new nest of squabs begging for their milky formula. This "pigeon milk" is produced from the lining of the parents' crop, a wide part of the esophagus (throat) where food can be stored for a short time. High in vitamins A and B and with more protein and fat than cow's milk, the cheesy-thick formula is just what young pigeons need for fast bone, muscle and feather growth. For the first days this is all the squabs eat. Seeds are then added more and more to the mix until the young find seeds on their own.

Today's Special

peas and corn

Habitat Café

Yumm . . . bring an order of seeds and a side order of fruit. Rock Pigeons are herbivores. Their food storage compartment, the crop, gives them a handy place to quickly load up a large amount of food and then fly off to digest their meal in a safe place.

SPRING, SUMMER, FALL, WINTER MENU:
 Seeds and some fruit

Life Cycle

NEST Nest building is not one of the skills of this adaptable bird. Rock Pigeons build a low, loose and skimpy platform nest with twigs, pine needles, straw, feathers, roots, grass and any other building material they can easily find. They may build a new nest on top of one from an earlier brood of squabs.

EGGS About 1½ inches long. The male and female incubate the clutch of 1–2 eggs for 17–19 days.

MOM! DAD! Altricial. Squabs hatch without feathers. Their parents spread their body or wings over the young to keep them warm.

NESTLING Parents spit up the "pigeon milk" into the open beaks of the begging squabs about 4 times a day in the beginning, and as they grow, just 2 times per day.

FLEDGLING The squabs leave the nest at about 1 month old during the summer but at 2 months old if they were raised during the colder months of the year.

JUVENILE The young stay near their parents for a week or two and then venture out on their own. In just 7–12 months they may nest and raise their own young squabs.

Did You Know?

Watch pigeons long enough and you could count up to 28 different color types, or morphs. Pigeons even wear a necklace of bright iridescent purple, green and yellow feathers, called a hackle. Count and record the different color morphs and note their behaviors to help scientists learn why pigeons can be found in so many different colors and which color morphs pigeons prefer for mates. Check out Project Pigeon Watch: www.birds.cornell.edu/pigeonwatch

When

Diurnal. Rock Pigeons are active during the day and rest at night.

Migration

Permanent resident. Rock Pigeons stay all year in the Rocky Mountain region of the U.S.

Nesting

Rock Pigeons begin nesting as early as February in the lower elevations and cities in the Rocky Mountain region of the U.S.

Getting Around

Pigeons have a streamlined body shape that aids them in flying at speeds of up to 82 miles per hour. They need to be fast to escape their natural predator and the fastest animal on earth, the Peregrine Falcon. Rock Pigeons also walk on the ground with their head moving forward and back and perch on branches with their long toes.

Where to Look

The natural wild habitat of the Rock Pigeon is on cliffs or in caves near water. They have adapted over time to living in cities and farms where they take to window ledges, bridges, barns and building crevices. Rock Pigeons are *Super Adaptors*.

Year-round
Migration

Summer
Winter

Grasslands, Cliffs and Canyons

Sharp-tailed Grouse

Tympanuchus phasianellus

Length: 16–18½ inches (41–47 cm)
Wingspan: 25 inches (64 cm)

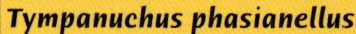

female

Males and females are similar with males heavier

White under-tail

Head, neck, back and wings barred with brown, black and buff

Round body with short legs

During courtship displays, the male puffs out his eye combs and purple neck sacs

Orange/yellow eye "combs"

Feathered nostril and legs

White upper belly marked with small dark "V"s

"Up-up-up." Both females and males give this call when taking flight. Males have six calls to attract females. Her favorite is his "bottle cork popping" sound.

Heartbeat of the Open Grasslands

The ground thumped and drummed. The air echoed clicks, cackles, coos and tail rattles. Arch-winged birds with ballooned orange brows and purple neck sacs circled invisible territories and battled for mere inches. Sharp-tailed Grouse have been performing this song and dance in the early morning each spring for hundreds of years on the open shrub land and prairies of the west. Male leks, courtship sites, include 40 acres of open area for dancing, with another 320 acres for nesting and feeding. Visit protected natural grasslands near you and witness the heartbeat of the grasslands firsthand.

Today's Special
clover & dandelions

Habitat Café

Yumm . . . bring an order of seeds, buds, insects and fruits with side orders of plants and flowers. Sharp-tailed Grouse are omnivorous. Food is often stored in their crop for digesting later. Once in the crop, food is ground into smaller pieces by small stones and chokecherry seeds—internal "teeth."

SPRING & SUMMER MENU:
Mostly insects, plants and fruit

FALL & WINTER MENU:
Seeds, buds, plants and fruit

Life Cycle

NEST The female makes the oval ground nest in thick plants and grasses, or under a shrub or small tree. The outer nest of grass, sedges, leaves and moss is lined with finer grasses and her soft feathers.

EGGS About ¾ inch long. The female incubates the clutch of 10–12 eggs for 21–23 days.

MOM! DAD! Precocial. The chicks hatch with downy feathers and their eyes fully open. They follow Mom and leave the nest to feed on their own. She protects the chicks from sun, rain and cold for the first few days. By 8 weeks of age, they are half the size of an adult, and by 12 weeks, full adult size. Everyone in this brood is on the lookout for predators: red fox, coyote, mink, Red-tailed Hawks and the stealth planes of the open grasslands, Northern Harriers.

JUVENILE The young stay close to the nest during the summer, but come September, the family members part. Young males may get a jump on the dating season and scout possible spring territories. They may practice battling with rushes, face-offs, standoffs and pecking.

Did You Know?

Watch the dance of the Sharp-tailed Grouse and you too could be dancing to the beat of the open prairies and grasslands. People have been inspired by nature throughout history, as evidenced in petroglyphs, carvings and art forms. The Rocky Mountain region of the U.S. is rich with connections to the deep cultural heritage of the people and wildlife that have long called the land home. Act with respect for the sacred meaning that cultures have for the area.

When

Diurnal. Sharp-tailed Grouse are active during the day and they rest at night.

Migration

Permanent resident. Sharp-tailed Grouse stay in the Rocky Mountain region all year.

Nesting

Sharp-tailed Grouse begin nesting in April–May in the Rocky Mountain region of the U.S.

Getting Around

Sharp-tailed Grouse travel short distances in a flight of 3 fast wing-beats and then a glide. They walk on the ground and "flight hop" from branch to branch. Their pectinae (fleshy knobs on their toes) grow longer and more numerous in the winter. This allows them to walk on the snow, as if they were wearing snowshoes.

Where to Look

Sharp-tailed Grouse live in open prairies, brush lands and clearings, often near a marshy area.

Year-round   Summer
Migration   Winter

Grasslands, Cliffs and Canyons

133

Prairie Falcon

Falco mexicanus

Length: 14½–18½ inches (37–47 cm)
Wingspan: 35½–44½ inches (90–113 cm)

Square-shaped head
with mustache feathers
called malars

White patch between eye
and dark ear patch

White throat

Male smaller than female
and with faster wingbeats

Pale brown above
and white with brown
speckles below

Dark "wing pit" (area
under wing) has black
patch at base of wing

Long, slender,
pointed wings

"Kik-kik-kik"
is a sharp-sounding
message from both the
male and female to
leave the area.

Order up: Ground Squirrels

When a Prairie Falcon is hungry in the open country of the Rocky Mountain region, you can bet they are on the lookout for tasty ground squirrels. Until, that is, ground squirrels head to underground burrows. Then, these stealthy aerial predators focus on the likes of Horned Larks, meadowlarks, and lizards. It's worth trekking to a place like the Snake River Birds of Prey National Conservation Area in SW Idaho to have a front row seat to see a falcon surprise its prey. Prairie Falcons have a hunting portfolio that includes a glide attack, a stoop (closing their wings and bulleting toward earth from 260 feet (80 meters) above the ground and a land-hugging power attack.

Habitat Café

Yumm . . . bring an order of medium-sized mammals and birds with a side order of insects and lizards. Prairie Falcons are carnivorous.

SPRING, SUMMER, FALL, WINTER MENU:
 Small mammals, birds, insects

Life Cycle

NEST They do not build a nest but lay the eggs directly on a scrape in the ground on cliffs with an overhang. Nests can be found on cliffs from 7 feet high up to 500 feet high. Most nests cannot be seen by anyone but the birds. In areas without cliffs, they may reuse a Red-tailed Hawk, a Golden Eagle, or a Common Raven nest.

 **EGGS** About 2 inches long. The female incubates the 4–5 eggs for about 29–39 days. The male may incubate at times during the day.

MOM! DAD! Altricial. The young hatch with downy white feathers.

NESTLING During the first three weeks Dad does the hunting and Mom then feeds juicy pieces of fresh meat to the hungry young.

FLEDGLING The young leave the nest at about one month of age and spend their time nearby. Mom and Dad bring food for another month.

JUVENILE At 2 years of age they are mature enough to nest and raise their own young falcons.

Birding Tip

The Snake River Birds of Prey National Conservation Area is home to many birds of the open country and birds in other sections of this book, including the Northern Saw-whet Owl, Western Screech-Owl, Great Blue Heron, Black-chinned Hummingbird, and more. It is just one stop along the Idaho Birding Trail. There are birding trails throughout the Rocky Mountain region of the U.S. to experience birds. Where is the closest trail to you? Check out the links to birding trails on pages 196–197.

When

Diurnal. Prairie Falcons are active during the day and they rest at night.

Migration

Permanent resident. Prairie Falcons remain in the Rocky Mountain region of the U.S. throughout the year. They may move to areas with better nesting habitat and more available prey according to the season.

Nesting

Prairie Falcons begin nesting as early as March, but generally April–May in the Rocky Mountain region of the U.S. They may share their nesting cliffs with Red-tailed Hawks, Golden Eagles and Common Ravens.

Getting Around

Watch for the short and fast wing strokes that power the Prairie Falcon's quick and direct flight.

Where to Look

Prairie Falcons live in the open prairies, plains, mountain canyons, cliffs and bluffs of the Rocky Mountain region.

Year-round | Summer
Migration | Winter

Grasslands, Cliffs and Canyons

Black-billed Magpie

Pica hudsonia

Length: 18–23½ inches (45–60 cm)
Wingspan: 22–24 inches (56–61 cm)

Black with white belly

Female and male markings are similar, male is larger

Metallic blue-green wings with white patch (in flight)

Black legs, feet, claws

Metallic blue-green long flowing tail

"Chatter" or "Sound the alarm, danger." The chatter notes grow faster as the danger becomes greater.

A Story to Tell

If magpies perched around your campfire they might sample your marshmallows and join in the story-telling. Magpies have been around a long time—there are magpie fossils from before the last glacial period, they have appeared in artwork created by Native Americans of the buffalo-speckled plains, and magpies stole food from the tents of Lewis and Clark in 1804. Magpies have the ability to change their behavior to the changes in the western landscape: they can adapt. There are very few buffalo to pick tasty ticks from these days, but magpies have found a new host from which to lasso ticks—cattle. Being able to adapt has given the Black-billed Magpie an ongoing story to tell.

Today's Special
grasshoppers

Habitat Café

Yumm . . . bring an order of insects, seeds and carrion with a side order of eggs and the nestlings of other birds. Black-billed Magpies are omnivorous. They eat both plant and animal matter.

SPRING, SUMMER, FALL, WINTER MENU:
Insects, carrion, seeds

Life Cycle

NEST Black-billed Magpies work on their layered nest for over a month. The nest is often built in a thorny bush or tree. Twigs are layered on the outside and a thick mud cup is made in the very center. Soft rootlets or pine needles line the cup making a cozy crib for the eggs.

EGGS About 1¼ inches long. The female incubates the clutch of 6–9 eggs for about 18 days.

MOM! DAD! Altricial. The pink and featherless chicks are kept warm (brooded) by Mom until their feathers grow in.

NESTLING Mom and Dad feed the young protein-packed insects and the meat of dead animals (carrion). They are one of nature's recyclers.

FLEDGLING The young leave the nest about 1 month after hatching.

JUVENILE They stay near the nest for another 3–4 weeks. During fall and winter they join a flock of magpie families. Magpies are mature enough at 1–2 years of age to raise their own young.

Unsolved Mystery

Magpies can make a game out of getting a meal. One tactic is for a magpie to distract an eagle, coyote or red fox by pulling on its tail while other magpies sneak in to steal the food (a ground squirrel or fish). Tail pulling isn't always to get food however. Magpies were observed pulling on the tails of hawks that did not have any food for the taking. Were they simply showing off to other magpies? Find the tail end of this mystery!

When
Diurnal. Black-billed Magpies are active during the day and they rest at night.

Migration
Permanent resident. Black-billed Magpies stay in the Rocky Mountain region of the U.S. throughout the year. Some may move to different elevations during different seasons.

Nesting
Black-billed Magpies begin nesting in April in the Rocky Mountain region of the U.S.

Getting Around
Black-billed Magpies walk with a swagger (sway back and forth). Look for them to swoop when they are flying down from a height and for their long tail to help them change direction quickly in flight.

Where to Look
Black-billed Magpies often live near waterways with brushy areas. They also live in agricultural areas with some tree and brush cover, as well as in open coniferous forests at low elevations.

Year-round   Summer
Migration   Winter

Grasslands, Cliffs and Canyons

Northern Harrier

Circus cyaneus

Length: 18–20 inches (46–50 cm)
Wingspan: 40–46½ inches (102–118 cm)

wheeling

White rump patch

Males are silver-gray above and lighter below

female

The females are brown above and cream and brown streaked below, with a banded tail

Juveniles look similar to females but are darker brown above and russet below

Black wingtips

"Kek, kek, kek" means "Stay away!"

Long, square tail

Flying Food Pass

Watch Northern Harriers during the summer. Watch closely. You may see the male perform a flying food pass. When he has a juicy mouse, he signals to the female on the nest below, "purrduk." She flies just under him, turns over and catches the mouse in her talons. A speedy delivery is made to the hungry chicks. Keep watch for Northern Harriers to pick up a mouse nest, shake it, then drop the nest. A litter of young mice and their parents are snatched up for a quick snack. How do they know the nest is full of mice? As they glide over grassy fields and prairies, harriers hear prey before they see it. Their hearing is aided by a facial disk that funnels sound to their enlarged ear openings.

Today's Special
gophers

Habitat Café

Yumm . . . Bring an order of mice, voles, shrews, frogs, lizards and small perching birds. Northern Harriers are carnivorous. They eat only animal matter. When their main prey, meadow voles, increase in great numbers in a given year, the number of young harriers produced increases. Supply-side food economics!

SPRING, SUMMER, FALL, WINTER MENU:
Entirely animal matter

Life Cycle

NEST The female builds a pile of grass and weeds on the ground, hollowed in the top with a few sticks or twigs as the base.

EGGS About 1¾ inches long. The female incubates 4–6 eggs for 30 days. The male brings her food and may shade or guard the eggs while she takes a break.

MOM! DAD! Altricial. Dad brings the food to Mom. She feeds the chicks by tearing the food into pieces as they take it from her bill. Unlike their quiet parents, the chicks use noisy screech calls to scare predators.

NESTLING When a chick strays from the nest, Mom carries it back home in her bill by the nape (back of neck). After two weeks of age, the young take paths through the grass to raised feeding and resting areas.

FLEDGLING As heavy as an adult, they can fly at 1 month of age and their meals come in an aerial pass from their parents. To practice capturing prey, the young pounce on objects on the ground.

JUVENILE Juveniles join with others their age, feeding and preparing for migration. It takes 2–3 years for them to gain their adult plumage and be mature enough to raise their own young.

History Hangout

The Migratory Bird Treaty Act of 1918 protects all migratory birds (and any part of the bird) wherever they spend their time. In addition, state laws protect all wild birds with the exception of the Rock Pigeon, European Starling and House Sparrow. You may not collect bird feathers, nests, or eggs. You can however keep the memory of what you find with a photograph, drawing or painting, and by keeping notes in Journal Pages at the back of this book (pages 188–189). Birds will benefit from your safe wildlife souvenirs!

When

Northern Harriers are diurnal. They can spend 40 percent of their day in flight, logging up to 100 miles per day!

Migration

Spring Arrival: March–May
Fall Departure: Sep–Nov
Permanent resident to mid-distance migrant. Flying alone, some migrate to Texas, Mexico, Costa Rica and Panama. Others stay all year in the Rocky Mountain region of the U.S.

Nesting

Northern Harriers begin nesting in April–May in the Rocky Mountain region of the U.S.

Getting Around

Look for Northern Harriers in an open field flying low (10–13 feet) over the ground with their slim, lightweight body and long wings. They fly with a series of flaps and tilting glides, their wings held in a spread-out "V." Their outer 3–5 primary flight feathers are notched for aerodynamic soaring.

Where to Look

Grasslands, prairies, wet meadows and marshes in the Rocky Mountain region of the U.S.

Year-round   Summer
Migration   Winter

Grasslands, Cliffs and Canyons

Red-tailed Hawk

Buteo jamaicensis

Length: 18–25 inches (46–63 cm)
Wingspan: 4–5 feet (122–152 cm)

soaring

Dark head and upper side, lighter underside

White underside with brown streaks on belly that may resemble a band

Male and female look the same, but the female is larger, stronger

Tail is "red" on upper side with a narrow, dark band

"Kee-eee-arr!" or, "This is my territory."

Only adult hawks have red tails

Roadside Snack Bar

Rust-colored tails flash overhead along country and city roadways in the Rocky Mountain region. Look for Red-tailed Hawks perched on power lines, in trees, and on billboards and roadway signs. They are likely scanning the ditch for a meal of rabbit, mouse or another mammal. Add to their roadside menu scrumptious snakes, tasty toads, frantic frogs, luscious lizards, fantastic pheasants, and go-to gophers, and grassy roadside stretches become a potluck. Red-tailed Hawks have learned to survive in many different habitats; they are adaptable. On your next road trip make a game of keeping count of the number of red-tails you see. What time of day do you see the most? Roadside science is fun!

Today's Special
muskrats

Habitat Café

Yumm . . . bring an order of rabbits, mice, voles, chipmunks, squirrels, snakes, gophers, skinks and pheasants. Red-tailed Hawks are carnivorous. Sharp, hooked beak and talons are used for capturing and tearing apart prey. Taken to a feeding perch, small mammals are swallowed whole and birds are beheaded, plucked and eaten. Bill-licking good.

SPRING, SUMMER, FALL, WINTER MENU:

 Mostly mammals, some reptiles, birds and amphibians

Life Cycle

NEST The male and female build a bulky nest in a large tree, 30–90 feet from the ground. They may return to the same nest for several years, adding more sticks and lining it with moss, evergreen twigs and grapevine bark. Nests that are reused for years can be over three feet deep!

EGGS Slightly more than 2¼ inches long. The female and male incubate the 2–3 dull, creamy white eggs for 28–35 days.

MOM! DAD! Altricial. Both Mom and Dad feed the young. At first the parents tear off pieces of prey for the chicks, but as they grow, the parents leave the food for the young to tear apart on their own. Learning to be independent is a big deal in the bird world!

NESTLING Fluffy down begins to be replaced by new feathers when the chicks are about two weeks of age.

FLEDGLING Young Red-tailed Hawks leave the nest and fly when they are 6–7 weeks old.

JUVENILE Immature hawks have a gray-brown tail with dark bands. It takes two years to develop the red tail. Immature Red-tailed Hawks begin to migrate south before the adults in the fall.

Unsolved Mystery

Several species of hawks regularly place a fresh, leafy branch in the nest with the chicks every day. Why? To shade the young? To hide the young from predators? Do the aromatic oils in the leaves help control parasites on the chicks' skin? To solve this mystery use a spotting scope from far away. Parent hawks will not go near the nest if they suspect it is being watched.

When

Red-tailed Hawks are diurnal, feeding during the day and resting at night.

Migration

Spring Arrival: April
Fall Departure: Sep–Oct
Permanent resident to short-distance migrant to the southern U.S. and Mexico. Red-tailed Hawks stay in the region throughout the year with some regional migration taking place.

Nesting

Red-tailed Hawks begin nesting in May–June in the Rocky Mountain region of the U.S.

Getting Around

Red-tailed Hawks soar, perch and fly low to the ground to find prey with their keen eyesight. Once they spot it, they dive or pounce on their prey, carrying it away in their strong talons. Look high in the sky for a soaring red-tail with its tail and wings spread out. They can look like a paper kite on a mild day.

Where to Look

Red-tailed Hawks prefer open areas with large trees nearby for perching, but also hunt for prey along both country and city roadsides throughout the region, including interstate highways.
· *Super Adaptor*

Year-round / Migration

Summer / Winter

Golden Eagle

Aquila chrysaetos

Length: 27½–33 inches (70–84 cm)
Wingspan: 73–86½ inches (185–220 cm)

Dark brown all over
with golden nape
(back of the neck)

Long broad wings

Long tail with gray
band underneath

"Wonk" is the "hello"
of one eagle partner
to the other.
"Skonk" is given when an
eagle feels in danger.

Yellow feet with heavy claws for
catching, holding and killing prey

Aquila, the Eagle

A jackrabbit is munching on plants over a mile from a Golden Eagle. It has been had. The eagle sees the rabbit's movement and zeroes in on its next meal. Eagles are built for the hunt. Their leg and wing bones are massive. Their large hooked bill, used to pull apart and eat prey, is equally as large. The Golden Eagle can hunt from a perch or from a soaring flight so high it is a mere speck against the backdrop of sky. This is fitting. The Latin name for eagle, *Aquila*, is a constellation in our Milky Way galaxy. Set out to an open area where Golden Eagles are at home and watch them on the hunt. Stay long enough and you can also watch Aquila in the night sky.

Today's Special

prairie dogs

Habitat Café

Yumm . . . bring an order of rabbits, hares, ground squirrels and prairie dogs. Golden Eagles are carnivores. They eat only meat.

SPRING, SUMMER, FALL, WINTER MENU:
Mammals and birds

Life Cycle

NEST The huge nest of sticks, roots and stems is made 10–90 feet high in a tree or rocky cliff. It is lined with moss, leaves and grass. The nest may be added to and reused in other years, reaching 4–5 feet high and with a diameter of 5–6 feet!

EGGS About 3 inches long. It is mostly the female that incubates the clutch of 1–3 eggs for 43–45 days.

MOM! DAD! Altricial. Chicks hatch with white down.

NESTLING The two chicks compete for food; sometimes this results in only one chick surviving.

FLEDGLING It takes 52–72 pounds of food to raise an eagle chick from hatching to fledgling (10 weeks). Ground squirrels have 4–17 times more fat and nearly 2 times the energy content of rabbits. Guess what parent eagles try to capture and feed to their chicks first!

JUVENILE They are about six months old when they are independent from their parents. It will be about 4 years until they have their own nesting territory and 5 years until they look like adults.

History Hangout

The eagle has a sacred place in the cultures of the native peoples of North America. The eagle is included in the dances of the Iroquois, Shawnee, Pueblo, Seneca, Choctaw, Natchez, Fox, Chippewa and other indigenous cultures. Golden and Bald Eagles and all their parts are protected under state and federal law. The U.S. Fish and Wildlife Service recognizes the sacred importance to Native Americans. For more information see: www.fws.gov/le/pdffiles/Possession%20 of%20Eagle%20Feathers%20Fact%20Sheet.pdf

When

Diurnal. Golden Eagles are active during the day and rest at night.

Migration

Permanent resident. Golden Eagles often stay in their nesting territory all year. They defend their 20–30 square kilometer (7–11 square mile) territory from other eagles. Some may move to alpine tundra areas in late summer when the chicks of alpine bird species are available for the hunt.

Nesting

Golden Eagles begin nesting in April in the Rocky Mountain region of the U.S. The pair may build up to 14 nests in their territory during courtship, ultimately using just one for the eggs. They may maintain another as a reserve nest.

Getting Around

Golden Eagles soar, glide, and use a flapping flight with 6–8 deep wingbeats with short glides. Their wings in soaring profile are stretched straight out and flat. They use their large wings to fly slow enough to scan and hunt prey while in flight.

Where to Look

Mountains, open forests, brush lands and rangelands with open spaces for hunting and cliffs for nesting.

Year-round **Summer**
Migration Winter

Grasslands, Cliffs and Canyons

Turkey Vulture

Cathartes aura

Length: 25–32 inches (64–81 cm)
Wingspan: 55–79 inches (140–200 cm)

Bright red skin on bare head and neck

Short, pale curved bill

All black with silver under wings

Slotted wing tips look like long black fingers

"Hisss." They make this sound when edgy. Turkey Vultures do not have a syrinx (voicebox) and cannot sing.

Long tail

Soaring Superstars

Turkey Vultures are soaring superstars. Soaring is similar to gliding, but it often involves riding on streams (currents) of air. When the sun comes up in the morning it heats the air, causing the air to rise. Turkey Vultures then take to the sky and soar on the rising warm air currents, called thermals. Birds use far less energy in soaring than they do in flapping flight. With so little energy put into flight, vultures can spend a good deal of their day in the air. When sniffing out their next meal (they find food by smelling it) vultures need to fly low to the ground. To soar at ground-hugging level, Turkey Vultures rock from side to side with their wings held in an upward "V" shape.

Habitat Café

Yumm . . . bring an order of small to large dead and decaying animals. Turkey Vultures are carnivorous (meat-eaters). They use their strong sense of smell to find dead meat. Their long middle toe acts like a fork to hold the meat down. The lack of feathers on their head allows vultures to dig in without need of a napkin.

SPRING, SUMMER, FALL, WINTER MENU:

 All animal matter

Life Cycle

NEST Once a nesting location is found in the darkness of a cave, cliff or a hillside ledge, a hollow tree, a log or an abandoned building, the rest is a cinch. Turkey Vultures do not build a nest or add material, they simply lay the eggs and snuggle one egg under each of their two bare and warm brood patches.

EGGS About 2½ to 3 inches long. The parents both incubate the 2 eggs for 28–38 days.

MOM! DAD! Altricial. The chicks are covered with long, white warm down except for their bare face, throat and neck. At first, chicks are fed spit up food by their parents. By two weeks of age, they eat solid food.

NESTLING Nest intruders are in for a surprise. Nestlings scare jump—leap forward and hiss loudly. If the intruder does not get the point, the young stomp their feet, hiss, shoot vomit and then escape to a dark corner of the nest.

FLEDGLING The young venture from the nest bit by bit. By 3 months of age they completely leave the nest.

JUVENILE They roost with a group of other juvenile Turkey Vultures before heading out for their first migration journey to wintering areas.

Gross Factor

Stink is supreme to the Turkey Vulture; it's how they find their next meal. They can't tear open large bodied prey so they wait until the body rots and is soft. Phew! They may also wait for another hungry animal to tear open the body first, or if they cannot wait, they enter through any body opening. They will even eat the stinky scent glands of a skunk. Gross!

When

Diurnal. Turkey Vultures are active during the day and roost at night in a group of other vultures.

Migration

Fall Arrival: Mar–Apr
Spring Departure: Sep–Oct
Short-distance migrant to southeastern U.S., using a gliding, soaring flight. A group of soaring vultures is called a "kettle" of vultures.

Nesting

Turkey Vultures begin nesting in April in the Rocky Mountain region of the U.S.

Getting Around

Turkey Vultures soar on thermals, a current of warm rising air, with their large wings held in an uplifted "V." When wingbeats are used, they are deep and slow. Their slotted wings have narrow wingtip feathers and look like long black fingers.

Where to Look

Turkey Vultures are found in grassland areas with open sites for feeding and open forested or man-made structures (towers, grain elevators) for perching and group roosting sites. Cliff areas near a river are commonly used for their updrafts.

Year-round	Summer
Migration	Winter

Grasslands, Cliffs and Canyons

Sandhill Crane

Grus canadensis

Height 4 feet (122 cm)
Wingspan: 6–7 feet (183–213 cm)

Yellow eyes

Red patch on crest of head

Long, stout bill

White cheek and long gray neck

Males are larger than females and their plumage is similar

The long trachea (windpipe) coils into the sternum to produce a very loud bugle call.

Long black legs, black feet

Do the Hokey-Pokey!

To a Sandhill Crane it's all in the dance. A pair of cranes bonds with each other with a spring dance that rivals any hokey-pokey. "You leap up high, you spread your wings out wide, you put your bill up and you shake it all about. You do the Sandhill-Pokey, and you turn around your partner. That's the spring crane dance!" They provide their own music with bugles and unison calls that can be heard two miles away. After the dance the tune changes. Nesting begins and the pair brings as little attention to themselves as possible. The mud they spread on their feathers is not a spa treatment but acts as a camouflage to blend into the brown grasses and sedges of their nesting area.

Today's Special
grasshoppers

Habitat Café

Yumm . . . bring an order of invertebrates, aquatic plant tubers (roots), and grains with side orders of small mammals and reptiles. Sandhill Cranes are omnivorous, eating both plant and animal matter.

SPRING, SUMMER, FALL MENU:
Lots of seeds, some insects

WINTER MENU:
More seeds and fewer insects than during spring, summer and fall

Life Cycle

NEST Both the male and female build the nest in an area with cattails, sedges and other marsh grass. While one is collecting plant material and tossing it over its shoulder onto a pile, the other is arranging it into a five-foot-diameter nest. The inner nesting cup is lined with small, fine plant stems and twigs.

EGGS About 3½ inches long. Both the female and male incubate the 1–3 eggs for 29–30 days. (There are usually 2 eggs.) Toward the end of incubation, parents may make a purr sound. Does this stimulate hatching or is it a response to hatching? It's a purr-fect mystery!

MOM! DAD! Precocial. The fluffy, yellow-brown chicks leave the nest within one day of hatching. By the second day, the chicks are battling it out to be number one. This aggression often results in the survival of only one chick. Chicks can fly at about 7 weeks of age.

JUVENILE The family stays together for the first 9–10 months, until about March. Groups of up to 20 young males migrate and feed together in a "bachelor flock." They look for a lifelong mate generally after 4 years of age. Sandhill Cranes can live to be 25–30 years old.

Did You Know?

Night in a museum? Try morning on the marsh. Listen to fall marsh sounds and experience thousands of waterfowl as they prepare for migration at Grays Lake National Wildlife Refuge and Teton Basin in Idaho. Visit a crane migration stopover such as Monte Vista National Wildlife Refuge, Colorado, in spring and experience dancing cranes. More wildlife adventures await, so bring your family and explore. See pages 196–197.

When

Sandhill Cranes are diurnal. They are active during the day and rest at night.

Migration
Fall Arrival: April
Spring Departure: Sep–Nov
Short-distance migrant from the greater Yellowstone area to New Mexico wintering areas of the middle and lower Rio Grande valley. This includes Bosque del Apache National Wildlife Refuge. The San Luis Valley in Colorado is the site of their spring and fall migration stopovers.

Nesting
In the Greater Yellowstone area of the Rocky Mountain region, Sandhill Cranes begin nesting in April in the marshes, meadows, and river valleys with nearby grasslands, shrubs or wooded areas.

Getting Around
Sandhill Cranes have a distinct wing stroke pattern; quick and snappy on the upstroke and slow on the down stroke. Their neck is held out straight in flight (Great Blue Herons bend their neck in an "S" in flight).

Where to Look
Open grasslands, prairies, river valleys, meadows and marshes of the greater Yellowstone area during the summer.

Year-round	Summer
Migration	Winter

Grasslands, Cliffs and Canyons

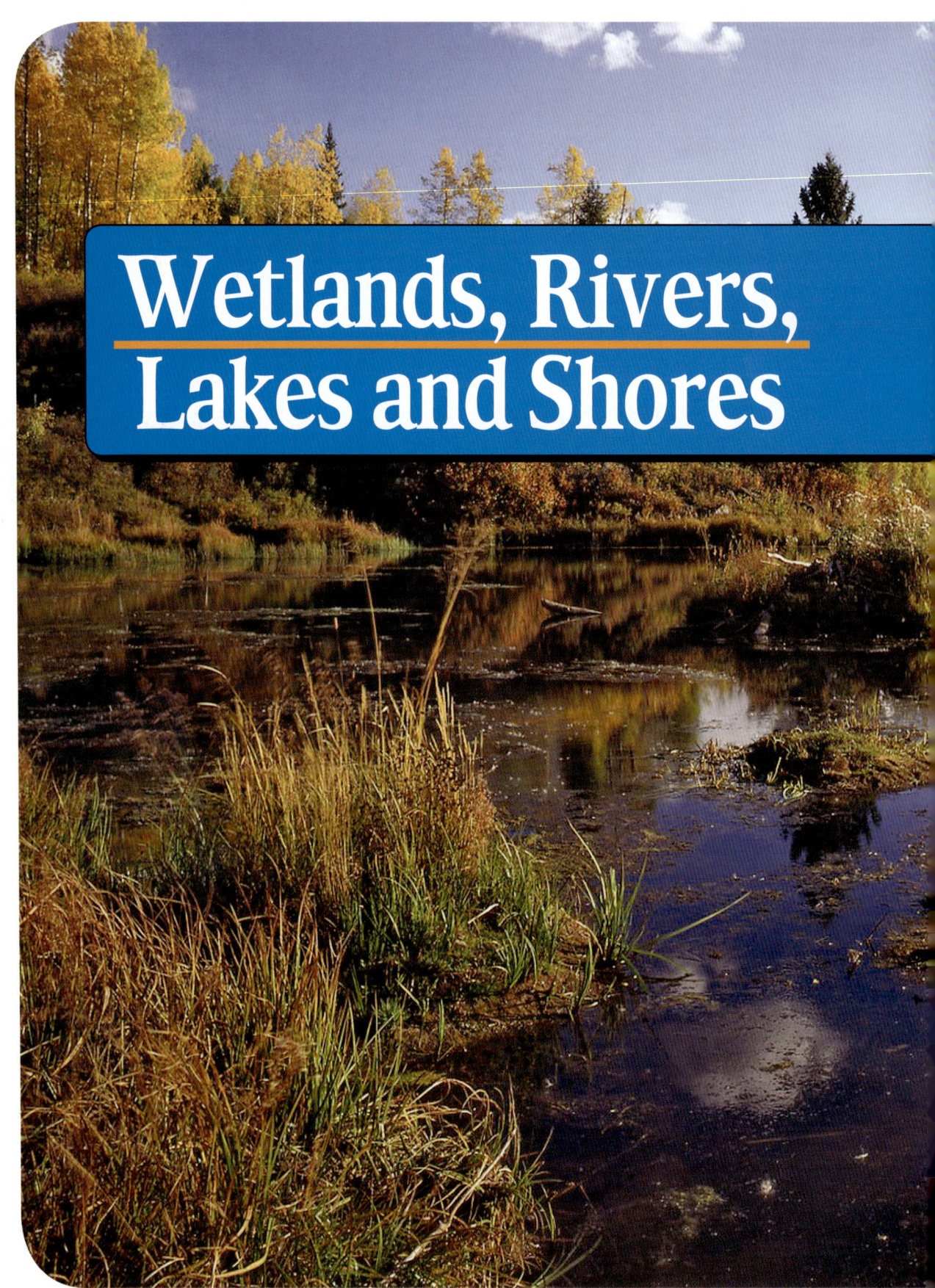

Wetlands, Rivers, Lakes and Shores

Our region has many wet habitats for birds. Snow-capped mountains send down meltwater in cool, fresh streams. Mountain lakes are tucked between peaks. Nesting and staging for migration are the main events in meadows and marshes. Great rivers wind through valleys, etching through stone. Set out for exciting adventures in the wetlands, marshes, lakes and shores across the region.

Rising Earth, Changing Earth

We can thank millions of years of volcanic and glacial action for much of the water in the Rocky Mountain region. The land bears evidence of the most recent glacial activity that took place 10,000–35,000 years ago. The

massive Canadian Laurentide Ice Sheets moved over the western areas of the Rocky Mountain region. The giant glaciers spun their magic over the area, altering the landscape and leaving icy glacial meltwater that, in time, formed rivers and wetlands.

Glacial watery remains filled sunken areas as well, producing Montana's 27-mile-long Flathead Lake. Today, these aquatic (water) areas are important to people and birds alike. They provide birds with major migration flyways and stopovers. Visit the Green River, as well as the Salmon, Snake, Yellowstone, Lochsa, Colorado and Missouri Rivers and the region's many national wildlife refuges for close-up views of local and migrating birds.

Wade Into Aquatic Areas

Pull on your boots and take a pal to a wetland, river, lake or shore. Aquatic areas are great places to find tadpoles, giant water bugs, dragonflies, crayfish, beavers, river otters, muskrats and birds. Look for the unexpected, rare animals, too. Nearly half of threatened or endangered species live in or depend on water habitats.

Wetland habitats are important for other reasons, too. They help filter pollutants from runoff, help recharge groundwater supplies, and reduce flooding by slowing the flow of rainwater on its way to streams and rivers. Water habitats are also super places to have fun. People canoe, kayak, hunt, fish, scout for water-polished rocks and enjoy nature. Public and private conservation and sporting groups and private citizens are working hard to protect the region's water habitats.

Great Blue Heron

Water habitats come in many shapes, types and sizes. Other habitats include shorelines and beaches, marshes, wooded swamps and river floodplains. Each kind of habitat has a special place in the Rocky Mountains' ecosystems.

female Common Merganser

Where Do Water Birds Live?

Just as forests have different levels that support different species of birds, a shore, lake, wetland or river has different areas, or zones, that support various plants and animals that birds in turn use for shelter and food.

Dipping up and down on a rock along a mountain stream, an American Dipper gets ready to plunge into the cool water after its prey.

Perched on an overhanging branch, the Belted Kingfisher scans the clear water for small fish to spear, while Common Yellowthroats flit among the cattails and reeds. With legs nearly as tall as the marsh grasses they wade through, Great Blue Herons silently stalk small fish, crayfish, frogs and giant water beetles.

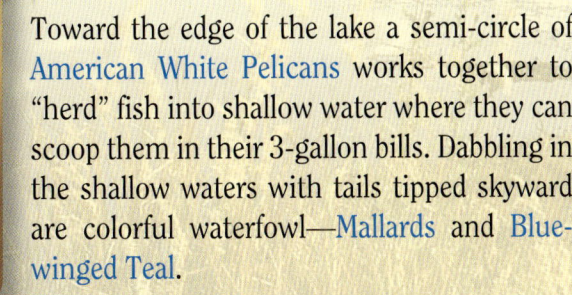
Belted Kingfisher

Toward the edge of the lake a semi-circle of American White Pelicans works together to "herd" fish into shallow water where they can scoop them in their 3-gallon bills. Dabbling in the shallow waters with tails tipped skyward are colorful waterfowl—Mallards and Blue-winged Teal.

The divers in the group are in the deeper waters. Pied-billed Grebes sink like mini-submarines and Common Mergansers snatch unsuspecting fish with their long, saw-toothed bills.

Watching from a throne high in a waterside tree is the Osprey, ready to dive feet-first and with talons outstretched for a fish.

Some species, such as the Red-winged Blackbird, have adapted to living along roadways where there are cattails to perch on and insects to eat. Wildlife is everywhere!

Check Off the Wetlands, Rivers, Lakes and Shores Birds You See!

When you spot wetland birds, use these pages to check them off. The locations of these illustrations indicate where you might see them (air, water, edge or shore).

Common Yellowthroat

Geothlypis trichas

Length: 4–5 inches (11–13 cm)
Wingspan: 6–7½ inches (15–19 cm)

Black mask with
white upper band

Females do not wear a
black mask and are more
dull than males

Males have
an olive-green
back, wings
and tail

Bright yellow
throat and
upper chest

Immature yellowthroats
resemble an adult female

"Where-is-it,
Where-is-it." Males sing this
song to say this is where my territory is. Then, if you are too
close for comfort they call out,
"Tchat!"

Masked Super Bird of the Wetlands

"Faster than a speeding bullet, able to leap tall buildings in a single bound"—probably not, but this black-masked superbird can down over 80 aphids in a mere minute! Nearly always on the move, Common Yellowthroats dodge detection in damp areas of cattails, shrubs and grasses. You won't need x-ray vision to find them, just follow the sound and visual clues. Warblers warble—their song has a rhythmic move to it. Yellowthroats are warblers built for maneuvering through tight spaces. They glean insects in low plants with their short, thin bill. Have you heard the latest marsh buzz? Clark Kent has something in common with this tiny superhero, but keep it under cover.

Habitat Café

Yumm . . . bring an order of small insects with side orders of spiders and caterpillars. Common Yellowthroats are insectivores. They are a friend to plants: they chow on leaf-eating insects. But watch out. Bigger birds like Northern Shrikes will make a meal of Common Yellowthroats!

SPRING, SUMMER, FALL, WINTER MENU:

 Mostly insects and spiders with a few seeds

Life Cycle

NEST The female builds the loose nest cup on or near the marshy ground where it is hidden from predators and shaded from the sun. The soft inner lining is made with finer grass.

EGGS About ½ to ¾ inch long. The female incubates the clutch of 3–5 eggs for 12 days.

MOM! DAD! Altricial. The orange-skinned, naked chicks are about 1 inch long and weigh less than a penny when they hatch—and that includes their black egg-tooth.

NESTLING "Chac-chac-chac" coming from the nest means the chicks are begging for more food. Mom and Dad take different routes to and from the nest to deter any lurking predators.

FLEDGLING At only 10–12 days of age, the young leave the nest. Mom and Dad chip in groceries for a couple more weeks and then the juveniles are on their own.

JUVENILE By fall, young males begin to practice their beginning song before the family heads out on migration.

Birding Tip

Get a close-up view of birds by using binoculars. (A pair with a large field of vision, 8 x 40 plus, works well.) First spot the bird without binoculars. Then, keep your eyes on the bird while you lift the binoculars to your eyes. Think of the binoculars as now being attached like a pair of eyeglasses and move them directly with your head. With practice you will be able to zoom in on quick-winged warblers! Tip: Spotting scopes in public wildlife viewing areas are free to use during your visits.

When

Diurnal. Common Yellowthroats are active during the day and rest at night.

Migration

Spring Arrival: Apr–May
Fall Departure: Aug–Oct
Short- to mid-distance migrant by night to wintering areas located along the Gulf Coast of the southern United States and northeastern Mexico.

Nesting

Common Yellowthroats begin nesting in the Rocky Mountain region of the U.S. in May–June.

Getting Around

Common Yellowthroats hop and climb through thickets, grasses and sedges for spiders, insects and caterpillars. Their flight is flitting, short and direct. Flight song: Males fly up with their tail bobbing and wings quivering to each note in their song. They come back down silently to land near their starting point.

Where to Look

Cattail marshes, thickets, river edges, damp fields and shrub areas over most of the Rocky Mountain region of the U.S.

Year-round Summer
Migration Winter

American Dipper

Cinclus mexicanus

Length: 5½–8 inches (14–20 cm)
Wingspan: 11 inches (28 cm)

White-eyelid feathers make a flash when blinking

Short wings and tail

Male and female look similar with female smaller

Gray

Long legs

"Jik, jik, jik, jik, jik."
Both the male and female make this call to each other.

Taking a Dip

American Dippers dip. They dip their head up and down into the water while they blink and flash their white eyelids. They also take a headfirst dip into a mountain stream to walk, dive and swim underwater in search of insects to eat. They are the only North American songbird and perching bird (passerine) that takes to the water. They propel themselves through the water with a 1-2 thrust from their short wings. To stay on the stream bottom rather than floating to the top, they keep their wings moving. A wet suit made of a thick layer of feathers holds in their body heat and sharp underwater vision is made possible with enlarged eye muscles. Visit a stream to see this remarkable bird dip into action!

Habitat Café

Yumm . . . bring an order of water insects in the larval (worm) stage: mayflies, caddisflies and stoneflies. American Dippers are insectivores. They dive into mountain streams and rivers to hunt for insects on the bottom.

SPRING, SUMMER, FALL, WINTER MENU:
Water insects

Today's Special

dragonfly larvae

Life Cycle

NEST The male and female make the nest facing a stream and fastened to a large boulder, under roots, or other support. A thick dome of living mosses with grass and roots shelters an inside nest cup of grass and leaves. For coming and going, a 3-inch by 2-inch side entrance is included. The nest may be reused.

EGGS About 1 inch long. The female incubates the 4–5 eggs for 14–17 days.

MOM! DAD! Altricial. The orange and pink-skinned chicks are featherless and dependent on their parents for warmth for the first two weeks, and are fed for a month or more.

NESTLING By day 16, they can run and stand, and if necessary, dip into the water for safety.

FLEDGLING At 24–25 days of age they leave the nest and explore their new surroundings. In another week they find streamside food on their own. They begin searching for food on the stream bottom when their full set of feathers grows in making them more water repellent—a bird wet suit.

JUVENILE They stay with their siblings for the first week out of the nest. The following spring they are mature enough to nest.

Unsolved Mystery

Dippers have curious habits. Take a plunge into their mysteries: Is dipping a way to communicate in a noisy streamside habitat? Why do they blink their white eyelids while dipping? Why do they lose all of their feathers at once, becoming flightless? Most birds molt one feather or so at a time. The American Dipper loses all of its feathers at once and becomes flightless. A naked dipper may avoid a predator by escaping into the water and hiding under a log or streamside plants!

When
Diurnal. The American Dipper is active during the day and rests at night.

Migration
Permanent resident where streams do not freeze in the winter. When their resident stream freezes, the bird will move lower down the mountain to a stream or river with open water. Adapted to living in cool mountain streams, the dipper lives where temperatures do not rise above 36° C (97° F).

Nesting
American Dippers begin nesting as early as March in the Rocky Mountain region of the U.S. They may raise two broods during the nesting season.

Getting Around
American Dippers walk from rock to rock, dive headfirst into water and move in a running motion on the stream bottom. Their wings propel them through the water in a 1-2 stroke and lift them in a low flight over water.

Where to Look
Fast-flowing clear and unpolluted mountain streams. They prefer streams with movement from waterfalls and other natural structures.

Year-round Summer
Migration Winter

Spotted Sandpiper

Actitis macularius

Length: 7–8 inches (18–20 cm)
Wingspan: 14½–16 inches (37–40 cm)

winter

Females and males look the same

White eye-ring

Black line from bill across eye

Brown back

Long, thin orange bill with black tip

White breast and belly with black spots

Orange-pink legs

"Peet-weet."
This soft call is made when flying away from danger.

Teeter-Totter Shorebirds

Up and down, teeter-totter, Spotted Sandpipers bob their tails as they pick and glean insects, snails and crayfish along the Rocky Mountain region's shorelines. The reason for the tail bobbing is a mystery. We do know both chicks and adults bob their tails. At the least alarm, the motion may increase until the entire lower half of the bird's body is in a fast teeter-totter. With a little more alarm, the bird may take to the air calling *peet-weet-weet*. This action by Spotted Sandpipers is repeated along shorelines in spring and summer. With a buddy, binoculars and bird watching manners, explore bird playgrounds near you for teeter-tottering sandpipers!

Habitat Café

Today's Special
grasshoppers

Yumm . . . bring an order of aquatic (water) and land insects, tadpoles, small frogs, mollusks and crayfish. Spotted Sandpipers are omnivorous.

SPRING, SUMMER, FALL, WINTER MENU:
Almost equal amounts of insects, amphibians and crustaceans

Life Cycle

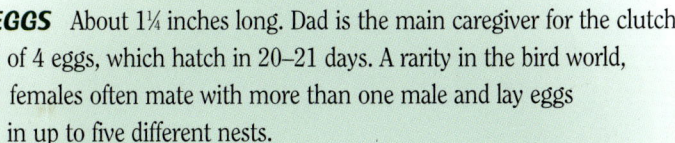

NEST Both parents build the 5-inch-diameter nest in a shallow depression in the ground, hidden under grass or a small bush and lined with dry grass.

EGGS About 1¼ inches long. Dad is the main caregiver for the clutch of 4 eggs, which hatch in 20–21 days. A rarity in the bird world, females often mate with more than one male and lay eggs in up to five different nests.

MOM! DAD! Precocial. As soon as the chicks hatch, they walk to shore, usually with Dad—wee balls of bobbing fluff. They don't have tails at this point, just tiny rumps of fuzz. Their gray down is nearly invisible against pebbles and gravel. When in danger they either flatten and become part of the beach, or hurry to the water and dive for cover. One of the parents will spread its wings around the brood during the first week to keep the chicks warm and safe.

FLEDGLING Flight becomes routine when they are just weeks old.

JUVENILE At one year of age the birds are mature enough to date, mate and raise their own young.

Did You Know?

Spotted Sandpipers change their fashion each season. Just before fall migration, Spotted Sandpipers become unspotted. They molt, or lose their old feathers, and grow in new white feathers without spots. Their bill and legs turn to a dull yellow color during the winter. When it is time for spring and the nesting season to begin, they molt into spotted feathers again!

When

Spotted Sandpipers are diurnal. They feed during the day and rest at night.

Migration

Spring Arrival: Apr–May
Fall Departure: Jul–Sep
Short- to long-distance migrant. Solitary (alone) bird, even in migration. Migrates by night to wintering areas in southern U.S. and as far south as Bolivia and Brazil.

Nesting

Spotted Sandpipers nest in late May–June in the Rocky Mountain region of the U.S.

Getting Around

Spotted Sandpipers fly directly up from shore in a burst of takeoff energy. In flight, their wings are stiff and flap only halfway up. This gives them their short, flickering flight. Look for their white wing stripe in flight. They dive straight into the water for safety and then straight out again from underneath the water!

Where to Look

Spotted Sandpipers live along the shorelines of lakes, ponds, streams, rivers and wetlands.

| Year-round | Summer |
| Migration | Winter |

Red-winged Blackbird

Agelaius phoeniceus

Length: 7–9 inches (17–19 cm)
Wingspan: 12–16 inches (31–40 cm)

Males are glossy black

Females have a light eyebrow stripe; they are brown above with streaks of brown below

Red shoulder patch with a yellow border

It takes young males two years to become black like Dad—called "delayed maturation"

"O-ka-lee!" means "Guys, stay away from my territory! But gals come on over—I have room for 3 or 4."

Safety in Numbers

Red-winged Blackbirds practice safety in numbers. It's harder for predators to capture prey in a large group. In late summer, redwings attend the annual family reunion with their cousins: starlings, grackles and cowbirds. Look for a flying river of blackbirds above the fields and across the sky at dawn and dusk in September to November. It can take more than 10 minutes for a massive flock of 10,000 birds to pass. Flocks feed in the fields during the day and roost at night. Female redwings migrate south in the fall before males. In the spring, males return first to the region's wetlands and roadsides to perch on a cattail, spread their red wing patches, and sing, "O-ka-lee . . ."

Habitat Café

Yumm . . . bring an order of dragonflies, grasshoppers, spiders, beetles, moths and seeds like sunflowers. Their slender brown bill is designed to pick up insects and seeds. Red-winged Blackbirds are omnivorous.

Today's Special
snails

SPRING, SUMMER MENU:
 Mainly insects, some seeds and berries

FALL, WINTER MENU:
More seeds and berries, fewer insects than during spring and summer

Life Cycle

NEST The female builds the nest cup 3–10 feet above the ground in cattails, reeds and bushes over or near water. She weaves the leaves of water plants through the cattail stalks to make a nest cup. The inside of the nest is lined with soft, fine grasses.

EGGS About 1 inch long. The female incubates the 3–4 blue-green eggs with brown markings for 11 days.

MOM! DAD! Altricial. The female feeds the young and removes the fecal sacs (chick diapers) from the nest. If a predator comes too close to the nest, the female does a "flip-wing act" 5–10 feet from the nest.

NESTLING The chicks' eyes open when they are about one week old.

FLEDGLING Both parents feed the young for up to two weeks after they leave the nest.

JUVENILE Juveniles join a flock with other "teens." They feed during the day and roost at night. By fall they join a large group of both males and females and prepare to migrate to wintering areas.

Do the Math

Red-winged Blackbird chicks are fed insects. Insects are much higher in muscle- and bone-building protein than seeds and berries. A male chick will increase in size by ten times in its first ten days. Multiply your birth weight by ten and you would be huge in only ten days. Do the math! But then, you don't need to grow into an adult your first year like a Red-winged Blackbird does. Answer on pages 194–195.

When

Red-winged Blackbirds are diurnal. They feed during the day and rest at night.

Migration

Spring Arrival: late Feb–Apr
Fall Departure: Sep–Nov
Short- to long-distance migrant. Red-winged Blackbirds gather in large groups of up to 100,000 birds before migrating to the southern U.S. and as far south as Mexico and South America. Some may stay all year in the Rocky Mountain region.

Nesting

Red-winged Blackbirds begin nesting in April and May.

Getting Around

The region's most common summer roadside bird, it is often found sitting on top of signs, mile markers and fence posts. They walk on the ground to search for seeds and insects. Redwings fly in a pattern of closing their wings, dipping down, and then rising again with a few wingbeats.

Where to Look

Red-winged Blackbirds are found in all of the Rocky Mountain region of the U.S.; look for them in wet roadsides and fields, marshes, and along the reedy edges of lakes and shores.

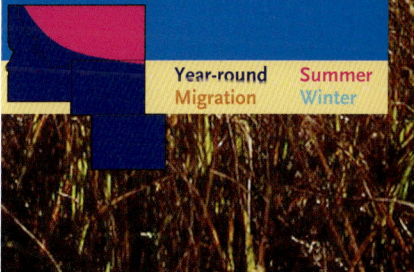

Year-round
Migration
Summer
Winter

Wilson's Snipe

Gallinago gallinago

Length: 10½–12½ inches (27–32 cm)
Wingspan: 16–17 inches (41–44 cm)

Camouflaged brown and patterned like the old marsh grasses it hides in

Rusty red tail

Long, straight bill

Short legs

"Scaipe." This call is made when flying zigzag up from cover and also made during nighttime migration.

Winnowing Ways

Claiming a nesting territory requires a male Wilson's Snipe to vamp-up his flight. The land area under claim starts large and is honed down to just the nesting site. In what is called winnowing flight, he climbs high over his potential nesting territory in a wide circle, performing back and forth and climbing to over 150 feet. He then bullets toward the earth in a daring skydive. To ensure that other males and a female partner are impressed, he spreads his vibrating tail feathers to make a humming or "winnowing" sound. In May, when the early evening light is low, trek to a marshy area and listen for the winnowing ways of the snipe.

Habitat Café

Today's Special
Fly larvae

Yumm . . . bring an order of insect larvae (worm-shaped stage) with a side salad of plants and seeds. Wilson's Snipe are omnivorous. The eyes of the snipe are set far back on its head. Even with its bill deep in the ground it has vision to both sides and the rear to watch for predators.

SPRING, SUMMER, FALL, WINTER MENU:
Insects and plant matter

Life Cycle

NEST The female weaves grass into a loose basket on a scrape in the ground. It is hidden in the plants at the edge of the marsh. She lines the nest with softer, finer grass.

EGGS About 1½ inches long. The female sits tight in the nest as she incubates the clutch of 2–4 eggs for 18–20 days.

MOM! DAD! Precocial. The downy young hatch with big feet, long legs and just the start of wings. Mom and Dad lead them to areas with soft wet soil and beak over food to them. By the time the chicks are 10 days old they can probe the soft soil for food too.

FLEDGLING The young leave their parents at about 3 weeks of age.

JUVENILE Hanging out with other young snipe at feeding areas is the thing to do when they are about 2 months of age. They are mature enough the following spring to raise their own young ones.

Did You Know?

Wilson's Snipe feel prey in the soil with the tip of their bill. This unusual tip has a very sensitive area called a sensory pit. Once prey is felt, the tips of the mandibles (jaws) can then be moved apart while the base of the bill is held together to grasp the prey (like a pair of pinchers or tweezers). To help find prey, a snipe may bounce up and down on top of the soil or stamp its feet. What a silly sight to see.

When
Crepuscular. Wilson's Snipes are active near sunrise and sunset.

Migration
Permanent resident to short-distance migrant. Wilson's Snipe may stay in the Rocky Mountain region during the winter where there is open water. Some migrate to the southern U.S., including Texas.

Nesting
Wilson's Snipe begin nesting in April in the Rocky Mountain region of the U.S.

Getting Around
Large pectoral (chest) muscles power the fast straight flight of the snipe. When it is surprised and springs up from the grass it flies in a zigzag pattern.

Where to Look
Look for Wilson's Snipe tucked in the grasses of marshes and meadows throughout the Rocky Mountain region during all or part of the year.

Year-round   Summer
Migration   Winter

Belted Kingfisher

Megaceryle alcyon

Length: 11–14 inches (28–35 cm)
Wingspan: 19–23 inches (48–58 cm)

female

Head crest can stick straight up or stay closer to the head

Females wear a rusty-orange-colored belt

Juveniles look like adults but with a much smaller bill

Blue-gray above with a white throat collar and a blue band across the chest

Males do not have a belt

"Rattle, rattle, rattle . . ." This rattle call echoes against streambanks and riverbanks.

Expert Angler

Scan the wires and tree branches over a stream or river for the big-crested head and broad bill of this expert angler. Then sit quietly and watch as the blue-gray kingfisher studies the shallow, clear water for the movement of small fish, frogs and crayfish. Once it spots dinner, it dives like an arrow, plunging its bill into the water. Captured! The prey is taken to a perch where the kingfisher shakes its head and pounds the fish. This stuns the fish and breaks the bones of some fish. The kingfisher then turns the fish to swallow it headfirst. Their two-part stomach is not equipped for scales and bones. Instead, these hard-to-digest items are formed into a pellet and coughed up.

Habitat Café

Today's Special

leopard frogs

Yumm . . . bring an order of tadpoles, small fish, crayfish and dragonflies. Belted Kingfishers are carnivorous. They most often eat small fish that live in shallow water or stay near the surface. A kingfisher uses its thick pincher bill to catch prey. Look for its white wing patches in flight.

SPRING, SUMMER, FALL, WINTER MENU:
Fish, frogs, tadpoles and aquatic insects

Life Cycle

NEST Both the male and female dig out a tunnel just a few feet from the top of a river or stream bank, a sand or gravel pit, or bluff. At the end of the 3- to 15-foot tunnel is a nesting room. The eggs are laid on fish bones and scales from spit-up food pellets that have fallen apart.

EGGS About 1¼ inches long. The female incubates the clutch of 6–7 eggs for 22–24 days. Dad sits in when Mom takes a break.

MOM! DAD! Altricial. Both parents bring a wad of regurgitated fish to feed the chicks during the first days.

NESTLING More like a cat in a litter box than a bird, nestlings back up and shoot their feces on the wall. They turn around and hammer soil from over the top of the wall with their bills.

FLEDGLING At four weeks of age, Mom or Dad sits on a nearby perch with a fish in its bill. When the chicks are hungry enough, they come out. Parents feed them less often as they grow.

JUVENILE Juveniles take ten days of fishing lessons. Their parents drop dead fish in the water for the young to capture.

Unsolved Mystery

What kind of fish did the kingfisher eat for dinner last week? To solve this mystery, first find their perch and look underneath for pellets. Inside the pellets are the answers to their recent menu. You may find bones and scales that will help you identify the species of fish they ate. You can even tell how old the fish were by counting the rings on the scales!

When

Kingfishers are diurnal. They feed during the day and rest at night.

Migration

Spring Arrival: Mar–Apr
Fall Departure: Sep–Nov
Short- to long-distance migrants as far south as Central or South America. Some may overwinter in the Rocky Mountain region where open water remains.

Nesting

They begin to dig the nest burrow in a bank or cliff near water as early as March (more commonly April–May) in the Rocky Mountain region of the U.S.

Getting Around

Kingfishers perch on a branch, rock outcrop or on a wire over a river, stream, or lake. Once they spot prey, they dive headfirst, catching it in their large bills. They also hover over an area for a short time to catch prey. Their short legs and feet with joined toes are not adapted for walking. They only need their feet for shuffling in and out of their burrow and perching.

Where to Look

Along the streams, rivers, wooded creeks, ponds, and lakes in much of the region.

Year-round
Migration
Summer
Winter

Pied-billed Grebe

Podilymbus podiceps

Length: 12–15 inches (30–38 cm)
Wingspan: 18–24½ inches (45–62 cm)

winter plumage

Square, flat head

White eye-rings

Dark brown with
a white patch
underneath

White bill with black ring

Females and males look
similar; males are larger

Flat green,
lobed toes

"Kuk-kuk-kuk-kuk-kuk-kuk-kuk, cow-cow-uh, cow-uh, cow-uh-cow-uh." Call begins soft and slow, but ends loud and fast.

Mini-submarines

Where did it go? Sinking in the water like a sneaky submarine, a Pied-billed Grebe can keep you waiting for its return. With its periscope eyes and camouflaged black-and-white bill the only parts above the water, it can stay hidden for a long time. The trick to sinking in the water at just the right level is the grebe's ability to force out and control the amount of air held in its feathers and body. Typical of diving birds, its legs are far back on its body and its wings are small. Don't let its small size fool you. It can sneak up on other birds in fierce attacks to claim its territory and protect its young. There it is—gone again!

Habitat Café

Today's Special
snails

Yumm . . . bring an order of fish, dragonflies and nymphs, beetles, bugs, snails, mussels, frogs and crayfish. Their chicken-like, arched bill is just right for catching prey or crushing crustaceans. Pied-billed Grebes are both insectivores and carnivores.

SPRING, SUMMER, FALL, WINTER MENU:
Equal amounts of fish and insects, some crustaceans

Life Cycle

NEST As soon as the winter ice is melted, the female and male build their nest on a floating mat of decayed vegetation held to plant stalks in water at least 1 foot deep.

EGGS About 1¾ inches long. The female incubates the clutch of 4–8 eggs for just 23 days. She covers the eggs with a layer of plant leaves when she takes a break.

MOM! DAD! Precocial. Chicks can leave the nest for brief periods as soon as they are dry. They are in danger of drowning so they hitch a ride on the back of Mom and Dad. This cozy ride also protects them from predators. In only a few weeks, these little black-and-white striped "water skunks" can swim, dive and sink like their parents.

FLEDGLING The young grebes are able to fly and become independent when they are 8–9 weeks of age.

JUVENILE On their spring migration return, they are mature enough to date, mate and raise their own young.

Gross Factor

Grebes eat their own feathers throughout their lifetime, at times filling nearly half their stomach capacity. Parents feed feathers to their chicks soon after hatching. Biologists theorize that the feathers act to strain the stomach contents, preventing fish bones from passing into the intestines. Periodically, grebes spit up pellets of undigested feathers and other hard matter. Gross!

When
Pied-billed Grebes are diurnal. Normally, they are active during the day and rest at night. But during migration they are shy, nighttime fliers.

Migration
Spring Arrival: Mar–Apr
Fall Departure: Oct–Nov
Permanent resident to short-distance migrant. Pied-billed Grebes in the western areas of the Rocky Mountain region may stay through the winter. Other nesting populations of pied-bills may migrate to wintering areas in the southern U.S.

Nesting
Pied-billed Grebes begin nesting in April and May in the Rocky Mountain region of the U.S.

Getting Around
Being wary birds, Pied-billed Grebes crash-dive into the water when they sense danger. This causes a spray of water several feet into the air, blocking the vision of the predator. By the time the spray is gone, so is the sneaky grebe!

Where to Look
Pied-billed Grebes live in wetlands, shallow lakes, and ponds that have thick stands of plants, including cattails, and areas of open water.

Year-round   Summer
Migration   Winter

American Coot

Fulica americana

Length: 13–16 inches (33–41 cm)
Wingspan: 24 inches (60 cm)

diving

Females and males look alike

White forehead shield with bright red spot

Red eyes

Chicken-like white bill with black ring

Black all over

Stubby, upturned tail

Nickname: Mud Hen

Green-lobed toes and green legs

"Kuk-kuk-kuk!" means "This is my territory!"

Dare to be Different

American Coots are a bit like the comical flip books that combine different body parts to make a truly one-of-a-kind bird. They act like ducks but they are in a shorebird family, the rails. Most rails spend their time wading along shores. Coots have adapted to being a shorebird and a duck, or nearly so. Their body shape is flat, like a duck. Their dense (thickly spaced) feathers on their underside are made for being in the water like a duck. To get around on both land and water their green feet are partly webbed, called lobed. Their interesting chicken-like bill comes in handy for cracking open snails and other crustaceans. What a combination!

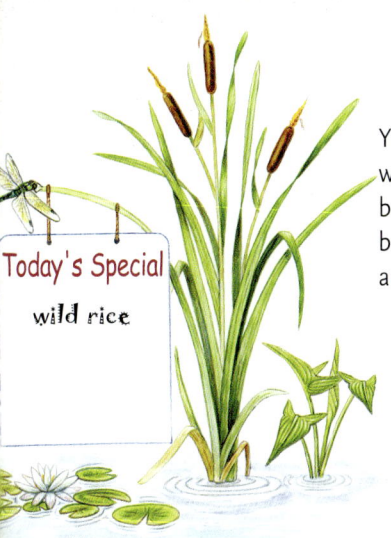

Habitat Café

Yumm . . . bring an order of aquatic insects, worms, tadpoles, snails and crayfish during breeding season. During non-breeding season bring an order of aquatic seeds, plant tubers and leaves. American Coots are omnivorous.

 SPRING, SUMMER MENU:
Plant matter, with equal amounts of insects and crustaceans on the side

 FALL, WINTER MENU:
Mostly plant matter, some insects and crustaceans

Today's Special
wild rice

Life Cycle

NEST The female builds the floating nest of plant leaves attached a few inches above the water to cattail and reed stalks. The nest is hidden in the edges of shallow lakes, ponds and wetlands.

EGGS About 2 inches long. Dad incubates the clutch of 6–12 eggs for 22–24 days. Mom pitches in at times.

MOM! DAD! Precocial. The black, downy chicks leave the nest soon after their down is dry. Frosted with white and wearing bright red patches on their heads, the chicks could be in a Dr. Seuss book!

Dad builds a brooding platform on a muskrat house, a mat of floating plants or a repaired nest. When the chicks are cold from the night air or storms, Dad or Mom keep them warm on the platform.

The chicks are fed insects during the first weeks by their parents. They feed themselves at 4–5 weeks of age and later add plants to their diet.

JUVENILE Juveniles leave the family group to join a flock of coots. When they are three months of age, they have grown to adult size.

Did You Know?

How many eyelids do birds have? Three. They have an upper and lower lid and a third, usually clear, lid between the two lids and the cornea. The third lid is the nictitating membrane. This lid is used for blinking and keeps their eyes clean, moist and protected from their chicks while they feed them. In diving birds, the nictitating membrane has a clear center, which acts like a contact lens underwater.

When

America Coots are diurnal. They feed during the day and rest at night.

Migration

Spring Arrival: late Apr–May
Fall Departure: Sept–Nov
Short- to- mid-distance migrant. In the fall, they fly by night to winter in the southern U.S, Mexico, and at times, Central America.

Nesting

American Coots begin nesting in April–July in the Rocky Mountain region of the U.S. They may have more than one brood per season.

Getting Around

Like many diving ducks, the coot's bones are solid and their legs are positioned far back on their body. Solid bones give them the extra weight they need to dive fast and deep. This helps them swim and dive, but makes for a clumsy take-off from the water.

Where to Look

American Coots live over much of the region in small bodies of water with reedy edges, including marshes, ponds and reedy lakes.

Year-round   Summer
Migration   Winter

Blue-winged Teal

Anas discors

Length: 14–16 inches (36–41 cm)
Wingspan: 23 inches (58 cm)

male

Look for blue wing patches and white wing bars

female

Females are brown with a faint white patch at the base of their bill; no white band on forewing

In flight, the top of wings are blue, white and green with a brown outer half

Males have a blue-gray head

A white, half-moon crescent between the bill and eye

White wing bars

Orange legs and feet

"Quack" is a protection and defense call by the female during nesting season.

Dabblers

Is the duck stuck? No, the bird with its rump sticking up from the water is a dabbling duck. There are two groups of ducks: dabblers and divers. Dabbling ducks tip up as they reach down through the water with their bill and neck to forage for plant and animal food on the pond bottom. This is called dabbling. Just under the water, their feet paddle to keep them partly underwater. Blue-winged Teal and Mallards are dabblers. They live in shallow water. Diving ducks live in deep water and have small wings, square heads, legs located far back on their body and swim low in the water. Whether you are watching dabblers or divers, it is certain that you are dabbling in a super way to spend a day!

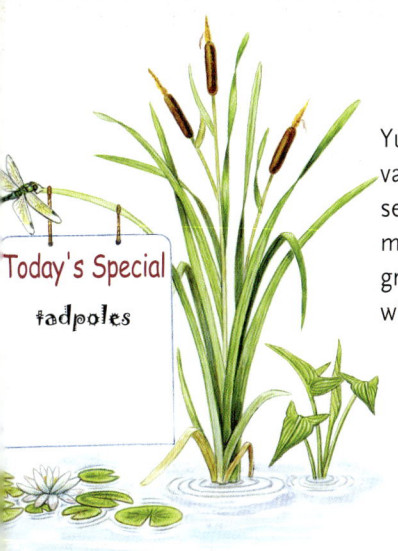

Habitat Café

Yumm . . . bring an order of insects, larvae and worms during the spring breeding season. In late summer through the winter months, it eats soft plant parts, wild rice, grasses, sedges and pond weeds. Blue-winged Teals are omnivorous.

Today's Special
tadpoles

SPRING & SUMMER MENU:
Mostly insects and larvae, some seeds

FALL & WINTER MENU:
Plants and seeds with some insects

Life Cycle

NEST The female weaves cattail leaves and dry grasses into a basket-like nest on dry ground near water. She lines the nest with her down feathers and arches nearby grasses over the top, making the nest nearly invisible.

EGGS About 1¾ inches long. The female incubates the clutch of 8–13 white eggs for 21–24 days.

MOM! DAD! Precocial. Soon after hatching, Mom leads the downy ducklings from the nest to water. They do not come back to the nest, but for the first two weeks, Mom broods them on chilly nights. The ducklings find insects on land and water on their own.

FLEDGLING Early nesters with an early fall migration departure, Blue-winged Teal mature very quickly. The young take flight at six weeks of age.

JUVENILE Mom goes her own way and the juveniles prepare for fall migration. When they return in the spring they are mature enough to date, mate and raise their own young.

Did You Know?

A migrating bird is busy with 4–5 major events in a year. Each event has to happen in order for the bird to survive. Between spring and fall flights, they have a breeding season and one or two molting periods. A female Blue-winged Teal must molt her feathers between the time she finishes her parenting duties and fall migration. Birds generally do not migrate with missing feathers. Males molt earlier and migrate south before females.

When

Blue-winged Teal are diurnal, active during the day and resting at night.

Migration

Spring Arrival: Mar–May
Fall Departure: Aug–Oct
Short- to long-distance migrant. Blue-winged Teal are among the first waterfowl to leave in the fall and the last to return in spring from wintering grounds in the southern U.S. through South America, including Brazil and central Chile. They fly in small flocks of 10–40 birds.

Nesting

Blue-winged Teal begin nesting in the Rocky Mountain region of the U.S. in April–May.

Getting Around

Blue-winged Teal take flight straight from the water! They fly at speeds of 30–50 miles per hour, and reach 60 mph during migration.

Where to Look

Watch for Blue-winged Teal in shallow marshes, ponds and mud flats near land with a lot of short- and medium-height grasses that they use for nesting.

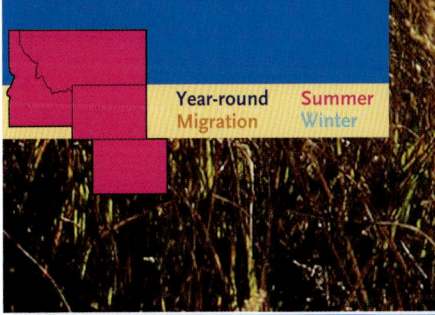

Year-round
Migration
Summer
Winter

Mallard

Anas platyrhynchos

Length: 20–25½ inches (50–65 cm)
Wingspan: 32½–37½ inches (82–95 cm)

female

Females, or hens, are streaked brown with an orange bill with small black spots; the speculum, a band of wing color, is metallic blue edged with white

Male (drake) has a green head with a white neck ring and a red-brown chest

Male has a black tail curl

Orange, webbed feet paddle water and push the body down to reach plants

"Quack, quack" is made only by females. Males have two calls of their own, a nasal warning "rhaeb" and a short courtship whistle.

From Marshes to Malls—Mallards Are All Over!

Mallards are *Super Adaptors*! In cities, they have been seen nesting in downtown flower planters and balconies of buildings. Close to people or not, as long as there is shallow water and food nearby, Mallards are content. They eat everything from insects to frogs, plants that live under and on top of water, seeds from farm crops and wild plants. Watch for Mallards eating cracked corn under bird feeders. Mallards are also big eaters of mosquito larvae and pupae that live on the top of shallow water. With Mallards near, you can enjoy being outdoors with fewer mosquitoes to swat.

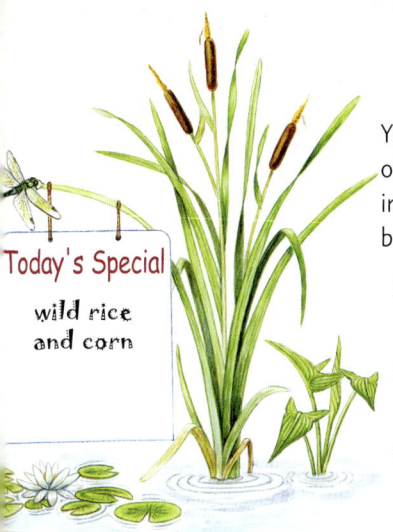

Today's Special

wild rice and corn

Habitat Café

Yumm . . . bring an order of seeds and shoots of aquatic plants, grass, snails, worms and insects. Mallards are *omnivorous*. They eat both plant and animal matter.

SPRING BREEDING SEASON MENU:
Lots of insects and animal matter

SUMMER, FALL MENU:
Includes aquatic plants and seeds

WINTER MENU:
Can include grains from farm crops

Life Cycle

NEST Built near water at the base of tall wetland plants or under a woody shrub. The female makes a few scrapes in the ground and lays her eggs. She then adds grass, reeds and leaves from nearby plants to make a nest rim around her body. Soft down feathers line the inside.

EGGS About 2¼ inches long. The female incubates the clutch of 9–13 eggs for 26–30 days.

MOM! DAD! Precocial. Mallard ducklings hatch covered with fluffy down and their eyes fully open. Mom is on her own with her large brood. The hatchlings are out of the nest after the first day and follow her to water.

Mallards dive for food during the first weeks after hatching, but this behavior disappears with the arrival of their flight feathers. Until they can fly at two months of age, they still need Mom's protection from snapping turtles, bass and raccoons.

JUVENILE At 10 weeks of age, young Mallards leave the family group to join a mixed flock of adults and juveniles. When they return in the spring, they are mature enough to raise their own family.

Did You Know?

While Mom is taking care of the ducklings, Dad joins a flock and stays very quiet. Male Mallards molt, or lose the old feathers and grow new ones, before fall migration. The bright breeding season feathers are replaced by dull camouflaged brown feathers called "eclipse plumage." During this time, they are unable to fly for a short period until the new feathers grow in.

When
Diurnal. They feed during the day and rest at night.

Migration
Spring Arrival: Mar–Apr
Fall Departure: Sep–Nov
Short- to mid-distance migrant to the southern United States and Mexico. Some Mallards stay in the Rocky Mountain region of the U.S. during the winter, wherever they find suitable open water within a reasonable "commuting distance" of feeding areas.

Nesting
Mallards begin nesting in April–May in our region.

Getting Around
Mallards are strong and direct fliers capable of reaching speeds up to 45–60 miles per hour. When they are alarmed they can spring straight up from the water. They use their wings and feet as brakes when making a landing into water! Mallards are also excellent swimmers.

Where to Look
Lakes, wetlands, rivers, parks and farm ponds. Explore city, county and state parks, and public areas or nature centers. Mallards may even eat cracked corn under bird feeders!
· *Super Adaptor*

Year-round	Summer
Migration	Winter

Common Merganser

Mergus merganser

Length: 21–28 inches (54–71 cm)
Wingspan: 34 inches (86 cm)

Female is gray with a rust-brown head, a short head crest and a white chin patch; male looks like female during much of the year

Long, orange bill

Black, iridescent green head

Gray back and tail

White neck and under parts

"Grrr." This is the male calling an alarm. Females make a "gruk gruk gruk" call.

Time for a Check-up

It's time for an environmental check-up. What is the health of the aquatic food chain? For a general idea, we can check the pulse of the Common Merganser. This large, slender diving duck uses its saw-toothed bill to get a grip on fish and then gulp them down. Mergansers are at the top end of the lake food chain. If there is a weak link further down in the food chain, then the merganser will likely show signs of it. The health of an aquatic food chain can be affected by toxic (poisonous) chemicals that get into the water, due to soil erosion, run-off, or acid rain (created from air pollution). Taking care of the land, water and air that wildlife share with us means a healthy check-up for all.

Habitat Café

Yumm . . . bring an order of small fish with a side order of water insects, mollusks and crustaceans. Garnish the top with a few frogs, please. Common Mergansers are carnivorous. The fish captured for dinner may be from over 50 different species and about 4–12 inches long.

SPRING, SUMMER, FALL, WINTER MENU:
Mostly fish and a few invertebrates

Life Cycle

NEST The simple nest is often in the cavity of a tree or a nest box. Less often it will be on the ground. The female may take some of her own down feathers to add to the materials already in the nest cavity. The parents may use the site again in other years. They will also nest in nesting boxes placed near a river or lake that supports fish.

EGGS About 2½ inches long. The female incubates the clutch of 6–17 eggs for about 32 days.

MOM! DAD! Precocial. Mom calls for the downy chicks to leap from the nest hole on the first or second day after they hatch. She takes them to the water where they are soon diving for their own lunch.

The young are independent by the second month. They can fly and practice take-off and landing maneuvers.

JUVENILE Females are mature enough during their second year to mate and raise their own merganser chicks.

Birding Tip

If you like to fish, then you and mergansers have something in common. The next time you're ready to cast a line, consider using a nonlead sinker. Water diving birds can get ill from ingesting lead fishing sinkers. The lead is poisonous to the birds. Many state fish and game departments have programs to help you get started with safe nonlead sinkers. Find the connection to your state on pages 196–197. Have fun catching the big one!

When
Common Mergansers are diurnal. They are active during the day and rest at night.

Migration
Spring Arrival: Mar–Apr
Fall Departure: Oct–Nov
Permanent resident to short-distance migrant. Mergansers stay the winter in the Rocky Mountain region where there is open water to catch a fish lunch.

Nesting
Common Mergansers begin nesting in May in forested areas close to lakes in the Rocky Mountain region of the U.S.

Getting Around
Common Mergansers fly fast at about 43 mph. To recognize them in flight, look for their flat, pointed shape skimming along the water like a dart towards a bull's-eye.

Where to Look
Common Mergansers live where there are forests with tree cavities for nesting, lakes and rivers for fishing, and downstream water systems to take their chicks to. They can be seen in lake and river areas throughout much of the Rocky Mountain region.

Year-round   Summer
Migration   Winter

Osprey

Pandion haliaetus

Length: 21½–23 inches (54–58 cm)
Wingspan: 59–71 inches (150–180 cm)

White crown
and forehead

Dark line
through eye

Long wings
with dark patch
at bend in wing

Brown back and
upper wings

Mostly white
breast and belly

"Tiooop, tioooop, tiooop."
Males and females make this
whistle call when guarding
the nest.

The female is larger
than the male, and
generally has a
more marked band
of brown feathers
across the breast

Olympic-style Adaptations . . .

Ospreys dive in and escape with the prize—however wiggly and slippery it may be. They have Olympic-style adaptations for surviving along waterways. Equipped with feathers so closely spaced and well oiled they are waterproof, they race into the clear water feet first to pluck their prize from the top few feet. Long and curved talons, barbed foot pads and reversible outer toes secure the desperate fish. If that isn't enough, two toes positioned forward and two backward lock the fish in a headfirst hold that makes for an aerodynamic getaway. Take to the waterways and cheer the performance of this wild champion.

Habitat Café

Yumm . . . bring an order of fresh, wiggling, living fish, with a side order of fish. Ospreys are carnivorous. They dive feet first into shallow water for fish. Their catch is taken to a perch, often near the nest, where it is devoured with enthusiasm.

SPRING, SUMMER, FALL, WINTER MENU:
Fish

Life Cycle

NEST Ospreys build their nest on top of a tall living or dead tree or a cliff along lakes and streams. They have also adapted to nesting on nest poles placed close to water. The male brings in large sticks for the base and smaller sticks, grass and wetland materials for the inside. To keep the eggs from falling through cracks, the female adds flat objects last. Once a sturdy nest is built, the pair may reuse it year to year.

EGGS About 2½ inches long. The female incubates the clutch of 1–4 eggs for 37 days.

MOM! DAD! Semi-precocial. The downy young beg loudly with the prize (food) going to the loudest. The third chick to hatch is generally smaller than the first chicks, making survival a challenge.

FLEDGLING At 7 weeks of age, the young exercise their wings at the nest rim and then leave the nest.

JUVENILE Ospreys do not leave their wintering areas until their second or third spring, when they often return to the area where they were raised. They are mature enough at 3–5 years of age to nest.

Did You Know?

Ospreys are near the top of the lake food chain. In the 1950s, pesticides leaked into water supplies and were absorbed by fish that were in turn eaten by Ospreys. The chemicals weakened the shells of their eggs and fewer chicks hatched. The Osprey population plummeted. With the banning of some pesticides, the number of Ospreys has steadily increased but it remains a species to keep a close watch on. Welcome back!

When

Ospreys are diurnal. They are active during the day and rest at night.

Migration

Spring Arrival: Mar–Apr
Fall Departure: Sep–Oct
Mid- to long-distance migrant. Ospreys migrate by day south of the U.S. to Central and South America. Females migrate earlier in the fall and travel farther than males.

Nesting

The male Osprey arrives before the female to locate the nest. They begin nesting in April and May in the Rocky Mountain region of the U.S.

Getting Around

Look for the dark patch at the bend of their long, narrow wings. Flight is steady and rowing with stiff wingbeats. They soar high on thermals to save energy. Ospreys don't wear nose plugs when diving, but they almost do. Their nasal valves close and prevent them from drowning when they dive into water.

Where to Look

Ospreys fish in the clear, shallow waters along lakes, rivers, streams and coasts. Ospreys are a threatened species in some states.

Year-round   Summer
Migration   Winter

Bald Eagle

Haliaeetus leucocephalus

Length: 28–38 inches (71–96 cm)
Wingspan: 6½ feet (204 cm)

adult feeding juvenile

fishing

Large, yellow hooked beak for tearing apart prey

Dark brown-black with a white head

Females and males look the same; females are often larger than males

Large yellow legs and feet with curved talons for capturing and carrying prey

White tail

"Kwit kwit kwit kwit, kee-kee-kee-kee-ker!" This is fair warning to "Stay out of my territory!"

National Symbol of the USA

The lakes and rivers of the Rocky Mountain region are an important home to Bald Eagles. However, in 1963 there were only 800 nesting Bald Eagle pairs in the lower 48 states. Thanks to regulation, the banning of DDT, and restoration efforts, the population has been moved from federally endangered to federally threatened. To continue to nest successfully in the region, Bald Eagles need tall trees, open water within one mile of the nest, food, roosting areas, and to not be disturbed. With more buildings placed near the water's edge, habitat is lost. You can be part of the Bald Eagle's success story by making choices that consider the needs of this fascinating wild bird of prey!

Habitat Café

Today's Special
coots

Yumm . . . bring an order of fish caught at the water's surface, carrion (dead meat) and water birds, including gulls and ducks. Bald Eagles are carnivorous. Eagles can eat large amounts of food and store it in their crop to digest over several days.

SPRING, SUMMER, FALL, WINTER MENU:
Mostly fish, some birds and a few mammals and reptiles

Life Cycle

NEST Both parents build the nest, or eyrie, in the top of a large tree (cottonwood or pine). The nest is a deep pile of large branches and sticks, lined with smaller twigs, grass, moss and weeds.

EGGS About 3 inches long. Both the female and male incubate the clutch of 2 eggs for 34–36 days.

MOM! DAD! Altricial. Covered with down for the first 5–6 weeks. Parents bring fresh food. The first chick to hatch is generally larger and may kill or starve the second, smaller chick.

NESTLING Feathers grow in at 5 weeks of age but young stay in the nest for 8–14 weeks. Before leaving the nest they practice. Half of all nest takeoffs fall short, leaving the bird vulnerable to predators. Mom and Dad come to the rescue and bring food until it can fly.

FLEDGLING Fledge at 3–4 months of age.

JUVENILE Juveniles gain their full adult plumage at 5 years of age. They stay with the same mate for life and remain in the same nesting territory each breeding season.

History Hangout

The National Emblem Law of 1940 made it illegal to kill any Bald Eagle in the lower 48 states. They are also protected under the Migratory Bird Treaty Act and are listed as a federally threatened species. Celebrate the Bald Eagle and other wildlife with kids from all over our nation by joining in the activities of National Wildlife Week sponsored by the National Wildlife Federation, http://www.nwf.org/nationalwildlifeweek/. You can celebrate eagles with a wild song too, www.birdsforkids.com.

When

Bald Eagles can be found throughout the Rocky Mountain region with the greatest numbers in areas along lakes and rivers.

Migration

Spring Arrival: Mar–Apr
Fall Departure: Sep–Nov
Permanent resident to short-distance migrant. Some stay in the region all winter near open water and food sources (especially in the greater Yellowstone area), while others migrate to states to the south. Overwintering eagles group up and need habitat with roosting trees near open-water feeding areas.

Nesting

Bald Eagles begin egg laying and incubation in April in the Rocky Mountain region of the U.S.

Getting Around

Bald Eagles use their powerful, broad wings to climb, soar and glide.

Where to Look

Bald Eagles can be found region wide with the greatest numbers in areas along lakes, rivers and coasts.

Year-round
Migration
Summer
Winter

Wetlands, Rivers, Lakes and Shores

179

Canada Goose

Branta canadensis

Length: 30–43½ inches (76–110 cm)
Wingspan: 50–67 inches (127–170 cm)

in flight

gosling

Bill: Small saw-like points on the edges of the upper and lower mandibles help the goose grip plants and strip seeds from standing grasses

Look for their white underside and dark tail when they take flight

Long, black neck with white throat patch

Females and males look similar, but the males are slightly larger

"Ha-roonk, ha-roonk!"

It's a Family Affair

Honk, honk . . . the family is touching down. For Canada Geese, it's a family affair from the time they hatch through adulthood. During their first year, the young stay with their parents, traveling in a family flock that may join up with other family groups. When they are mature enough to start their own family at age 2–5 years, they pair up and stay with the same mate for life. Pairs return to the same breeding area each year and so do their daughters. The family group then continues to increase its territory, leading to some challenges in urban areas. Wildlife biologists and managers work toward balancing both the needs of wildlife and people.

Habitat Café

Yumm . . . bring an order of roots, stems, leaves, fruits, berries and seeds. Canada Geese are herbivores. They also like to eat bluegrass—the kind of grass found on lake-shore lawns and golf courses.

 Today's Special
field corn

SPRING, SUMMER, FALL MENU:

 Aquatic plants high in protein

WINTER MENU:

Grass, agricultural crops, fruit, berries and seeds

Life Cycle

NEST Geese nest on muskrat houses, beaver lodges and floating mats of vegetation, or build their own nest, usually on the ground.

It's best to stay far away from nests. Females will lay their neck flat and lie motionless on the nest. Males defend the nest with gusto. They have been known to attack intruders with their strong neck, bill and wings. Spotting scopes, binoculars and a camera with a zoom lens are great for safe, close-up views of wildlife!

EGGS About 3½ inches long. The female incubates the clutch of 4–7 eggs for 28 days. Dad sits on the nest when Mom takes a break.

MOM! DAD! Precocial. The down-covered goslings are able to walk, swim, feed and dive just one day after hatching. They instinctively spread their webbed feet out to push through the water and then close the web when the foot comes forward again. The goslings are fully fledged with strong flight feathers at 7–9 weeks of age.

JUVENILE Juveniles stay with their parents through the first year and are mature enough at 2–5 years of age to mate and raise their own young.

Birding Tip

Draw for Ducks! You can be a part of waterfowl conservation efforts by creating your own artwork featuring ducks in their natural habitat. Enter your artwork in the U.S. Fish & Wildlife Service's Junior Duck Stamp Contest. Eligible species include Common Merganser (page 174), Mallard (page 172), Canada Goose and Trumpeter Swan (page 184). To learn more, visit www.fws.gov/juniorduck/ArtContest.htm.

When

Canada Geese are diurnal, active during the day and resting at night.

Migration

Spring Arrival: Mar–Apr
Fall Departure: Sep–Nov
Short- to mid-distance migrant to southern portions of the Rocky Mountain region, southeast Colorado and Texas. Some overwinter in the greater Rocky Mountain region of the U.S. where they find open water.

Nesting

Canada Geese begin nesting in March–April in the Rocky Mountain region of the U.S.

Getting Around

Canada Geese can move fast for large birds, flying at speeds of 40–60 mph. Their "V" formation is energy efficient, too. Flying in the slipstream of the leader, the other geese face less wind resistance and use less energy. When the lead goose tires, it changes place with another goose. Now that's teamwork.

Where to Look

Canada Geese live in open country with wetlands, ponds and lakeshores—even golf courses and city parks.

Year-round / Migration   Summer / Winter

Great Blue Heron

Ardea herodias

Length: 38–54 inches (97–137 cm)
Wingspan: 5½–6½ feet (167–201 cm)

in flight

Feather plume

Yellow bill

Adults have a white crown
and black areas on their
wing (shoulders)

Blue-gray with
a white throat
and head

Male and female
look alike

"Rok-rok"
means
"This is my space!"

Rok-Rok, Rookeries

Great Blue Herons nest in colonies of often 100 or more birds, called rookeries. Some heron rookeries are located along large rivers and forested islands. Oxbow Bend on the Snake River (in Grand Teton National Park) has a history of hosting a heron rookery. Going near heron colonies during nesting is not a good idea. You might cause the herons to abandon their young. Besides, a heron colony is a very smelly place. Together, many birds create a lot of droppings! Heron colonies are best enjoyed at a distance. Herons may fly out to feeding areas in wetlands over 30 miles from a colony. They are much easier to find and watch as they slowly stalk shoreline shallows in search of fish and other prey.

Habitat Café

Yumm . . . bring an order of fish, frogs, crayfish, lizards, grasshoppers, mice and shrews. Herons grip or spear prey with their 6-inch pointed bill. Great Blue Herons are carnivorous. They eat only animal matter.

Today's Special

snakes

SPRING, SUMMER, FALL, WINTER MENU:
Lots of fish, with fewer insects, reptiles and amphibians

Life Cycle

NEST Hundreds of Great Blue Herons nest together in the tops of tall trees in a colony called a rookery. The nest is built of large sticks. Herons will use the same rookery for many years. Some heron rookeries have been used for nearly 100 years!

EGGS About 2½ inches long. Both the female and male incubate the clutch of 4 eggs for 28 days.

MOM! DAD! Altricial. Both help feed the young.

NESTLING The chicks stay in the nest for about 7–8 weeks.

FLEDGLING They are about the same size as their parents when they leave the nest. The parents continue to feed them for 2–3 weeks.

JUVENILE The juveniles join with others their age, feeding and preparing for migration. They have a black crown, but it takes 2 years to grow a full feather plume. At 3 years they are mature enough to nest and raise young.

Gross Factor

Parents catch, eat and partially digest fish, frogs and other small animals, and deliver the baby food by spitting it up into the chick's open beak. As chicks grow, they take the food out of the parent's beak. Finally, the parents spit the food into the nest and the older chicks fight over the juiciest pieces. Chicks ward off threats from below by leaning over the nest and spitting half-digested fish on the intruder. Gross!

When

Great Blue Herons are diurnal, feeding during the day and resting at night.

Migration

Spring Arrival: Feb–Apr
Fall Departure: Sep–Oct
Short- to mid-distance migrant to the southern U.S. and as far south as Panama.

Nesting

Great Blue Herons begin nesting in April–May in the Rocky Mountain region of the U.S.

Getting Around

Herons wade in shallow water, and sometimes stalk on dry land. Their toes spread out as they step on the ground, leaving tracks in the mud 6–8 inches long and 4–6 inches wide. Herons fly with slow, deep, steady wingbeats, legs stretched out behind, and their neck bent into a tight "S" shape.

Where to Look

Great Blue Herons can be found near rivers, streams, wetlands and lakes throughout the Rocky Mountain region.

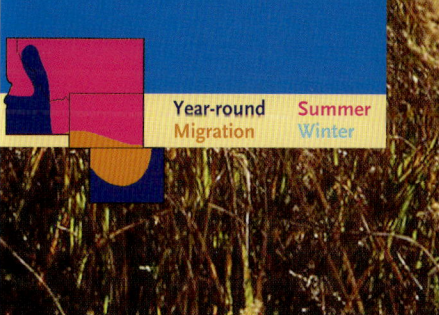

Year-round   Summer
Migration   Winter

Trumpeter Swan

Cygnus buccinator

Length: 3¼ feet (99 cm)
Wingspan: 5 feet (152 cm)

takeoff

Black bill

Males, called cobs, and females, called pens, are both white

The largest waterfowl in the region

The orange color on the birds' feathers is from iron salt deposits in their feeding areas

Black legs and feet

Juveniles are gray for the first few years, reaching full adult white at four years of age

The windpipe (trachea) coils through the keel of the breastbone (sternum) to make a sound like the trumpet of a French horn.

Trumpeting Toward Success

Imagine finding webbed footprints the size of a party plate along a wetland. Trumpeter Swans were leaving very few footprints in the early 1900s. By 1935, only 69 individual Trumpeter Swans remained in the lower 48 states. They were the Trumpeter Swans of the Greater Yellowstone area. It takes teamwork to bring a species back from the edge of extinction. A team of local, state and federal wildlife experts and volunteers have worked hard since then to bring the Rocky Mountain population of nesting Trumpeter Swans to over 400 in 2008. You are part of the team, too, when you make choices that consider the environment and leave only a green footprint. That is something to trumpet about!

Today's Special

wild celery

Habitat Café

Yumm . . . bring an order of roots, seeds, leaves and tubers of plants that grow at the bottom and float on top of marshes and lakes. Cygnets (young swans) eat insects and snails for the first 2–5 weeks, finding their meal by the color and movement of their prey. Adult Trumpeter Swans are herbivores.

SPRING, SUMMER, FALL, WINTER MENU:

🌱 Mostly plants, with a few fish and invertebrates

Life Cycle

NEST The male and female build the nest on a muskrat house, beaver dam, on a small island, a floating mat of plants, or they may build up enough plants to make their own nesting platform.

EGGS Nearly 4½ inches long. The female incubates the clutch of 4–6 eggs for 34 days. Dad may help. One day before hatching, the chicks begin to peep inside the egg. Mom and Dad stay close to the nest.

MOM! DAD! Precocial. Cygnets can swim as soon as their down is dry, but they stay on the nest for a few days. They are brooded by their parents for the next three weeks until their new feathers grow in. Mom and Dad stir up snails and insects from the bottom of the marsh for them by pumping their feet up and down under water. Fast-growing cygnets need the extra protein found in insects and crustaceans. It takes nearly 4 months for them to take their first flight.

JUVENILE Young swans stay with their parents through their first winter until they return in the spring to the breeding area. Teens hang out with their siblings until they are mature enough to mate and raise their own young at 4–6 years of age.

Birding Tip

A plan is in place to make certain this majestic bird has a future. The 2008 Pacific Flyway Management Plan set a goal for a population of 540 adult swans in our region by 2013. The Trumpeter Swan Society is a group of dedicated volunteers and experts hard at work toward this goal. Roll up your sleeves and join in—to join, visit: www.trumpeter-swansociety.org/rocky-mountain-population.html

When

Trumpeter Swans are diurnal, active during the day and resting at night.

Migration

Permanent resident. The swans of Greater Yellowstone stay in the area during the winter in the warm waters caused by the area's unique geothermal activity, including hot springs and geysers. In winter, they are joined by the western Canadian populations of Trumpeter Swans. In 2009, the combined count was over 5,000 swans.

Nesting

Trumpeter Swans begin nesting in May in the Rocky Mountain region of the U.S.

Getting Around

Swans fly low over the water. They run on top of the water with their wings flapping to take off. Just after takeoff they pull their neck into an "S" and then straighten it out. They sleep with their head tucked under their wing.

Where to Look

The wetlands and lakes of the greater Yellowstone area, which includes southeast Idaho, southwest Montana and north-west Wyoming.

| Year-round | Summer |
| Migration | Winter |

American White Pelican

Pelecanus erythrorhynchos

Height: 50–65 inches (127–165 cm)
Wingspan: 96–114 inches (244–290 cm)

Yellow-orange skin around eye

11–15 inch bill has a deep pouch for scooping food—it can hold 3 gallons of water

dinner

in flight

White with black wing tips and black along edges of wings

Females and males look similar

Orange legs and webbed feet

Hey, Good-looking!

What does a pelican find good-looking? Bring on the nuptial tubercles and yellow crest feathers! For American White Pelicans, spring dating and mating season calls for chic outerwear. From late winter until after eggs are laid, the top of a pelican's bill has ridges, called nuptial tubercles. These look like a large knob. Pelicans also grow a spring crest of pale-yellow feathers on the back of their head. Wearing black wingtips is not just about style. Pigment adds color to feathers (white feathers have no pigment). The pigment that gives a black color, melanin, adds strength to feathers. Wearing black wingtips gives a pelican a strong leading edge to its flight feathers.

Habitat Café

Yumm . . . bring an order of small fish with a side order of salamanders and crayfish. American White Pelicans are carnivorous, eating only meat. They work together by making a semi-circle on the water and "herding" the fish into shallow water. To eat fish, a pelican first points its beak down to drain out the water and then lifts its beak and head up—swallow!

SPRING, SUMMER, FALL, WINTER MENU:

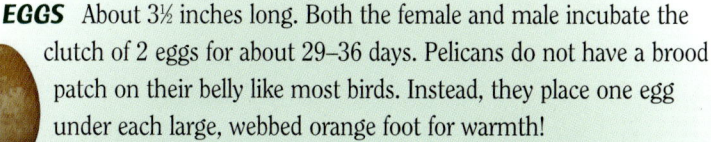 Almost entirely fish, some amphibians and crustaceans

Today's Special
fish

Life Cycle

NEST The simple nest is often in the cavity of a tree or a nest box. Less often it will be on the ground. The parents may use the site again.

EGGS About 3½ inches long. Both the female and male incubate the clutch of 2 eggs for about 29–36 days. Pelicans do not have a brood patch on their belly like most birds. Instead, they place one egg under each large, webbed orange foot for warmth!

MOM! DAD! Semi-altricial. Hatched out of the egg naked and flesh-colored (some even look green), the new chicks are covered with thick, white down within ten days.

NESTLING The chicks leave the nest at three weeks to huddle in groups. Mom and Dad visit the group to deliver food and then leave until the next mealtime.

FLEDGLING The short-legged young are ready for take-off flights by 2 months of age.

JUVENILE Juveniles have gray to flesh-colored bills and brown streaks on their white feathers. They migrate south in the fall and are mature enough to mate and raise young at 3–4 years of age.

Gross Factor

Young chicks eat regurgitated liquid food from the front part of their parents' throat pouch. As they grow, they reach farther back into the pouch for regurgitated food with larger pieces of fish. This transition to larger food pieces prepares them for the time when they feed themselves. Bill-smacking tasty!

When
American White Pelicans are diurnal. They are active during the day and rest at night.

Migration
Spring Arrival: Apr–May
Fall Departure: Sep–Oct
Short-distance to mid-distance migrant. American White Pelicans from the Molly Islands of Yellowstone Lake and the Canyon Ferry and Arod colonies of western Montana winter mostly along the Pacific coastline. Others migrate to the east, and south to Mexico and as far as Honduras.

Nesting
American White Pelicans nest in colonies on bare islands and sandbars. If the nest site is disturbed, they may not return the next year. They begin nesting in May.

Getting Around
Their long, broad and slotted wings help them to soar. They use rising flows of warm air, called thermals, to soar up, drifting down to the bottom of the next thermal. Soaring saves energy on long trips.

Where to Look
Pelicans prefer large lakes and rivers. Visit the Yellowstone, Teton and the Snake River areas to see pelicans.

Year-round | Summer
Migration | Winter

YOU MIGHT INCLUDE:
- size, shape, field marks
- type of bill and feet
- shape of wings and tail
- feather color and pattern

Sample Journal Entry

Today I was looking in my binoculars and I saw a female robin feeding her chicks. They were in my neighbor's tree on 5/13/12. The chicks were small and gray. They had bright yellow beaks. The female was brown with an orange belly, feet and beak. Her nest was made of sticks and twigs. She was very cool.

OTHER NOTES YOU MAY WANT TO INCLUDE:
- Date, time and habitat
- What the bird was doing (behavior)
- Song/call
- Alone, pair or group of birds
- Flight pattern
- Other signs, like tracks, scat (droppings), nests, eggs, wood chips, wing marks in snow, ice crystals from a snow burrow

Glossary

Brainy Bird Words and Their Meanings

adaptation A physical feature, behavior or trait that a bird has developed to help it take full advantage of its habitat. American Robins are found all over the Rocky Mountain region because they have adapted to a variety of habitats for shelter, nesting and raising their young. They have also adapted to eating a variety of foods. A robin's diet includes worms, insects, seeds, berries and fruits. These meals can be found in rural, city or suburban habitats around the region.

altricial Baby birds that hatch from the egg helpless. They are naked, unable to see, walk, hop, fly, or feed themselves, and need to be cared for by one or both parents.

anting Some birds, such as the Blue Jay, will place ants between their skin and their feathers with their beak. At times, some birds actually stand on an anthill and allow the ants to crawl up into their feathers!

binomial nomenclature A system of classifying and giving scientific names to plants and animals based on similar identifying characteristics. It is used to group birds together by which body characteristics they have in common. Scientific names originate in Latin and Greek and remain the same all over the world. The scientific name for the American Robin is *Turdus migratorius*.

boreal migrant Birds that breed in Canada, but come south into the Rocky Mountain region of the U.S. during some years when their northern food supply is scarce.

bristle feathers Stiff, hair-like feathers made up of a firm central shaft (rachis). They usually grow near the eyes, nostrils and beak opening. Bristle feathers may protect the eyes from insects, dust and dirt, or help the bird funnel food into its mouth.

brood patch A bare spot on the chest or belly of a parent bird that is used to incubate eggs. The feathers in this area either fall off or are plucked out. Blood vessels next to the brood patch help keep the eggs warm. In most bird species, feathers regrow after the nesting season.

camouflage A bird's shape, or the color and pattern of its feathers (plumage), that helps it hide from predators or prey. The Wilson's Snipe's plumage is similar in color and pattern to the brown grasses of the marsh and wetlands where it lives.

coniferous trees Trees that bear their seeds in a cone.

contour feathers These feathers overlap each other to give birds a streamlined body shape (a contour) for less friction. This helps birds fly faster through the air and dive faster in the water. Contour feathers are found on the body, wings and tail. They have a central shaft (rachis) with vanes on each side. Attached to the vanes are barbs. On each side of the barbs are small barbules that make a "zipper" to hold the feather barbs together. When the barbs unzip, the bird uses its beak to zip them back together while preening.

courtship behavior The actions that a bird does to attract a mate. Some birds stomp the ground and turn in circles in a courtship dance. Others perform amazing aerial dances, and some drum on hollow trees. Courtship is the "dating" behavior of birds.

crepuscular Active during the twilight hours, which include the hours of dawn just before the sun rises, and dusk just after the sun sets. Crepuscular birds are active during the time between day and night when the faint light of sunrise and sunset provides them with protection from predators. Common Nighthawks are mostly crepuscular.

deciduous trees Trees that lose all their leaves each year are called deciduous trees. Aspen are deciduous.

diurnal Active during the daytime, or the hours that the sun is up. Diurnal birds feed, build their nests and preen during the day. American Robins are diurnal.

down feathers These feathers do not "zip" together like contour feathers, but stay fluffy. The air spaces hold the bird's body heat close like a warm blanket. Young birds often have down first to keep their small bodies warm until their contour and other body feathers grow in. Adult birds' down feathers are located under their contour feathers.

egg tooth A newly hatched chick has an egg tooth. This small, sharp projection on its upper mandible (bill) helps it to chip through the egg's shell during hatching. The egg tooth is no longer needed after hatching and soon falls off.

field marks Each bird species has physical features that make it unique (one of a kind). These unique features can help you to identify it. Field marks include feather color, feather pattern, a bird's basic body shape and size. Other field marks include the shape and size of the bird's bill, feet, wings and tail. An eye-ring (which gives the bird the appearance of wearing a pair of glasses) or a crest on the top of its head are also field marks.

fledgling Young birds that have just learned to fly on their own and have left the family nest are called fledglings. To fledge is to be fully feathered and be able to sustain flight.

filoplume feather Delicate, hair-like feathers that help a bird adjust the position of its contour feathers for better flight. Filoplume feathers are scattered over a bird's body. They are sensitive enough to move with the slightest breeze, and send information to nerve cells at their bases.

foraging Gathering food.

game wildlife Birds and other wildlife that can be legally hunted under the laws of the Rocky Mountain region during designated times of the year. Hunting seasons and limits are specific to each species.

glean To collect or pick up, often referring to gathering food. When a bird picks insect larvae from cracks in tree bark, or spilled grain from a harvested farm field, it is said to be "gleaning."

habitat The place where a bird lives. For a Mallard, home is a shallow lake or wetland habitat where it can reach for the plants and animals on the lake or wetland bottom with its long neck and bill. For a Northern Flicker home is in a forest habitat with trees large enough for it to make nesting holes.

hawking The act of catching insects where the bird sits very still on a perch until it sees a flying insect. It flies out, snatches the insect in mid-air and then returns to the perch to devour the insect or deliver it to its young.

juvenile A young bird that has grown to be independent of its parents (it can fly and find food, water and shelter on its own) but is not yet mature enough to breed. Many smaller birds pass through this stage in their first year; larger birds can remain a juvenile for four or five years. They are the adolescents and teenagers of the bird world.

lift This is what allows a bird to defy gravity and get off the ground. Lift is made by the force of the air pressure underneath the wings, which is greater than the air pressure above the wings, and results in a raising force. The shape of a bird's wings is what makes this work. The top side of the wing is convex (curved), and the bottom is flatter. The air rushing past the wing is divided in two flows: one over the top of the wing and the other past the bottom of the wing. The top air moves faster. This causes the air beneath the wing to go slower and increases the air pressure under the wing—the bird is lifted off the ground. The Swiss scientist **Daniel Bernoulli** (1700–1782) discovered this principle of flight, which is now called **Bernoulli's Principle**.

migration The seasonal movement of birds or animals from one region to another. Cliff Swallows migrate to wintering grounds in South America in the fall and return to the Rocky Mountain region of the U.S. the following spring to nest and raise their young.

molt When a bird sheds its old feathers and grows new ones to replace them.

navigation How a bird finds its way, such as during migration.

neotropical migrant A bird that breeds in the Rocky Mountain region of the U.S., but migrates to wintering areas in Central and South America. Includes both mid-distance Central American and long-distance South American migrants.

nocturnal Active during the night. Birds that are nocturnal actively feed, build nests and preen during the night. Great Horned Owls are nocturnal birds.

nongame wildlife Birds and animals protected by state or national laws from trapping and hunting. Most birds in this book are nongame birds. There is no designated time or "season" to legally hunt them. Game birds, however, can be legally hunted.

ornithology The study of birds. The segment "ology" in a word means the study of, and "ornith" is associated with birds. An ornithologist is a scientist who studies birds.

overwinter To spend the winter. Some Red-tailed Hawks overwinter in the Rocky Mountain region of the U.S.

permanent resident Birds that breed and remain in the Rocky Mountain region of the U.S. all year. Black-capped Chickadees and Gray Jays are permanent residents in the Rocky Mountain region of the U.S.

phenology The study of the changing seasons.

plumage A bird's plumage refers to all of its feathers together.

precocial Chicks that hatch able to see, walk, hop, or fly and feed themselves. They need only limited care by one or both parents. The role of the parents in precocial birds is usually to lead the young to food, offer protection from predators, and provide brooding in weather and temperature extremes. The young of many ground-nesting birds such as the Killdeer and Canada Goose are precocial.

predator A bird or animal that captures other living creatures to eat. A Cooper's Hawk is a predator of small mammals that it catches for lunch.

preening When a bird arranges, cleans, fluffs and straightens its feathers.

prey A bird or animal that is captured and eaten by a predator. The small mammals captured for lunch by a Cooper's Hawk are considered its prey.

semiplume feather A combination of a contour feather and a down feather. It has a stiff shaft and soft down vanes that serve as extra insulation to keep a bird warm.

short-distance migrant A bird that breeds in the Rocky Mountain region but winters just far enough south or west to avoid extreme temperatures and snowfall.

super adaptor A bird that is able to live in a variety of habitats.

syrinx The vocal organ of a bird similar to the larynx (voicebox) in humans. Birds use the syrinx to call and sing.

territory A bird's territory is the space that it defends from other birds (and sometimes mammals such as squirrels) for feeding, courtship, nesting and raising its young.

undulating To move in waves, in an up-and-down way.

uropygium gland A gland located above a bird's tail that holds oil. The bird squeezes the gland with its bill to get the oil and then spreads the oil onto its feathers for conditioning.

warm-blooded All birds are warm-blooded. They can keep a constant body temperature no matter how hot or cold the weather. Mammals like you are also warm-blooded. Reptiles and amphibians are cold-blooded. They take on the temperature of their surroundings.

webbed feet When a bird's toes are connected to one another by thick skin, the bird is said to have webbed feet. Mallards and Canada Geese have webbed feet that help them paddle through the water.

wetlands Areas of land that hold water in the soil or are covered with water during all or part of the year. Wetlands can be found separate from other bodies of water, or associated with the shallow edges of a river or lake. Plants and animals living in wetland habitats have special adaptations to make the most of the watery conditions.

Do the Math Answer Key

Do the math on your own first and then check if the answer is figured correctly. If not, review the equations in this answer key to find where you worked the math differently. Use your brain power, you can do it!

Clark's Nutcracker (pg. 51)

A Clark's Nutcracker can hold up to 150 pine seeds in its throat pouch that adds up to about 20% of its total weight. If you weigh 90 pounds and had a pouch of seeds that was about 20% of your total weight, what would the weight of the pouch be?

Step #1: Change the percent to a decimal

$$20\% = 20 \div 100 = .20$$

Step #2: .20 x 90 lbs = the pouch would weigh 18 pounds

White-tailed Ptarmigan (pg. 55)

From -27° at the snow's surface to +24° seven inches under the snow = 51 degrees of difference between the temperature at the surface of the snow and the temperature seven inches under the snow. Wow, snow is an efficient insulator.

Hairy Woodpecker (pg. 89)

How many drumbeats can a woodpecker drum? If a woodpecker makes 15 drumbeats in one second, how many drumbeats can it make in one minute?

15 drum beats per second X 60 seconds in one minute = 900 drumbeats in one minute

Ten minutes?
900 drumbeats in one minute X 10 minutes = 9,000 drumbeats in 10 minutes

American Robin (pg. 90)

14 feet of earthworms per day x 7 days = A robin can eat 98 feet of earthworms in one week! Line up 98 feet of gummy worms, pipe cleaners or string on your sidewalk or driveway to see this amazing feat for yourself!

Gray Catbird (pg. 93)

If you were to increase your body mass, or in this case, weight, at the end of the summer, so you weighed one-and-a-half times as much, like a Gray Catbird does, how much would you weigh?

Step #1   Your weight in pounds ____ X 1.5 = ____ total pounds in weight

Cooper's Hawk (pg. 101)

66 prey X 3 chicks = 198 prey needed to feed 3 young hawks for six weeks

66 prey X 4 chicks = 264 prey needed to feed 4 young hawks for six weeks

66 prey X 5 chicks = 330 prey needed to feed 5 young hawks for six weeks

Brown-headed Cowbird (pg. 121)

Cowbirds travel 500 miles between their summer and winter areas. A flock of mixed blackbirds (including Brown-headed Cowbirds) travels at about 30 miles per hour (mph). At this speed, how long does it take a flock to travel 500 miles?

500 miles ÷ 30 miles per hour = 16.6 hours or an estimation of between 16 and 17 hours

Red-winged Blackbird (pg. 161)

This solution is based on a birth weight of 8 pounds. Place your birth weight in and rework the problem.

8 pounds birth weight X 10 days = A weight gain of 80 pounds in just 10 days!

Wildlife Near and Far: Where to Find Birds

The Rocky Mountain region includes four states: Colorado, Idaho, Montana and Wyoming. There are many places to experience wildlife first-hand: over 35 national forests, 5 national parks, over 30 national wildlife refuges, over 100 state parks and countless acres of land preserved by private conservation organizations open to the public.

The following state and national resources are great places to learn where bird species may be observed, and the list includes nature and environmental centers. Be a citizen scientist and send your observations in to state and national databases listed on these pages.

State Resources

COLORADO
Colorado Department of Natural Resources

http://dnr.state.co.us/Pages/DNRDefault.aspx

http://wildlife.state.co.us/WILDLIFESPECIES/Pages/WildlifeSpecies.aspx

IDAHO
Idaho Department of Fish and Game

http://fishandgame.idaho.gov/

http://fishandgame.idaho.gov/public/wildlife/

MONTANA
Montana Fish, Wildlife and Parks

http://fwp.mt.gov/

http://fwp.mt.gov/wildthings/

WYOMING
Wyoming Game and Fish Department

http://gf.state.wy.us/wildlife/nongame/index.asp

http://gf.state.wy.us/

Citizen Science Resources

Birds for Kids:
www.birdsforkids.com

Christmas/Holiday Bird Count:
www.audubon.org/bird/cbc/index.html

Great Backyard Bird Count:
www.birdsource.org/gbbcApps/kids

International Migratory Bird Day:
http://www.birdday.org/

Cornell Lab: Macaulay Library of Sounds:
http://macaulaylibrary.org/index.do

National Bird Feeding Society:
http://www.birdfeeding.org/

National Wildlife Federation:
National Wildlife Week:
http://www.nwf.org/Get-Outside/Be-Out-There/EventsNational-Wildlife-Week.aspx

The Nature Conservancy:
http://www.nature.org/tncscience/?src=l10

North American Bluebird Society:
http://www.nabluebirdsociety.org/

North American Breeding Bird Survey:
http://www.pwrc.usgs.gov/BBS/

Cornell Lab of Ornithology:
http://www.birds.cornell.edu/

Partners in Flight:
http://www.partnersinflight.org/

Project Feeder Watch:
www.birds.cornell.edu/pfw/

Project Pigeon Watch:
www.birds.cornell.edu/pigeonwatch

U.S. Fish & Wildlife Service:
http://www.fws.gov/educators/E_birds.html

Wild About Science:
http://www.wildaboutscience.net

The Trumpeter Swan Society
www.trumpeterswansociety.org/citizen-science-projects.html

Greater Yellowstone Trumpeter Swan Initiative
www.trumpeterswansociety.org/csp-greater-yellowstone.html

National Resources

American Birding Association:
Birding Trails:
http://www.aba.org/resources/birdingtrails.html

Birding Festivals:
http://www.aba.org/festivals/index.php

National Audubon Society:
General Information:
http://www.audubon.org/

Birding Trails:
http://www.audubon.org/bird_trails/backseat_birder.html

Important Bird Areas:
http://www.audubon.org/bird/iba/

National Wildlife Federation:
http://www.nwf.org/naturefind/

Watchable Wildlife:
http://www.wildlifeviewingareas.com/

Also visit the websites for your local, state and national parks and forests

Birding Trails in the Rocky Mountain region of the U.S.

Hit the trails and get to know the birds in this book first-hand. There are many birding trails throughout the region, but there is only space to list the main trails here. Explore them all, big and small!

• Birding Trail updates: www.birdtrail.org

• Colorado Birding Trail: www.coloradobirdingtrail.com

• Great Pikes Peak Birding Trail: www.greatpikespeakbirdingtrail.org/

• Idaho Birding Trail: www.idahobirdingtrail.org

• Great Montana Birding and Wildlife Trail: www.montanabirdingtrail.org

Bird Species by Taxonomic Order

This taxonomic list draws from the common Linnean system, which classifies birds and other living things by their morphological (physical) features. It was developed over two hundred years ago by Carl Linnaeus, a Swedish naturalist. Learn more about scientific names on page 13, in "What's In a Name? Binomial Nomenclature."

ANSERIFORMES: DUCKS, GEESE, SWANS, WATERFOWL
Canada Goose
Trumpeter Swan
Mallard
Blue-winged Teal
Common Merganser

GALLIFORMES: CHICKENS, QUAIL, TURKEYS, PHEASANTS
White-tailed Ptarmigan
Sharp-tailed Grouse

PODICIPEDIFORMES: GREBES
Pied-billed Grebe

PELCECANIFORMES: PELICANS
American White Pelican

CICONIIFORMES: HERONS, BITTERNS, EGRETS
Great Blue Heron

FALCONIFORMES: EAGLES, HAWKS, FALCONS
Turkey Vulture
Osprey
Bald Eagle
Northern Harrier
Cooper's Hawk
Red-tailed Hawk
Golden Eagle
American Kestrel
Prairie Falcon

GRUIFORMES
American Coot
Sandhill Crane

CHARADRIIFORMES: SHOREBIRDS, GULLS, TERNS, PLOVERS, SANDPIPERS
Killdeer
Spotted Sandpiper
Wilson's Snipe

COLUMBIFORMES: DOVES, PIGEONS
Rock Pigeon
Mourning Dove

STRIGIFORMES: OWLS
Western Screech-Owl
Great Horned Owl
Northern Saw-whet Owl

CAPRIMULGIFORMES
Common Nighthawk

APODIFORMES: HUMMINGBIRDS, SWIFTS
Broad-tailed Hummingbird

CORACIIFORMES: KINGFISHERS
Belted Kingfisher

PICIFORMES: WOODPECKERS
Williamson's Sapsucker
Hairy Woodpecker
Northern Flicker

PASSERIFORMES: PERCHINGS BIRDS, SONGBIRDS
Western Wood-Pewee
Western Kingbird
Warbling Vireo
Gray Jay
Steller's Jay
Clark's Nutcracker
Black-billed Magpie
Common Raven
Cliff Swallow
Black-capped Chickadee
Mountain Chickadee
Red-breasted Nuthatch
Rock Wren
House Wren
American Dipper
Golden-crowned Kinglet
Mountain Bluebird
American Robin
Gray Catbird
American Pipit
Yellow-rumped Warbler
Common Yellowthroat
Chipping Sparrow
Vesper Sparrow
Song Sparrow
White-crowned Sparrow
Dark-eyed Junco
Western Tanager
Black-headed Grosbeak
Red-winged Blackbird
Western Meadowlark
Brown-headed Cowbird
Bullock's Oriole
American Goldfinch
Evening Grosbeak

This order follows the most recent version accepted by the American Ornithologists' Union, recently revised to include DNA evidence.

References

The resources used to prepare this book include numerous reports and surveys, many from state breeding bird atlases, the Important Bird Areas Program (IBA) of The National Audubon Society and state Wildlife Action Plans including the data associated with identified Species of Greatest Conservation Need. A complete reference list can be found at Adele Porter's author website: www.adeleporter.com.

General references and sources of additional information include the following books, reports, and publications:

Gill, F., and Poole, A., eds. *The Birds of North America, volumes 1–18*. Philadelphia: Academy of Natural Sciences; Washington, D.C.: American Ornithologists' Union; Ithaca: Cornell Lab of Ornithology, 2002.

Lynch, Patrick J., and Proctor, Noble S. *Manual of Ornithology, Avian Structure and Function*. New Haven: Yale University Press, 1993.

Partners in Flight. North American Landbird Conservation Plan, 2005. www.partnersinflight.org/cont_plan/PIF3_Part2WEB.pdf

Perrins C.M., ed. *Oxford Ornithology Series*. New York: Oxford University Press, 2002.

Podulka, S., Rohrbaugh, R.W. Jr., Bonny, R., eds. *Handbook of Bird Biology, Second Edition*. Ithaca: Cornell Lab of Ornithology; Princeton: Princeton University Press, 2004.

Poole, A., ed. *The Birds of North America Online*: http://bna.birds.cornell.edu/BNA/. Ithaca: Cornell Laboratory of Ornithology, 2005.

Sauer, J. R., J. E. Hines, J. E. Fallon, K. L. Pardieck, D. J. Ziolkowski, Jr., and W. A. Link. 2011. *The North American Breeding Bird Survey, Results and Analysis 1966–2009*. Version 3.23.2011 USGS Patuxent Wildlife Research Center, www.pwrc.usgs.gov, Laurel, MD.

About the Author

Award-winning author and science educator Adele Porter combines her passion for science and dedication to children in her new books. In fact, the students that Adele has worked with during 20 years as an educator inspired *Wild About Rocky Mountain Birds*. Adele has also written educational materials for the Minnesota Department of Natural Resources, the U.S. Forest Service and various publications. She is a member of the National Science Teachers' Association, the American Ornithologists' Union, and the Society of Children's Book Writers and Illustrators.

For Adele, one of the best parts of being an author is meeting the readers of her books at author programs and book signings and hearing their enthusiastic outdoor adventure stories. She looks forward to hearing of your new wildlife adventures!

A native of Minnesota, Adele enjoys the time she and her three children spend together more than anything else. Visit her website, www.adeleporter.com, for information about school programs on-site with Adele, as well as classes via Skype.

Go to www.birdsforkids.com to download and print a free bookmark that features a life-size Black-capped Chickadee and tells how to use your book to identify a bird!